MY PARANORMAL LIFE

Supernatural Stories from
A Hollywood Insider

Dan Harary

BearManor Media.com

Typesetting and layout by PKJ Passion Global

Published in the USA by
BearManor Media
1317 Edgewater Dr #110
Orlando FL 32804
www.BearManorMedia.com

Softcover Edition
ISBN-10:
ISBN-13: 979-8-88771-463-9

Printed in the United States.

FOR MY MOTHER, JOAN, WHO BELIEVES
NOT ONE OF THE STORIES IN THIS BOOK

Table of Contents

"An interesting read. This is a paranormal memoir with enthusiastic experiences told by Dan Harary. I enjoyed his experiences with the supernatural!" -- G.L. Davies, Author of the worldwide bestselling *A Most Haunted House* and creator of *TheParanormalChronicles.com*

"A hugely successful and sometimes hilarious Hollywood businessman, Dan Harary's new book presents stories about an unshakable darkness and paranormal experiences that have long loomed over his life. In many of his stories, beautiful bouts of selfless compassion backfire like the death rattle of a tricked out 1957 Chevy. Other-worldly chandeliers speak to him, manifestations from the dearly departed visit him, and precognitive visions permeate dramatic moments from his life. Is he cursed to suffer in darkness? Did he enter into a prebirth contract to repay an enormous karmic debt from a past life? Will he ever find inner peace? This hugely entertaining book leads the reader down several pathways, but one hopes that Dan will eventually find the one infused with sunlight… the one that will penetrate the seemingly pervasive dark cloud that he describes in remarkably frank and candid detail." - Kathleen Marden, Founder of the Mutual UFO Network's Experiencer Resource Team; award-winning UFO researcher; seeker of esoteric knowledge through social research and experimentation; author of *Forbidden Knowledge: A Personal Journey from Alien Abduction to Spiritual Transformation;* and co-author of *Captured: The Betty and Barney Hill UFO Experience*

"Dan's emails to me are always PUNCTUATED with words in ALL CAPS, and now I understand why! He's had a WILD life! His book is a fascinating rollercoaster of supernatural close-calls, thoroughly ENTERTAINING, and more than a little bit CHILLING. A must-read for paranormal enthusiasts!" – Steve Kostanski, Film Writer/Director/Producer, Credits Include: *Leprechaun, Psycho Goreman, The Void* and *Syfy's Day of the Dead*

"I met Dan Harary at a UFO/paranormal conference in San Francisco in 2023. But after reading his new book, *MY PARANORMAL*

LIFE, I feel like we've been friends forever. The similarities/ synchronicities in our early lives were striking at times. He shares completely fascinating - sometimes funny and often intensely frank - stories of how one guy manages to live with all the weirdness he's experienced throughout his life! This is a thoroughly captivating, entertaining read, one you won't want to put down until the last sentence." – Debra Jordan-Kauble, aka "Kathie Davis" in Budd Hopkins' New York Times Best-Selling Book, *Intruders: The Incredible Visitation at Copely Woods*. Kauble is also the author of *Abducted: The Story of Intruders Continues*, and of *Extraordinary Contact: Life Beyond Intruders*

Introduction

I have been extremely fortunate to have worked in Hollywood's entertainment industry for well over 40 years as a noted Publicist. I have owned and managed a well-respected company, The Asbury PR Agency, for coming up on thirty years. I have worked alongside many dozens of the world's biggest stars from film, TV, rock and pop music, since 1972 at the age of 15. For reasons that seem almost a bit supernatural to me now, I have been something of a "Celebrity Adjacent Magnet" for most of my life.

For example: I worked with Bruce Springsteen when I was 16 (years before "Born to Run"); attended college with Howard Stern; and was told by Jerry Seinfeld in 1981 (ten years before his TV show debuted) that I was his "very first fan." I watched the film *The Blue Lagoon* (1980) alone in a private screening room with actress Brooke Shields and her mother -- the film launched her acting career; became Jay Leon's publicist just as he was hired to helm *The Tonight Show* (1954) in 1987; called Meryl Streep by the wrong name while shaking her hand in 1990; told an unknown waitress named Katrina Lenk in 2008 she'd become a big star one day (she'd win a Tony Award exactly ten years later); and discussed Jewish deli foods with Steven Spielberg.

To read about my adventures in Hollywood, please be sure to check out my first book from Bear Manor Media, *FLIRTING WITH FAME,* which was released in 2022.

I came to Los Angeles at the tender age of 24 in Fall 1980, with six dollars in my pocket. My original dream at that time was to become a comedy writer for television. And while that goal was never attained, I was able to transform myself into a working Publicist, which allowed me to survive, send my two children through college, and not have to sleep on the sidewalk along Wilshire Blvd. inside a large refrigerator box.

Intertwined with my entire life story, including my "Hollywood Years," oddly, have been numerous moments of what's now termed "high strangeness" -- inexplicable events that I simply brushed aside, ignored, or forgot about completely. It wasn't until my late Grandpa Joseph Harary (1896–1967) began haunting my Beverly Hills apartment during the Spring of 2003, however, that I began to take notice! That experience was so profound, it was then I became convinced that "Supernatural Stuff" *really can happen* to normal people in everyday life. The evidence of "His" existence was so powerful, it could not be denied or simply explained away as something else.

My beloved dead grandpa had become a Poltergeist!

It was around that same time I began to reflect upon the various supernatural, paranormal, off-the-wall, and simply peculiar events that I'd experienced since my childhood along the New Jersey Shore. These started in the early '60s and continued for decades thereafter. I wrote down a list of those moments, then misplaced it.

Twenty-years later – in 2023 – I re-discovered that list, updated it, and came to the conclusion that there was probably enough "meat" on the bones of my wild and wacky, supernatural life experiences to compile into a book of short tales of the bizarre.

Welcome to *MY PARANORMAL LIFE!* Everything you are about to read is true. I hope you enjoy these tales. Please contact me if you have any similar stories of your own, I'd love to read them: DanHararyAuthor@gmail.com

DJH/Beverly Hills, CA/2024

Chapter One

The Gargoyle (1961)

I was born in Neptune, New Jersey, during the summer of 1956 -- the product of two brilliant parents who'd met in Brooklyn and relocated to the Jersey Shore upon their marriage in 1952. We lived one town west of the famous resort city Asbury Park. My parents took me there often to enjoy the kiddie rides, eat frozen custard, swim in the Atlantic, play Skeeball, and stroll the famous Asbury Boardwalk. (I still have these home movies.)

My father was an Electronics Engineer/Physicist for the U.S. Department of the Army at Fort Monmouth in Belmar, N.J., for 45 years, working on top secret military projects. In his free time, he had a beloved hobby -- playing the trombone in big bands and dance bands, large and small. My mother, professionally both a teacher and later a probation officer, was also a noted singer, accordionist, actress, pianist, playwright, poet, artist, and stage producer. Each of my parents performed musically for many decades in front of live audiences throughout Monmouth County, New Jersey, occasionally atop the Howard Johnson's Restaurant on the Asbury Boardwalk. They most often appeared in separate bands and shows, but for several years they performed together in the SAME combo -- Harry Hurley's Big Band. Asbury Park's WJLK Radio broadcast several of their concerts live. I still have those recordings.

We were the only Jewish family in our Neptune neighborhood, and all my little friends at that time were young Catholic or Protestant females. One day in 1961 when I was five, two, cute, older Catholic/Italian girls who lived directly across the street came over to my house and asked my mother if I could come out to play. She agreed, and the sisters led me one block down the street, around the corner, and into the parking lot of a drugstore. Situated within that parking lot was a three-story tall billboard sign promoting that business.

Kathy and Lizzie began climbing up inside the cross-beamed wooden lattice of that large billboard sign -- they were casually swinging from beam to beam like George of the Jungle. I was watching from the ground. "Hey Danny, it's easy," shouted Lizzie. "Just do what we're doing." When I looked up inside its skeleton, I was scared. But not wanting to be taunted by the sisters, I began to climb the beams, very slowly.

At the point when we were probably near the very top of the sign, Kathy shouted, "Hey Danny, look at me!" and blew me a kiss. Startled, I FELL OFF THE SIGN! I distinctly remember floating as though in slow-motion through the air, face up, watching the looks of horror on the faces of my two little girlfriends.

I must have landed on my back with a thud. I have no memory of that.

Within an hour, I awoke on a couch inside a strange house, about two blocks away from the sign. I sat up and looked around, called out "Hello?" but no one was home. The living room of this house was completely foreign to me. I knew I'd never been there before in my life.

I distinctly recall thinking maybe I'd died, and that my body had somehow been rescued and brought back to life. As that remarkable thought was zapping across the synapses of my little boy's brain, I glanced over to the front door of the house, which was located at the south end of the living room. There, I saw a very tall, slightly deformed CREATURE, with very angular shoulders (possibly the stumps of wings) and a BEASTLY-LOOKING FACE, leaving the living room. He was the color of white chocolate…sort of light beige. He glanced over his left shoulder to look at me, his face appearing bull-like. He snorted, then walked out through the front screen door of the building and disappeared.

As I watched this "Being" walk outside, I vividly recall assessing the idea that this "Thing" may have just saved my life. Was "he" an Angel?

This was NOT a dream. I was awake and witnessed this in "real life." It's among the earliest of my memories. I can still recall this sight today, well over 60 years later.

I was never told how I got to that house. Foolishly, I never asked Kathy or Lizzie what had happened after I fell. So, clearly, I'll never know precisely what took place. But as God is my witness, I can clearly remember the look on the heinous face of this Creature as he was about to leave. His expression was almost one of disgust, as if to say to me: "Yeah, I saved your life. But I had no choice They made me do it."

When I told my daughter, Anjuli, this story in 2023, she suggested that perhaps the creature that saved me was a Gargoyle! And possibly, since Lizzie and Kathy were hard-core Catholics, they might have been so frightened by my "dead" body on the ground after my fall, that they prayed over me, thus summoning this other-worldly being into existence!?

According to various websites:

- "Gargoyles are said to protect what they guard from any evil or harm."

- "Gargoyles can take on human form."

- "Gargoyles go way back to Ancient Egypt."

- "The primary purpose in Gargoyle life is to protect."

- "Gargoyles on the ground use their wings as a projection of their size -- they will frequently slap their enemies with their wings or use the back of their wings as a shield. They also use their wings as humans use our arms."

- "When a Gargoyle protects a person, it usually stays within a quarter mile of the person or the person's home."

And: "There can be few anguishes greater for a Gargoyle than failing to protect someone from harm. When Gargoyles choose to protect a person or an area, they will do so steadfastly, even when the humans whom they are protecting respond to them with fear or hatred."

Bottom Line: I'll never know what that Thing was that saved my life and carried me inside a stranger's house. I've been unable to find Lizzie or Kathy via the Internet in adult life. But I do know that my Creature did exist and that something truly supernatural had happened to me on that sunny afternoon back in 1961.

Chapter Two

The Past Life Curse: The Early Years
(1960 – 1968)

I was cursed in a past life. Concurrent with my birth, it had been predestined by the universe that I was never meant to find happiness with a woman.

A truer statement I have never made. It's something I have lived with every single day for nearly 70 years -- a phenomenon that has been proven to me, hundreds of times, to be interwoven into the fabric of my particular DNA. A few people who know me well believe this, including Dr. Kathryn Uzunov, a renowned, LA-based therapist, who, after reading my book *Carrots: True Confessions of a Hollywood Sex Addict* (Bear Manor Media, 2022) said, "I have to wonder how one man can have SO MUCH bad luck his entire life with the opposite sex? It's enough to make me a believer in his wild idea that he really is the unfortunate bearer of a past life curse!"

However, most people with whom I've shared my curse theory think I'm bat-shit crazy. For some reason, "whoever" or "whatever" I was during a past life was evil incarnate (Hitler? Pol Pot? Stalin? Attila the Hun? Genghis Kahn?) As a result, I am living out the consequences of a past life curse during this lifetime. The curse is interesting, though, because it only pertains to my ability to develop and secure happy, peaceful, loving, intimate relationships with romantically-targeted members of the opposite sex.

This curse, which is very specific to me, has clearly been designed to prevent me from ever finding happiness in the form of a female companion. I simply do not have a Soul Mate.

The only way I can prove this theory to you, my dear reader, is to weave a retelling of numerous, real-life experiences from my life with girls and women throughout this book. These stories will serve as my evidence:

My very first memory -- I'm four. My best friend and next-door neighbor, adorable, blonde Donna, and I were on the lawn in front of my house, kicking a ball. Without warning, Donna decided to stop playing. In a sudden burst of rage, I picked up a rock and hurled it, striking her in the forehead. It caused quite a gash. She put her hand to the wound, felt the blood, and stared at me for a second in silence, before letting out a scream that I can still hear today, 60-plus years later.

Donna's mother flew through her kitchen door, racing to her daughter's aid. She saw the blood and the rock, then shot me a terrifying glare. "Look what you did!" she screamed. "What's wrong with you? Such a bad little boy!"

The woman grabbed my arm and shouted through the screen to my mother. "Joan, Joan, come quick," she cried. "Look what your son did to my daughter!" My mother's face conveyed it all -- despair and disappointment. "I'll talk to him," she said. As we heard, "I don't want him playing with my Donna again" through the screen door, my mother told me it was never OK to hurt a girl.

Having been banned from seeing Donna, I next turned my attention to Mary-Barbara (MB), a rambunctious, chubby brunette. When I was five and she was about seven, MB said, "Let's take off our clothes." I had no idea why anyone would want to do that. Standing behind the large bushes in the front yard of her house, MB removed her shirt and pulled down her skirt, until she stood in just panties and shoes. My heart pounding, I was frozen, awaiting her further instructions.

Suddenly from nowhere, MB's mother (a short, little Italian powerhouse with glasses,) appeared, parted the bushes like Moses at the Red Sea, and shrieked, "What on Earth are you doing to my daughter? You little pervert!" My shame, fear, and confusion were overwhelming.

Pulling me by the ear, the woman rushed me down the street to my house. Once again: "Joan, Joan come quick! We have a problem!" My poor mother answered the door and learned the news. "Stay away from the little girls, Danny. They are not your friends," she admonished. I was so utterly embarrassed. *What had I done wrong?* MB was the criminal here, *not me*! Yet, because I was the boy caught with a nearly naked girl, I was the evil one. The sicko. Clearly, the savage neighborhood rapist.

After this one-two punch, I decided my mother was right -- neighborhood girls were trouble. I started palling around with a young boy named Gus who had a train set. We'd ring doorbells then ran away, and insult an ancient woman named Elsie (calling her 'Elsie the Cow,') whenever she pushed her walker past us on the sidewalk.

At six, I met a new neighbor -- a young boy playing in his front yard. He invited me inside to see his Etch-a-Sketch. We played with several of his wonderful toys, and his mother brought in milk and cookies. I was in heaven. This was a wonderland. While we played, my pal's baby sister walked into his room, clad only in a diaper. Drinking from a bottle, she was probably about two.

Flashing back to the incident with MB in the bushes, I realized I needed resolution: "What on Earth do girls have 'down there'?" I pondered. Deciding this baby wouldn't pose much of a challenge, I pulled down her diaper, and took a good long look. "Interesting," I thought. "I wonder what that thing is?"

My luck with mothers-of-friends having not changed even for this briefest instant, my buddy's mom walked in, saw what I'd done, and became hysterical. She swooped up the little girl, shouting, "You little bastard! Get out of my house and don't ever come back!" I quickly made my escape, but remember thinking, quite clearly, that at least I saw a naked girl that time.

Third Grade. Two situations that have haunted me for decades:

During recess, a buddy and I wanted to play "catch the girls," a running game. A pair of identical twins, Wendy and Robyn, were willing, so I selected Wendy and began my chase. I was an extremely fast runner as a child, so I zoomed after her, sure I could tag her quickly. Wendy managed to stay ahead of me the entire time -- I was never able to touch her. After a few minutes, Wendy sprinted away, turned her head over her left shoulder, and mocked, "You'll never get me, Danny," not noticing the fencepost railing dead ahead.

Wendy slammed her mouth, hard, into the railing, and came to a screeching halt. I stopped running when I heard that awful sound. Clearly in a daze, Wendy spat blood into her hand, then slowly lifted her face toward mine. Holding half of an adult front tooth in her open palm, her expression read, "Look what YOU did to me!" As she ran off to the school nurse, crying, accompanied by her twin, I stood alone in stunned silence. Once again, for whatever inexplicable reason, I'd "hurt" a little girl -- this time, one I never even touched. And once again, I experienced the same terrible feelings of guilt I'd become accustomed to from my earliest days of childhood.

Another third-grade trauma involved square dancing, of all things. In gym class, we had an unprecedented, "boy/girl" session taught by our male coach, a real hard-ass, former Marine, and our lovely, young, female teacher, who paired the boys off with the girls. My partner was a blonde cutie.

The coach had a record player at the front of the gym, and as the singer sang, "Swing your partners, Docie Doh, round and round and round you go," I did exactly as instructed, exuberantly swinging my gal pal. I distinctly recall her laughing -- I'd never been happier in my life. Suddenly, the coach stopped the record player, blew his whistle, grabbed me by the shirt collar, and screamed: "What do you think you're doing?"

"Do you know what we do to boys who are too rough with little girls?" he admonished, inches from my face. "We take them to the woodshed and BEAT THE CRAP out of them!" His rage was overwhelming. His face was bright red…steam was shooting out from his ears. I glanced to my teacher for help, but she simply turned away. Stunned and speechless, I worked up the courage to look at little blondie, but she'd begun to cry. The coach had me sit on the floor in front of the class. "Stay there, you little ass. Do not move."

I recall telling my mother about this event that same afternoon. I was particularly upset by two things: First, I had no idea what I'd done wrong -- and still don't, to this day. Second, I was startled to hear the words "crap" and "ass" -- the first "dirty words" I'd ever heard in my life. Unfortunately, my mother didn't believe my story, and I was forced, once again, to subjugate my abject humiliation.

****

At 12, I was quite popular in school. During these "glory days," I was elected president of my 6th grade class, which was led by an evil bitch of a teacher. She once asked me to deliver a report about Nasa's Gemini Space program in front of the class, criticizing me the entire time. This caused me to develop a fear of public speaking that would last for decades.

One night I got a phone call:

Me: "Hello?"

Caller: "Do you know who this is?"

Me: "No…"

Caller: "Stephanie" (a fellow sixth grader)

Me: "Why are you calling?"

Steph: "Who do you like?"

Me: "What?"

Steph: "Who do you like from school?"

Me: "What are you talking about?"

Steph: "What girl do you like?"

Me: "Girl? I don't like any girl…"

Steph: "You must like one girl in our class… Who is she?"

Me: "Nobody."

Steph: "We know you like somebody. What's her name?"

Me: Not wanting to sound like a total loser -- "Joanne, I guess."

Steph: (Giggling voices in the background) "Joanne, I knew it… Okay, bye."

Like a deer in the headlights, I had no idea what had just happened. I shrugged off the call, then went to watch Tiny Tim sing "Tiptoe Through the Tulips" on NBC's *Laugh-In* (1968). The next day, a gaggle of girls from my class cornered me on the playground during recess. They included Stephanie, and Joanne, a cute, round-faced blonde I'd only even noticed for the first time a few days earlier. Clearly the ringleader, Stephanie confronted me: "When are you going to ask Joanne to go steady?"

Poor Joanne was now the deer in the headlights. "What does that even mean?" I asked. Stephanie explained: "You get an ID bracelet with your name on it and give it to Joanne. Then she's your girlfriend. It's easy." As the geese gaggle fluttered away, Joanne looked over her shoulder, shooting me a seductive, parting glance. I instantly felt an electric twitch -- I'd like to say it came from my heart, but, to be honest, I believe it came from my pre-pubescent testes.

I asked my father for some cash, something I dreaded, due to his lifelong insecurities about money. (My dad and his family once lived for a week on a sidewalk in Brooklyn during the Great Depression, when his parents couldn't pay their rent or utility bills.) I told him there was a girl involved, and he reluctantly handed me five bucks. A friend of mine named Justin and I rode our bikes to a stationery store that always smelled like pencil erasers, and I bought an ID bracelet engraved with my first name. It was much too big for my wrist, and during the ride home, fell off me several times.

End of school the next day: Before we could be dismissed by her majesty, our teacher, we had to stand in two lines -- one for boys, one for girls -- and wait for the bell to ring. All eyes were now laser-honed onto my face. Stephanie whispered: "Do it, Danny, come on!" My heart racing, I removed the bracelet, turned to Joanne, and, in my best Don Juan impression, said, "Here, you want this stupid thing?" Tossing it, Joanne caught the bracelet, put it on, and gave me an enormous smile. The other kids were psyched. I was a pioneer, not just the 6th grade class president and the leader of my peers, but also the first kid in our class to be going steady. The bell rang, we all dispersed, and I realized I wasn't in Kansas anymore.

Joanne and I spent hours on the phone the next couple of nights, discussing the most inane topics imaginable.

A few days later, our shithead teacher called on Joanne to answer a very hard question. Joanne choked and had no response. The woman, devoid of one ounce of humanity, kept hounding her: "Why don't you know this material, Joanne? What's wrong with you? Didn't you study? Why are you in my class?" Joanne turned beet red and started to cry. Teacher: "Are you a crybaby now?" The eyes of every single student then shot over to ME, as if to say, "Your girlfriend is embarrassing YOU, Danny! What are YOU going to do about this?"

A very pretty brunette who sat just in front of me (and with whom I credit my first sexual fantasy based on a person I knew in real life,) turned and said, "Some girlfriend you picked! Good luck with HER!" For whatever reason, I didn't call Joanne that night, simply because I'm an inconsiderate putz.

That weekend, Stephanie threw a boy/girl party. I arrived with my best friend Justin and was instantly confronted by several guys from class. "Danny, Joanne really embarrassed you the other day. She can't be your girlfriend anymore, she's a crybaby. You need a different girlfriend. She's a loser." I was besieged by these brilliant words of wisdom. Feeling cocky, and egged on by Justin, I thought, "They're right. I don't want a crybaby for a girlfriend. She really DID embarrass me." Marching up to a smiling Joanne, I demanded my ID bracelet back.

Stunned, heartbroken, and crying once more, Joanne reluctantly handed the silver jangler back to me. My friends started laughing. My first relationship, which had lasted maybe two weeks, was now over.

I walked away thinking, "Why on Earth did I just do that? I really liked this girl."

Chapter Three

The Message from The Monkees (1966)

When I turned 10, my life took a dramatic turn. In the Fall of 1966, NBC presented *The Monkees* (1966-68) TV show and their music. As manufactured and "fake" as they may have been at the time, they rocked my world to its core. While I loved The Beatles' music, I was quite young when the Fab Four first conquered America in 1964. I had only two of their albums, had seen them perform just once on *The Ed Sullivan Show* (1948) when I was 7 – their historic, debut appearance in Feb. '64 -- and watched their film *HELP!* (1965) alone at an Asbury Park movie theater.

But now at the age of 10, The Monkees became something else entirely for me. Here was a rock band comprised of four funny guys with long hair, who cranked out hit song after hit song on a WEEKLY TV SHOW! They were instantly accessible in spite of the fact my family only had a black and white television set back then. I bought all their records, playing them until the grooves were scratched beyond repair.

My brother Bob (age 6) and I would dance to Monkees' records together in our den.

The arrival of The Monkees on TV had a second impact on me. I became obsessed with Micky Dolenz, their drummer. Watching Micky (pretend to) play the drums made me realize I no longer wanted to study classical piano (something my parents had forced upon me from the age of 7.) I HAD to enter the world of rock 'n roll.

During the second or third telecast of *The Monkees* on NBC, I was sitting cross-legged on the floor about a foot in front of our TV screen in the living room, watching the group perform one of their hit songs. As I was studying every move of Micky Dolenz's hands beating his drum kit, I HEARD A VOICE THAT SPOKE UNTO ME. It whispered into my right ear:

"DANNY, YOU MUST PLAY THE DRUMS!"

I shot up from my seated position like a Saturn V rocket and looked around the room to see if anyone else might have said those words to me.

I was completely alone at the time.

This "Message from The Monkees" had a profound and immediate impact on me, and in retrospect was the first step on the path that would eventually lead me into show business. (Side note: I would befriend Micky Dolenz exactly 20 years later in Hollywood. When I said to him, "I've been playing the drums my whole life because of you," he smiled, shook my hand and responded, "That's cool, man. I hear that a lot!")

After I heard the Voice, I began hounding my parents incessantly to buy me a drum set. Eventually the agreement became that I could start taking drum lessons along with my continued piano lessons, and IF I stuck with BOTH, I would get drums as a Bar Mitzvah present when I turned 13.

I initially took drum lessons for two years, learning all the rudiments on a little rubber drum pad and later, on a red sparkle-colored snare drum, all under the tutelage of local area professional drummer Bill Weir, who always smelled of bourbon. Finally bailing out on the piano, my parents realized that playing drums was my passion. One of the greatest moments of my life was the day my father took me into Brooklyn to a Sam Ash music store to order a sky-blue pearl Ludwig drum set. When he wrote out that check for $350.00, I was stunned to my core. That was a fortune as far as I was concerned! I honestly didn't know he had access to that kind of cash.

(Weird side story: When my dad bought my drums that day, he'd arranged for them to be shipped to my house. However, he did allow me to leave the store with a hi-hat -- the contraption a drummer works with his left foot that brings together two small cymbals, making a sound that accentuates the beat of a song. Since we were in Brooklyn, that same day we took a side trip to visit my mother's mother, my Grandma Bess, in her apartment in that city. My dad and

I rode up in the elevator in my grandmother's building -- I was holding the hi-hat stand in a long rectangular box. We arrived at her floor. The elevator doors opened. As I was about to walk out from the elevator, the long, thin, metal POLE that is the essential component of the hi-hat (the pole on which the two cymbals are connected) somehow SHOT THROUGH A TINY HOLE IN THE BOTTOM OF THE HI-HAT STAND BOX, AND FELL STRAIGHT DOWN, DIRECTLY AND VERTICALLY INTO THE ½ INCH CRACK BETWEEN THE ELEVATOR AND THE BUILDING'S 5TH FLOOR, AT THE EXACT SAME SECOND I STOOD OVER IT! THIS EVENT COULD NEVER HAVE BEEN PURPOSELY REPEATED IN A MILLION YEARS!

My dad and I watched this phenomenon happen in utter amazement -- this surely has never happened before or since in all of mankind's history. My father had to find the building's maintenance operator, who had to turn off the elevator in the building for an hour while he scoured the deepest recesses of the elevator's basement. Fortunately, the man found the pole, and my dad reluctantly handed him five bucks.)

At the age of 12, two years into my love affair with drums, a friend of mine gave me an extra ticket to attend a concert at Asbury Park's Convention Hall featuring the band Iron Butterfly. At the time, not only was their "In-A-Gadda-Da-Vida" the biggest "acid rock" song of 1968, but it also featured the first recorded rock and roll drum solo. While watching Iron Butterfly, I stood during that drum solo, trying to glean just how drummer Ron Bushy was able to accomplish such a remarkable feat.

From then on, I became obsessed with attending live rock concerts at Convention Hall, and during the next six years, would see dozens of shows there by such iconic bands as Mountain, YES, Chicago, Ten Years After, Black Sabbath, Humble Pie, The Eagles and Grand Funk Railroad. During a show by Emerson, Lake & Palmer, I leaned against the front of the stage, just feet in front of, and underneath, Greg Lake. A mesmerizing moment!

My beautiful Ludwig drum set was shipped to my house in the fall of 1968, ten months shy of my Jewish birthday milestone. As one of the very few kids my age with a professional-quality drum set, I was quickly sought out by the various guitar players from my neighborhood. I jammed, briefly, with a few local garage bands, before meeting Steve Walter in Hebrew School. Steve was to become a lifelong friend and noted guitarist. (Today, he is the owner of the world-famous Cutting Room nightclub in Manhattan -- Lady Gaga was discovered there in 2006!)

Starting in 6th grade, Steve and I put rock bands together with other fellow student guitarists, bassists, and keyboard players. Our bands had such names (taken from a dictionary) as Radiation, Grain, Eclipse, and later Mr. Spud, which our bass player Scott thought was the real name of the "Mr. Potato Head" toy. Our bands performed contemporary songs by iconic '60s and early '70s bands such as The Rolling Stones, The Young Rascals, Creedence Clearwater Revival, The Who, Led Zeppelin, The Allman Brothers Band, Mountain, Cream, Grand Funk Railroad, Jefferson Airplane, and many more.

Steve and I also built a "lightshow" which could accompany our band's performances -- this was comprised both of floodlights that would illuminate the front of the stage, as well as a "wet show" projected onto an enormous white sheet suspended behind our performing band. Called "Joe's Express Lights," our lightshow featured kaleidoscopes and colorful liquid "blobs" which pulsated in time with our music.

We also rented out our light show to other local area bands. My drumming career and light show work directly resulted in Steve and I becoming the Stage Managers and Lighting Directors at The Sunshine Inn, a legendary, now defunct, rock music hall in Asbury Park. We were employed there from 1972-1974, and worked with dozens of up-and-coming rock music acts, including Humble Pie, J. Geils Band, Deep Purple, Mott the Hoople, Slade, Renaissance, Edgar Winter, King Crimson, Procul Harum, and many others.

We also worked stage crew and stage lighting for three groups not yet famous -- KISS (their first ever, non-New York show); Fleetwood Mac (years before Stevie Nicks and Lindsey Buckingham joined); and a guy named Bruce Springsteen (pre E-Street Band) for a show in February 1973.

The bottom line is this: That "Message from The Monkees" led me to the drums, which led me to my friend Steve, which led me to building a light show, which led me to working at The Sunshine Inn, which became the foundation of my interest in show-business, which ultimately led me to a successful career in Hollywood.

"Whoever" or "Whatever" it was that spoke the words: "DANNY YOU MUST PLAY THE DRUMS!" into my right ear on that September evening in 1966, I say today with great humility and gratitude, "Thank you!"

Chapter Four

The Civil War Fever Dream (1967)

When I was 11, I had a bad flu with a high fever. I was sick in bed for several days, mostly sleeping and drinking orange juice.

One night, perhaps 2 am, while my parents were asleep in their room, and my two younger brothers were sleeping in theirs, I sat up in bed and saw standing before me a Civil War Soldier. He was in full Confederate grey attire. "Are you ready to serve?" he sternly asked me.

I hopped out of bed and saluted him. "Private Dan Harary reporting for duty, SIR!" I declared. I remember this, clearly, today.

The apparition walked out of my bedroom, through the kitchen, through our rec room and out the side door of our house which led to the garage. I ran after him and found myself outside. He'd vanished.

I stood on our front lawn in a stupor for a few minutes, before I woke up. It was snowing and I was barefoot.

Not understanding why I was outside in the middle of the night, I quickly returned inside the house, and snuggled back under my warm covers.

Sleep-Walking Dream? Perhaps. Ghost? Fever Hallucination? You tell me.

Chapter Five

The First UFO (1970)

One late afternoon during Spring 1970, my father, Jack, picked me up after Hebrew School class -- it must have been around 3 pm and was still daylight. We were in my dad's car approaching Dwight Drive in West Deal, New Jersey -- the street my family lived on from 1963 (having moved there from Neptune) until 1978. As we turned onto Dwight Drive from the adjacent Deal Road, we saw through the windshield an enormous silver "Flying V" shaped UFO craft very, very slowly hovering over the homes of our neighbors. The craft had three lights -- one red, one blue, and one silver -- one light on each of its tips (I think.)

I shouted "Dad, Stop the car! Stop the car!" My dad pulled his vehicle off to the side of the road -- I flew out of the passenger seat. Together, we watched the giant craft glide directly above us – silently -- perhaps 100 feet in the sky.

I was hyper-ventilating, jumping up and down in amazement. "Dad this is so cool! A UFO! Dad, we saw a UFO!" My father said nothing. As though the sighting was commonplace, he was completely and totally nonplussed by the entire experience. Bored, he looked like he was inspecting a head of lettuce at the supermarket. Once the craft had passed us overhead, my dad then said, "Let's go home now."

Once back inside the car, I said, "Dad! I'm gonna put this in my diary!" To which my brilliant genius father coolly responded, "What? You have diarrhea?"

Upon returning home, I ran into the kitchen and picked up the family's (rotary) phone to call *The Asbury Park Press* -- our local area newspaper. I remember distinctly the conversation. A woman answered. I said, "Hi, my name is Danny Harary. I live on Dwight Drive in West Deal. I want to report a UFO! My dad and I just saw a big silver UFO flying over our street!" The woman, sounding somewhat frantic, said, "Sonny, we're getting A LOT of phone calls about this right now. Sorry, but I don't have time to talk to you. I have to go." She hung up.

I searched that newspaper the next day and beyond and was greatly disappointed to see no mention of his encounter anywhere. No story ever ran.

Now, here's the most incredible part of this story: I completely forgot about this UFO sighting for 47 years!

And when I did finally remember, in 2017, it would change my life. I would discover things about my late father's career I never knew; I'd write a popular science-fiction novel; I'd befriend -- and become embraced by -- dozens of the world's leading UFO Researchers; I'd launch a new Hollywood organization; and I'd even host my own, national podcast about the paranormal and the unexplained!

Chapter Six

The Magical Zit, Part One (1970)

My friend Allan from 8th Grade approached me one day during recess at school: "Hey Danny, wanna have a boy/girl party at your house?" The idea stopped me in my tracks. I didn't have that kind of courage. The basement in his house had flooded, and he needed a new venue for his 14th birthday party.

"Mom, Dad, can I have a boy/girl party here Saturday night?" My parents were excited. "We've been waiting for you to show some interest in little girls," my mother replied. The party was a go.

Allan and I produced a joint venture at my house, comprised of six boys and six girls, among them a sultry little beauty named Bonnie, who I'd never seen before. Allan taught us how to play spin the bottle, and as we sat in a circle, I noticed Bonnie smiling at me. After a series of other party games, Allan told us about "Seven Minutes in Heaven." He'd pair each boy with a girl, and, together, each couple would then enter my garage for seven minutes of bliss. Allan designated me the timekeeper, as I was the only kid there with a watch.

Allan and a pixie little blonde went first, and then one couple, after the next, after the next, each had a full, solid, seven minutes of making out behind my garage door. Since I was clocking these sessions, I'd inadvertently become the last boy to participate. Finally, Allan took Bonnie's hand, placed it in mine, and said, "Okay, Romeo, have fun out there."

My heart pounding out of my chest, I was about to experience my "coming of age" -- the moment when I would forever leave behind my childhood and become a man.

Bonnie walked out into the garage ahead of me. I stopped for a few seconds to quickly glance at the mirror in our den to make sure my hair looked good. AS I WAS LOOKING IN THE MIRROR, MY

VERY FIRST ZIT BURST FORTH FROM MY SKIN! It appeared from out of nowhere -- right in the middle of my forehead, directly in-between my eyebrows.

Bonnie stood before me at the foot of our attic stairs in the garage, trembling slightly. Trying to ignore the zit, I stroked her hair and hugged her tight. Here was a real live girl, in my arms -- a first. I slowly and deliberately closed my eyes, and gently placed my lips against hers. She smelled like fresh linen. We kissed. Her lips were nice and moist. I "saw stars" from behind my closed eyes. I could swear that I also heard music playing. The kiss was heaven…it was bliss….

And it only lasted about 20 seconds.

Bonnie's father had arrived far too early -- and completely unexpectedly -- to pick her up. Allan raced into the garage, panicked, and grabbed my arm. "Danny! Bonnie's father's here!" I thought he was playing a particularly cruel joke. Why was my new best friend busting my chops? Then, through the open garage door, we saw a man in an overcoat. Bonnie: "Oh my God, my Dad! I am so sorry, Danny." Bonnie fled, hooked up with her father, and split the scene moments later.

After the party guests left, my parents entered the room. "So, did you meet any nice little girls?" my mother asked. How was I supposed to answer that question? I'd just experienced the most magical moment of my life. And then, in a flash, it was gone. In the blink of an eye. Just like that.

The Magical Zit on my forehead receded back into its birthplace about an hour after the party ended.

A few weeks later, Bonnie's father was transferred to another city, and her family moved away. I never saw or heard from her again.

In addition to this chapter being a story about an inexplicable and "magical" zit, this tale should also be considered an early, foundational "building block" of my "Past Life Curse" theory.

Chapter Seven

The Mind-Reading Incident (1973)

My best buddy Steve and I had been performing in rock bands since 1968 and continued to do so during our high school years in the early '70s. When we weren't performing or rehearsing, or building up our light show, or working with soon-to-be-famous rock bands at the Sunshine Inn, we hung out at each other's house, watching TV, listening to new records, eating pizza, or secretly scouring the copies of *Playboy* Magazine I'd regularly been stealing from a drugstore for years.

Prior to our junior year of high school, Steve and I were never alone with just one of the brunette "groupie girls" who used to follow our band around town. There was no hooking up -- or pairing off -- yet, just hanging out sessions en mass.

But all that changed after a remarkable event in the school cafeteria. A high school sophomore Steve and I both knew named Laura -- one of our band's little groupie girl followers -- and I were sitting together one day having lunch. "Can I talk to you?" she asked.

Looking at her face, I saw the word "STEVE" prominently displayed on her forehead. It appeared to me like a neon sign for about five seconds.

"If I wanted someone to ask me for a date, should I tell him?" Me: "You mean Steve, right?" Laura: "How could you possibly know that?" Me: "I just read your mind."

I am calling this a "Mind-Reading" Incident, but, in retrospect I'm not sure that's what it was. I don't think I read her "mind" -- I literally read her *forehead,* which was projecting the word "STEVE" to me like a Times Square billboard.

I relayed the message to my best friend, who was pretty taken aback. "Really? Laura wants to date me?" Up until that point, Steve and I lived for just one thing, Rock and Roll. Our bands, instruments,

LP collections, long hair, light shows, and stage crew work at The Sunshine Inn had consumed our every waking moment for the past five years. Now, suddenly, the dynamics between us were about to change forever.

Steve and Laura fell in love in about ten minutes. I helped him buy condoms at the local drugstore, so that the lovers could quickly lose their virginities to each other. Lucky me, since I was the first one with a driver's license, I was often asked to drive them to clandestine locations for their lovemaking sessions. That truly sucked. Suddenly, I was the "third wheel" to my best friend.

In retrospect, it was my crippling shyness -- a result of my undiagnosed clinical depression -- that was the true reason behind the fact I was unable to develop a relationship with any of the other brunette groupie girls in high school during my teen years (one of whom had a big crush on me, I'd discover many years later.)

My overwhelming depression would remain unaddressed for many decades hence.

Chapter Eight

The Past Life Connection (1974/75)

After the end of the long, tortuous summer which followed my high school graduation, my parents schlepped me an hour north to Rutgers University, in New Brunswick, New Jersey. Rutgers was the only college I applied to -- or had ever even heard of -- because, quite simply, my father went there. Now it was my turn to continue the family tradition.

It was Fall 1974. I was 18 years old, with incredibly long hair, and a drummer without a band. I was still a virgin, while all my friends had been getting laid for most of the previous year. My acne was beyond belief -- there were days when chunks of "salsa" seemed to be dripping from my face. To top things off, I'd become deeply, seriously depressed, while having no idea that biological depression ran in my family.

My parents brought my suitcases up to my dorm room, hugged me goodbye, and split. I watched their car pull away, realizing I was now in an alien universe. In my entire life, I'd only ever slept away from home one night -- at the age of 10, in the woods at summer camp -- an experience that scared me to death. Suddenly, my parents, my brothers, my drums, Steve, The Sunshine Inn, my music buddies, and the only girls I'd ever spoken to, had all vanished. I was utterly alone.

An older student popped his head into my room.

"Hey man, I'm Carlos. Wanna get high?" These were the very first words I ever heard at college. "No thanks, man. I don't smoke pot." Carlos stared at me in disbelief. "Oh, you're into acid? Pills? Coke? Whatever you need, let me know, I can get if for you." Me: "Sorry, Carlos, no, I don't believe in drugs." Carlos: "With that hair, are you serious? We were taking bets out here you were a heroin addict." It took me a while to convince him. "Okay, man, whatever," he said, retreating into his room at the end of the hall. Moments later, Jimi Hendrix blasted "Purple Haze" out from Carlos' room, as a massive cloud of marijuana smoke wafted through the cracks in his door.

That night, a "Welcome Freshmen" dance was held at the student union. Having been alone most of that day, I attended in hopes of making some new friends. A DJ played records before the large, assembled crowd. A bunch of overweight girls were dancing with each other, while several guys, none with hair anywhere near the length of mine, were drinking beer. A few couples danced.

And then I saw HER on the dance floor. Alone. Swaying to the music. Her eyes closed. Her *incredibly long red hair* flowing over her shoulders and breasts, and nearly down to her ass. I gasped -- electricity in my brain firing across all cylinders.

For a few, fleeting seconds, she looked at me from across the room. Our eyes locked. As though her brain were a telegraph, I instantly downloaded this message: "YOU KNOW ME." In my gut, I took that to mean that she and I had previously known each other in a past life.

Instantly in love, I named this wonder girl "Long Red." Staring at her -- from afar -- for over two hours, I never once approached her, nor spoke to her. I watched as a number of guys did dance with her, though, each giving her one or two songs, and then politely moving on. I was frozen in place. Mesmerized. No beer, no alcohol, no drugs. While watching this wondrous creature sway before me, I became completely and utterly catatonic.

The dance ended, the crowd scattered, and Long Red began walking – alone -- back to her dorm building. Like a mental patient, I trailed about 15 yards behind, stalking her, watching her hips sway and her hair flutter in the breeze. This woman was a vision to me, a goddess. I was certain "Long Red" was "The One."

Virtually every day for the next four months, I'd visually scan the gatherings at Rutgers, looking for my dream girl, and would see her quite often in the cafeteria. As I stood staring from a safe distance, food tray in hand, she and her girlfriends would be seated together, laughing. During one of these stalker sessions, Long Red looked up from across the room, and caught me staring. She shot me a quizzical smile, as if to say, *"Who are you? Why don't you come over and talk to me?"* Almost dropping my tray, I scurried off in another direction.

My roommate, Fred, and most of the other guys on my dorm floor knew about my obsession. I'd get Long Red "sighting reports" -- what she was wearing, who she was with, etc. A dorm friend, Keith (the first openly "gay guy" I ever met,) was eventually able to learn that her first name was Meryl.

A few months into my freshman year, my mother became concerned about my mental health. She'd call on the dorm's payphone and would hear me fighting back tears. I told her I was in love with a girl I couldn't even talk to, and was thinking, quite often, about suicide. Realizing I was having a mental breakdown, my mother made an appointment for me to see a shrink during the upcoming Thanksgiving break period.

Dr. L. asked me to draw a house, a family, and a tree. He also asked me to draw Long Red. I thought he was an imbecile. We only had one session together. Never explaining to me that I had clinical depression, a MEDICAL ILLNESS that ran in my family, he simply told me to take some of his pills. "You'll feel better."

"Drugs? I don't do drugs. Drugs are for losers," I snapped. Dr. L.: "These pills will elevate your mood. You don't need to feel sad all the time. You should try them." Me: "Yeah, sure whatever." My parents filled the prescription, and I went back to college, tossing the pills away.

"Fuck that bullshit," I thought. "I don't need any fucking drugs. Drugs are for losers. I'm no drug addict." In the naivety of youth, I didn't understand the difference between drugs as medicine and drugs as recreational distractions.

Without question, this decision was the single biggest mistake I would ever make in my life.

****

While most of the guys in my dorm were, like me, total losers with women, two were incredible exceptions. Not only were these guys both unbelievably good looking, but they played guitars together beautifully, and sang like angels. Billy and Ronny were our heroes – our teenaged Gods – while their girlfriends were among the prettiest women in all of Rutgers.

One evening while Fred and I were studying in our room, Keith knocked on my door. "Long Red's upstairs at the coffee house. Billy and Ronny are playing. She's alone." I looked up, my heart racing. "Oh my God, is tonight the night you actually meet this mystery woman?" Fred scoffed. Keith: "Come on. You have to talk with her. Now!" My pals had to literally pry me out from my desk chair and lead me upstairs to our dorm's social gathering.

As the elevator doors opened, I saw candles everywhere, and heard Billy and Ronny performing. Keith had me sit with his friends, and subtly pointed out Long Red. She was sitting alone, next to a cement column a fair distance away, chewing gum, and swaying her head to the music. Once again, her eyes were closed. "This is your chance," my roommate encouraged. "She'll like you. Go for it." Keith: "We're right here for you. Nothing bad will happen. You need to do this. Tonight is your night."

A million thoughts raced through my mind: "What's my opening line? What on earth can I possibly say to the woman I've been obsessed with for the past six months?" I re-positioned myself on the floor about four feet from where she sat, pretending not to notice her. However, I could see from the corner of my eye that she was keeping tabs on me as well.

With each new song, I managed to forcefully glide my ass a bit closer to my dream girl. After perhaps six tunes, I was finally in a position just inches from her right shoulder. I was sweating -- what should I say? "What's your name?" No, too stupid. "I'm Danny." Who cares? "Got another piece of gum?" Not bad… that one could work. "I love your hair." Too forward. "These guitar players live on my floor." So what? What the fuck? The lines were swirling like cotton candy, constricting any iteration of normal thought.

"Do it for God's sake!" Keith had insisted just a few moments earlier. "This is it. You will meet Long Red right now. You will talk to her. You will have a conversation. She smiled at you once, remember? You CAN do this. You will do this NOW." I turned to my left. Long Red turned to face me. Now scant millimeters apart, our eyes locked.

"Urghhhahhhuhmmmm." Nothing. No words. No semblance of anything resembling the English language -- a low, guttural, laryngitis-type noise emanated from my constricted voicebox. (Medically, this condition is called Dysphonia.) Six months planning this moment and the best I could do was make a virtually inaudible sound that I didn't even recognize. I'd never heard it before.

Long Red furrowed her brow, stared into my face, and tilted her head to one side like the RCA Victor dog. I stared helplessly into her eyes. Still nothing. No words or other sounds. I was a helpless fucking loser, madly in love with a goddess. She was a "Carrot on a Stick."

Mercifully, Long Red stood after not too long, and walked away. My friends came up to me. "She's not your type anyway. I don't see what the big deal about her is," said Keith. "I couldn't do it. I just couldn't," I croaked.

My obsession with Long Red continued throughout the rest of my freshman year. I never once – ever -- spoke to her. Keith took it upon himself to tell her I was in love with her but was just incredibly shy. "Yeah, I know," Long Red told him. "It's too bad, because I think he's cute, and I like his long hair. But I'm looking for a boyfriend with some courage. Apparently, he doesn't meet that criteria."

Throughout the remainder of my freshman year of shit, I confided solely to my mother the details of my horrifically painful life. Realizing my sanity was at risk, she insisted that I transfer colleges the next year.

I'd visited my friend, Steve, during that year at the Berklee School of Music in Boston and had a fantastic time there.

My next stop that fall would be Boston University.

Chapter Nine

The Doppelganger (1977)

I attended Boston University from 1975-78, enrolled in their School of Public Communications (today known as the College of Communications). I loved the city of Boston, had some great experiences there and made two new friends for life -- my roommate Brad, and a fellow student named Julie (more about her in a later chapter.)

During my sophomore year at BU, Brad and I lived in an enormous dorm building with the address 700 Commonwealth Ave. Since so many kids lived inside there, the building's nickname was "the Zoo" -- with the numbers "700" matching the look of that word.

The following year, Brad and I moved into our own apartment which was directly across the street from the School of Communications, where we'd live until our graduations. I could stumble out of bed and get to class in three minutes or less.

During my senior year at BU, the oddest thing began to happen. I'd be walking along Commonwealth Avenue to or from classes, minding my own business, when female BU students would come up to me, reach out their arms to hold my arms, appear truly stunned, stare intensely into my face, and say, "Jeffrey?" I'd reply, "Excuse me?" "Jeffrey, right?" these girls would say. "Urh, augh, no, sorry… not Jeffrey," I'd respond, and once actually heard, "Are you sure?"

Am I SURE that my name ISN'T JEFFREY? Yeah, I'm pretty sure, lady!

This phenomenon happened at least a dozen times, but only during 1977 and only in the city of Boston.

As each of the female students who stopped me on the sidewalk was attractive, I should probably, in retrospect, have ADMITTED TO BEING JEFFREY just so I could get to know them!

Obviously, whoever Jeffrey was and whatever Jeffrey was doing, he was doing it quite well with the ladies! I never met him or tracked him down, but clearly, he and I are doppelgangers of each other.

I only wish I'd had Jeffrey's magical allure and charisma with those beautiful girls during that painfully shy period of my life.

Chapter Ten

The "6-1-7" Experience (1978)

Need to backtrack a hair…at the end of my freshman year of college at Rutgers, I went to a dentist appointment for a cleaning. My mother was with me. At the end of the appointment, my dentist took my mother and I aside and said, "Are you aware that your jaw is slightly malformed, Dan?" "Huh?" I replied. "What are you talking about?" my mother asked.

The dentist went on to explain that my lower jaw protruded about a quarter of an inch out in front of the teeth in my upper jaw. "As you get older, your bite is going to get worse and worse," the dentist explained. "You should have jaw reduction surgery."

To make a very long story short, my parents arranged for me to see an oral surgeon, who explained to us that yes, he could perform jaw reduction surgery on me – the operation would push back my lower teeth so that they would much better mesh with my uppers. "During the surgery, we will break your jawbone in two places, push it back, then wire all of your teeth closed so that your jawbone can mend. You won't be able to open your mouth for 12 weeks," the surgeon explained.

I almost fainted.

After a great deal of thought, consideration, and my father checking to see if the operation would be covered under his medical insurance plan (it would be,) it was decided that I would have the operation done a month following my college graduation from Boston University in May 1978.

The last possible day that I was going to be covered under my father's insurance policy was going to be on my 22nd birthday -- June 17, 1978. That became the date for the planned operation.

EVERY SINGLE DAY for three solid years -- 1975-1978 -- I worried HOW IN THE NAME OF HOLY FUCK was I going to be able to survive HAVING MY FUCKING MOUTH WIRED SHUT FOR 12 WEEKS? That seemed literally impossible to me -- not to mention the fact that this incessant worry greatly contributed to my continuing, untreated clinical depression.

I became something of a basket case during those three years. And while I was able to get excellent grades in school, this worry certainly did nothing to aid in my asking girls out for dates. (In retrospect, it would have been better if I had simply fallen down a flight of stairs after college graduation and had my jaw broken that way -- at least it would have occurred quickly and without years of pre-meditated worry.)

I graduated on time from BU in May 1978, with a Bachelor of Science Degree in Communications, then relocated back to the Jersey Shore. My parents had just split up a few months earlier, so it was decided that after my operation, I would spend the first few weeks at my dad's new apartment (which he called "the hovel,") and later move in with my mother into HER new apartment, following the sale of our family home, which she was awarded as a result of the divorce proceedings.

So now it's June 17, 1978 -- the morning of my 22nd birthday. I had not seen both of my parents in the same room at the same time for quite a while by that point, but they stood on either side of my hospital gurney as the nurses pushed me into the operating room. I remember holding each parent's hand on either side of the gurney and thinking that, if I was about to die, at least I'd said goodbye to them both in dramatic fashion.

I'm told my surgery took about five hours. When I awoke from the anesthesia, I was in the ICU, and my head was wrapped up in gauze like a mummy. The bandages completely encircled my head except for my eyes and my nostrils. I was on morphine, and I remember how wonderful that felt.

I glanced across the ICU room to see, directly opposite me, a large wall clock that prominently read: 6:17 pm.

That evening, my parents came to my bedside, along with our family's Rabbi. The expressions of horror on those three faces, I'll never forget. They later said I looked like I'd just been on the wrong side of an argument with Muhammed Ali, circa 1972.

That same night, my nurses wheeled my bed into my private hospital room. The room number? 617.

So, let's recap this now, shall we?

I was in ROOM 617 on 6/17 (June 17, 1978), having awakened from my surgery at 6:17 pm IN THE SAME HOSPITAL WHERE I HAD BEEN BORN EXACTLY twenty-two YEARS EARLIER TO THE DAY, ON June 17, 1956.

Miraculously, I survived the recovery period following my surgery -- which thankfully became ten weeks instead of the planned-for-12. I never lost a pound of weight -- I blended everything imaginable for those ten weeks: steaks, hamburgers, hot dogs, tuna fish, chicken, spaghetti and meatballs, and pizza, not to mention, of course, a million milk shakes.

The three years of worry and dread about the operation were FAR, FAR WORSE than the operation itself and its aftermath.

Since the operation, I have "seen" the numbers "6-1-7" COUNTLESS times at various moments of my life: at cash registers, at gasoline pumps, on billboard signs, and most notably on clocks. I can be extremely busy at work, or entranced while reading a good book, or taking a nap, or sleeping for a full night, and be suddenly and urgently "compelled" to stop what I'm doing, or to wake up from a dead sleep, and glance across the room to notice the time on any clock.

You guessed it, this ONLY happens to me when it's either 6:17 am or 6:17 pm.

And to wind up this section, during the few times I have played the Lottery, I have, of course, integrated the numbers 6 and 17 into my picks. I'd love to say they have been "winning" lucky numbers for me, but that certainly has NOT been the case.

Chapter Eleven

The Southern Woman's Voice (1978)

Once I had recovered from the horrors of my jaw surgery, my friend, Steve, and I decided -- a few months after our college graduations in 1978 -- to rent a house along the New Jersey Shore in Belmar and put together a new rock band. (We'd not played together since 1974.)

As we were both completely unemployed at the time, our fathers were kind enough to front our rent.

If I recall correctly, Steve and I were driving through Belmar one day when we saw a "For Rent" sign on the lawn of a large, over-100-year-old, green house one block west of the Atlantic Ocean. We knocked on the door, met the owner, and she gave us a tour of the beautiful, two-story, dark-wood-paneled building.

At one point, the phone in the kitchen rang, and the woman excused herself to go answer it. Steve and I were standing side by side in the living room, in front of the fireplace, at the time.

Suddenly, and from literally NOWHERE, Steve's head quickly jerked far up and to the right -- so far up his chin was pointing toward the ceiling. He then said in a DISTINCT, SOUTHERN WOMAN's VOICE: "I surely do hope y'all like this HOW-ISSSS!"

"Steve! What the FUCK was THAT?" I asked, stunned.

"I have NO IDEA what just happened!" was his equally shocked reply.

If I had to guess at an explanation for this tale, I'd say that Steve had become possessed for a few seconds by a previous female owner of that same house -- a woman who clearly had been raised in the American South.

Steve and I lived in that house from September 1978 to May 1979. We did put together a new rock band there called Quick, but it never took off. After our one and only failed gig, I realized I was not meant to be a rock and roll drummer as a profession.

I met Steve's cousin, Paul, during that time frame, and, through him, landed a job as an art director at a local area magazine called *The New Jersey Boater*. It was my first job in "media," as well as the first rung on my future career ladder.

Paul was older than we were and truly hilarious. He became my new best friend during 1979 & 1980.

Steve never gave up on his love of music and his guitar. Twenty years later, he would go on to launch The Cutting Room nightclub in Manhattan. Today a famous rock music venue, The Cutting Room was the "birthplace" – quite literally -- of the "Lady Gaga" character created by Stefani Germanotta in 2006.

Paul would reappear by my side in the future -- many years after his passing.

Chapter Twelve

The Fortune Teller (1979)

Right after the lease on the Belmar House I was sharing with Steve ended, I turned 23 and moved -- by myself -- a few miles north to Long Branch, New Jersey, a few blocks from the Atlantic Ocean. At that time, there was a terrific boardwalk nearby with rides, restaurants, and novelty stores. One summer day, I noticed a shop with a sign that read "Spiritual Advisor." Having never encountered such a place before, and on a whim, I entered. A heavy-set, middle-aged woman said she'd tell my fortune for $20. Although that was a chunk of change, I paid her. We sat, and I stuck out my hand. She stared at it for an uncomfortably long minute or so.

Slowly, she looked up, stared into my eyes, and spoke firmly: *"Many women are attracted to you. But something GOES WRONG with EACH ONE you meet,"* she declared.

Then leaning closer into me, she added, *"The women you desire somehow elude you -- they remain just beyond your reach."*

Her words were so completely accurate, I almost fell off my chair. How could this total stranger know my entire life story with females? I'd just walked into her shop at random!

For all these many years since, I've been kicking myself in the ass. I never asked her "WHY?" Why did the women I desired most always seem to elude me? Why did things always "go wrong" for me with the opposite sex?

This event was the first, hard-core affirmation I ever experienced that had NOT come from my own, first-hand experiences, that my "Past Life Curse with Women" theory truly did have a great deal of merit.

There would be hundreds of more affirmations along these lines, during the decades yet to come.

Chapter Thirteen

The "Voice" on the Bus (1980)

In early 1980, I'd had enough of my small-potatoes job as the art director for *The New Jersey Boater,* and during my week-long vacation, I secretly decided to spend those precious five days "pounding the pavement" in the Big Apple to pursue a job in communications. During that week, I fell in love with the wonders of Manhattan. As a kid, my family and I would occasionally visit relatives in Brooklyn, but now in my 20s, I got to experience New York City really for the first time…the smells, the excitement, the too-many-people. I was enthralled.

During my week of job-hunting in NYC, I had a few interviews with personnel agencies, but nothing came of them. On the last day of that week, I called a friend of mine, Stu, from Boston University, who was now working at a movie company called Columbia Pictures. (I knew absolutely NOTHING WHATSOEVER about the entertainment industry. I could barely have named the three major television networks back then.) He'd just been promoted to Publicist and told me his old job as an assistant publicist was available.

I arrived at Columbia Pictures within a half-hour. The building was a beautiful, older one on Fifth Avenue, just a few blocks south of Central Park and the Plaza Hotel. Stu introduced me to Abe K., a legendary motion picture promotions guy, who made Methuselah look like one of the Olsen twins. Abe had been in the movie business for about sixty years. He used to play golf with the Warner Brothers (the ACTUAL Warner Brothers,) escorted President Truman around Hollywood, and once dated Jane Russell. Looking up from his clutter-filled desk, his eyes caught mine. Abe: "You as good as Stuart?" Me: "Uh, I don't know, maybe, I hope so." (I had NO IDEA WHO these people were or what they even did. Movie Publicity and Promotion? What the heck did that even mean? No fucking idea.)

Abe: "Well, if Stuart likes you, then I guess I like you. When can you start?" Me: "Uh, uhm, erh, two weeks?" Abe: "You're hired."

Stu led me to personnel, shook my hand, and said, "Welcome to Columbia Pictures, Dan. You're in the movie business now!"

I began work at Columbia Pictures, and, ironically, had I not completely fouled things up with a New York girl I was dating a mere few weeks earlier named Emily, I could most likely have lived with her, just a few blocks north of my new job. Instead, I had to commute by bus from my apartment in Long Branch, N.J., into the Big City. I rode that horrendous bus for four hours a day (two hours each way,) five days a week, for four months. It was true hell.

I had no idea what I was doing at that job. Basically, Abe was in charge of "field promotions" in the New York City area. He was constantly coming up with zany ideas. To promote the crappy film *Used Cars* (1980), Abe brought in a huge trash bag filled with greasy spark plugs, fan belts, and engine parts, and plopped it onto my desk. He told me to gift wrap them, one at a time, along with free screening passes, and messenger them off to local area film critics as presents. There I was in a new suit and tie, gift wrapping disgusting, oily car parts, and tying them up in ribbons. "This is the movie business?" I asked myself.

To promote the film *The Hollywood Knights* (1980,) Abe had printed up little white short shorts, with flesh-color painted "ass cheeks" on the back. He asked me if I knew any beautiful young girls. I told him about some of the more recent Asbury Park boat show queens I'd met when I'd worked at the *New Jersey Boater Magazine.* He had me hire two of them to walk around Manhattan wearing these shorts, while handing out promotional materials for the film. I hired a gorgeous blonde boat show queen, and her friend, a sweet brunette, both from New Jersey, to come into NYC and walk around with me. They were good sports about wearing Abe's "Ass Shorts." Construction workers hanging from steel girders in unfinished skyscrapers wolf whistled after them.

During the time I worked at Columbia, the studio's biggest hit film was *The Blue Lagoon* (1980,) starring Brooke Shields, then aged 15. Brooke and her mother were constantly hanging out in the PR department. Brooke's mom was nicknamed "Terrible Teri" by my co-workers, all of whom were scared to death of her. But, for some reason, *Teri seemed to like me!* One day in a panic, Abe called me into his office. "Dan, I need you to babysit Brooke Shields and her mom. 'Terrible Teri' specifically asked if you could bring them up to the screening room, and tell them to run her movie, ok? They haven't seen the finished film yet." I took the two ladies upstairs to the beautiful private screening room at Columbia, where, together, the three of us watched *The Blue Lagoon*. It was the first time they had seen the film in its entirety.

In the elevator back down to the PR offices, I said: "Brooke, you were terrific. You are a very talented actress." Brooke: "You really liked it? I hate it. I thought it was embarrassing."

One day, while I was busy filing, with my back facing toward the front of my desk, I could sense the "presence" of someone powerful standing there in silence -- directly behind me. Brooke Shield's charisma was literally magnetic -- it "pulled" me to turn around quickly. She was young and sweet, modest, and electric.

I adored her.

****

Commuting by bus every day into Manhattan from the Jersey Shore was killing me. I began shaking and trembling, and my asthma (which I'd overcome from childhood,) was acting up by my constantly inhaling bus fumes. I felt exhausted and depressed. Although I was making good money, and was, technically speaking, in "showbiz," the effort was more than I could manage.

To exacerbate matters, there was a beautiful woman who rode the same bus with me each morning. My age perhaps, dirty blonde hair, expensive business suit, briefcase -- I imagined she was a lawyer. However, any time I glanced in her direction, she would deflect my gaze and look away. I never once was able to catch her eye.

On one of my last days of commuting into New York, this elusive woman was unable to find any other seat, so she sat down right next to me. Still painfully shy with women, I was unable to speak to her -- so we both sat in silence for the entire two-hour journey. As I glanced out my bus window, wondering how and why my personal "interactions" with women were so consistently out-of-whack, a VOICE SPOKE UNDO ME. It said into my right ear: "WRITE *CARROTS.*"

I swear to God this is true.

It took me a minute to realize that the voice wanted me to write down the stories of the elusive women in my life -- all the *Carrots* that I had long been unable to connect with in real life, since childhood. You know, *Carrots* -- like carrots on a stick, which tempt and taunt an ignorant mule to perform a lifetime of labor for absolutely no possibility of any gain.

****

One day, Abe handed me a package. "These are film trailers for Brooklyn. They need to be put on the truck, today. It's important, OK? Take them down to the mail room." I completely fucked this assignment up, and had the trailers *mailed* instead of *delivered* by rush messenger. The next day Abe got a screaming phone call from the producer of one of our films. The trailers weren't showing in Brooklyn. Abe called me to his office. "You put those trailers on the truck yesterday, right?" Me: "Yeah, Abe, of course. The mail truck." Abe's face fell. "The MAIL truck? I wanted you to put them on the SPECIAL DELIVERY truck! They had to be there by last night!! Are you trying to get me fired??" He was beyond pissed. He was incredulous -- the only time I'd ever seen him angry. He skulked away and closed the door in my face. I knew, at that moment, my job there was doomed.

I stayed at Columbia another three weeks after that disaster, but Abe barely spoke to me any longer. This screw up of mine, on top of my growing medical ailments, and the ice queen on the bus, were all conspiring against me. This job was much too hard for me to maintain. I simply couldn't do it. I asked the head of the PR department if she could please lay me off, so I could get unemployment benefits. Both she and Abe agreed.

At the end of my last day at Columbia Pictures, Abe said, "You're a good kid, Dan. You mean well. I'm sure you'll find something out there better suited to your personality." We shook hands. I left, feeling enormous relief, but, also, huge disappointment.

Had I blown my one big "show business" break? Honestly, I couldn't have cared less. All I could think about, on that final bus ride home from Manhattan that night, in July 1980, was that I needed to sleep for a week.

Then I needed to write *Carrots.*

Very long story short: I originally wrote *Carrots* as a romantic/fantasy movie screenplay on my mother's dining room table in late Summer 1980. For the first few years I lived in LA, I "shopped it around" to producers. Remarkably, Jerry Seinfeld's agent took it on for a few weeks as a special project in 1980. But ultimately nothing ever happened.

Believe it or not, in 2022, FORTY-TWO YEARS LATER, what I'd originally written as a terrible screenplay morphed into an actual book. Entitled *Carrots: True Confessions of a Hollywood Sex Addict,* my book was published by BearManor Media. I'm not sure if the version of *Carrots* I wound up authoring was the same work the voice on the bus had intended for me to produce originally.

But at least I obeyed its command and did – eventually -- fulfill that supernatural voice's utterly bizarre request.

Chapter Fourteen

The Manifestation of Hugh Hefner (1980 & 1984)

During my lunch hours while working in New York for Columbia Pictures during Spring/Summer 1980, I would usually grab a quick sandwich someplace and walk a few blocks north to Central Park, where I would sit on the same rock every single day. Once during that walk, I watched Peter Bogdanovich directing actor John Ritter and *Playboy* model Dorothy Stratten during the making of the film, *They All Laughed* (1980.) (Stratten was infamously murdered by her husband just a few months later.)

One day while sitting on my Central Park rock, I glanced to my right to see movie actress Jill Clayburgh smoking a joint. It was so cool sitting next to a two-time Oscar nominated performer. We exchanged glances and she extended her hand to me, offering me a hit. I took it, inhaled, and handed the jay back to her. We never said a word to each other; instead, we just smiled during the very brief experience of sharing a high together.

During that summer of '80, I was miserable with my job and the commute, not to mention the fact that my romantic life was nil. While sitting in Central Park, I would daydream about writing *Playboy* Magazine founder Hugh Hefner a letter, asking him for his advice on how I could go about meeting attractive women in Manhattan.

I composed it in my head and wondered if, by some miracle in life, the famed sex guru would read my letter, reach out to me, and somehow "rescue" me from my celibate life. Alas, I never did write or send that letter.

I include this anecdote here because EXACTLY FOUR YEARS LATER, I would meet Hugh Hefner, after I became the first-ever

Publicist for the *Playboy* Channel in West Hollywood, CA. And not only would I hang out with "Hef" several times, but I would spend many hours of my life at his infamous *Playboy* Mansion in Bel Air.

There, I was often surrounded by unbelievably beautiful -- and quite often naked -- *Playboy* Bunnies, Playmate Centerfold girls, and *Playboy* Models!

Of course, I'd just gotten married at the time, so my timing, once again, couldn't have been worse.

Chapter Fifteen

The Pre-Destined Meeting of My Wife, Including: The Song in the Sky, the Friday the 13th, the Message in My Forehead, and the Ring in the Mud (1978 & 1982)

This chapter comes in two parts: Part One took place during my last year of college in Boston; Part Two happened just 15 months after I moved to Los Angeles:

PART ONE (1978): During the Xmas break from my senior year of study at Boston University, I was back in New Jersey for the holidays. Steve and I spent most of our nights during that era at our favorite place on earth -- a nightclub called "The Royal Manor." The hottest chicks on the planet danced there, the drinks were incredibly strong, and the band, "Holme," was our own Beatles. The place simply worked -- "Disneyland for Young Adults," we called it. Steve had scored with girls there a number of times, and even I managed to briefly kiss a few on the dance floor occasionally. (Invariably, though, one of us, Steve or I, would usually end up getting too drunk, and puking his guts out in the bushes at the front entrance.)

The highlight of our Royal Manor era took place that New Year's Eve, 1978. I was the designated driver that night. I arrived at Steve's house, and his younger brother, Dean, greeted me: "We've got a problem." Steve was sick. He had a 102-degree fever and had just thrown up. His Mom: "Steve's not going anywhere tonight, boys. He needs to stay home." His Dad: "I don't want Stevie out tonight. He stays in bed." Steve was hyper animated and pissed. "No way! It's New Year's Eve! I'm not staying home! I'll stay in bed tomorrow. I'm going to the Manor with Danny." Resigned to his decision,

Steve's mother said, "Please Danny, be sure Steven doesn't die tonight."

Steve, Dean, and I zoomed off to the Manor, and once inside, downed our first round of Long Island iced teas. The women at the club that night were super-hot, with skintight pants, low cut tops, and open toed heels, even though it was like 29 degrees outside. Steve, coughing his ass off, was determined that nothing was gonna slow him down, here in our magical escape from reality.

The place was packed solid. It was hard to move after about 10 o'clock, which was kinda fun, because it meant grinding bodies up against every girl that passed by. Steve, Dean, and I were all getting some terrific looks from the girls we were squished up against, and one French kissed Steve outright, probably dying of pneumonia the next day. The band was playing songs we all loved -- the greatest hits from The Beatles, The Beach Boys, Boz Scaggs, The Stones, and Van Morrison.

Around 11:30 pm, the three of us were dancing with an assortment of girls in every direction. Balloons and confetti were omnipresent -- people blew noisemakers wildly. From the corner of my eye, I saw Steve chatting up a girl with long, perfectly straight, white-blonde hair. He approached me: "There's a cute girl over there -- her name is Kim. You should talk to her." Steve started coughing again and walked off toward the bathroom. The girl he'd mentioned stood in the middle of the dance floor alone, sipping a cocktail. Completely out of character, I walked up: "Hey Kim, I'm Danny. Wanna dance?" Almost in slow motion, Kim looked up from her drink and stared into my eyes. "How'd you know my name?" "Tonight's magic," I said, "Just go with it." So, we danced.

Midnight: The lead singer from Holme announced the countdown: "Ten, Nine, Eight, Seven…" Kim and I were making out like bandits. If we'd squeezed each other any tighter, I would have been standing behind her. Kim's tongue was so far into my mouth, I almost choked. Her hands all over my ass, she was grinding herself against me. "Six, Five, Four, Three…" I led Kim to the back part of the dance floor and pressed her up against a wall. The chemistry we had was undeniable and overwhelming. I felt like I'd found my life partner -- my missing link. "Two, One, Happy New Year!" Holme played "A Hard Day's Night," and the place erupted. A few girls threw bras into the air. Dean was at the opposite end of the dance floor kissing his partner. I motioned to him, "Where's Steve?" Dean indicated he was in the bathroom, heaving his guts out.

"Listen, my best friend is really sick. Can you stay here for a minute?" Kim: "Of course. I'm not going anywhere. I won't leave you, Danny." Her smile was electric -- really phenomenal. Dean and I retrieved poor Steve, who'd been sitting next to a toilet on the men's room floor. "You better not fucking die tonight, buddy, I promised your mother," I said. Dean and I each grabbed one of Steve's arms and lifted him. Approaching Kim, I said, "I have to get my pal home. Give me your phone number. I want to see you tomorrow." Jotting on a napkin with lipstick, she stuffed it into my pocket. Kim: "Tomorrow. I can't wait. Feel better Steve."

Steve was incoherent. Miraculously, Dean and I managed to get him back home, before any permanent brain damage from his fever -- or alcohol poisoning -- had set in. I arrived at my mother's place about two in the morning. (My father, who'd been having an illicit affair with my mom's best friend, had moved out of our family house a few months earlier.)

Completely wired, a million thoughts swirled around my noggin. And then I remembered… I had to fly back to Boston on January 2, so I could start my internship at a TV station on the third! Fuck! I'd just met this sexy blonde girl who wasn't repulsed by my presence, and I only had another 24 hours to see her again!

January 1, 1978, saw an incredible blizzard hit New Jersey -- I didn't care. Fuck snow. There was no way on Planet Earth I wasn't going to see Kim that day. No way. I called her, got her address, and told her I'd see her "soon."

After somehow convincing my mother that I was capable of driving her car through supernaturally tall snowbanks, I shot out the door, and my little adventure began. I would have had a solid hour of driving in normal weather, but with this bullshit snowstorm, who even knew? The trip was hell. The snow and ice were so compacted, I didn't "drive" that night, I "slid" my mother's car across the Garden State Parkway and the New Jersey Turnpike. It took me two and a half hours to get to Kim's house, with virtually no other car in sight.

I finally arrived, parked, and trudged through a snowdrift to reach Kim's house. The moon was full, the air was incredibly cold, and the street was silent. Christmas tree lights shone through the windows of pretty much every house on her block. She greeted me at the door, wearing a fluffy white sweater and jeans. Her long blonde hair and sky-blue eyes were a sight to behold. She greeted me with: "I didn't think you'd make it!" Me: "No big deal." Kim: "Come on in, I want you to meet my folks."

Kim led me inside. In the kitchen, her father, cigarette dangling from his lips, was frying an enormous mound of bacon in a skillet. It occurred to me that he looked EXACTLY like Lee Harvey Oswald! He shook my hand and seemed nice enough. I then met Kim's mother and brothers, all of whom were watching TV.

Kim decided we should take a walk, so we could be alone. Her Mom: "Are you two seriously going outside? You'll freeze to death." Kim: "I want to show Danny the stables. We'll be right back." The night air hit us hard, and our smoky breaths were everywhere. I held Kim's mitten-clad hand, and together we walked the crunchy street. The moonlight was intensely bright, and the icy road beneath our feet twinkled from the reflection of multi-colored Christmas lights strewn on houses throughout her neighborhood. We didn't talk.

And then, I heard music -- I LITERALLY heard the song "There's A Kind of Hush" by Herman's Hermits, playing in the sky above:

"There's a Kind of Hush, all over the world, tonight.

All over the world, you can hear the sound, of lovers in love." (I swear this is true.)

Kim led me to the next block, where we entered stables, pet some horses, and sat on bales of hay. We were shivering… violently. I leaned in, we kissed. The looks in our eyes were magnetic-- hypnotic. We were mesmerized by just the sight of each other. Shaking from the intense cold, but mesmerized.

"Kim, I can't wait to make love to you. I can't take it. I want to be alone with you so badly," I somehow managed to say. Kim: "I know. I want you too. But we can't. Not here, not now. It's too cold. And my father will be looking for me if we don't get back soon. Sorry." Me: "I can't believe I met you -- this amazing girl -- and I have to go back to Boston tomorrow." I explained my internship situation to her -- that I needed to complete it as a requirement of my graduation. Silence followed. Kim: "That's not fair. I don't want to be here without you."

During those fleeting moments, I also learned that Kim, who had just turned 20, was a junior nurse in a local area hospital, and that her last name was "Will."

We sat on the hay bales for maybe 15 minutes, tops. Our kissing was deeply passionate, but our noses were getting frostbite. We stood, and slowly walked back to her house in silence.

I took Kim to her front door and kissed her goodnight. Her younger brothers were watching through the window, laughing. "When can I see you again?" she asked. Me: "I'll be back at my mother's place for spring break. I promise, we'll be together in April." Kim: "I can't wait to make love to you either." She winked. One last kiss for Dannyboy, and back into mommy's car I went, no longer aware of the shivering. The feelings I had at that moment were the most powerful I'd ever felt in my life. Kim waved goodbye, blew me a kiss, and shut her door. I skidded off, "slip sliding" away, honestly not knowing if I'd ever see my little blonde girl friend again. I'd been at her place for less than an hour. It took me almost three hours more to get back home, lost in conflict, emotion, and a blasting defogger the entire way.

****

I began my internship at the Boston TV station on January 3, 1978, as scheduled. Other than working there on weeknights, I was completely alone. It was still Christmas break, and everyone else at B.U. was away. When I got home each night after midnight, I'd lay in bed like a lox, wide awake, hour after hour.

After a sleepless week, my phone rang at 3 am one early morning. Kim: "Danny, I haven't slept in days. I can't take it. I need to see you." Me: "I can't sleep either. I can't stop thinking about you." Kim had saved enough money (she was working at a local, N.J., hospital) to fly up to Boston. I was ecstatic. I'd been completely alone and now a GIRL was flying to see ME??

Unheard of.

That Friday afternoon, after buying some condoms for the first time in my life for myself, I took a subway to Boston Airport, arriving hours early. I waited until Kim's flight landed, and when she walked through the gate, I saw she was carrying daisies. I stood still, in awe of her. She practically leapt into my arms and kissed me. "These are for you," she said. Kim accompanied me to my internship that night, and moments after the newscast ended, we took a taxi (a rare luxury) back to my apartment. The minute we got inside, clothes flew off in every direction. We jumped into my bed, where we would remain for the next 12 hours, straight.

That day was highly memorable to me for three reasons:
1) Hubert Humphrey died.
2) I'd finally lost my virginity.
3) It was a Friday, the 13th.

Kim and I made a "whole lotta love" that day. We had sex nine times, to be exact! The next morning, Kim said, "My God! I never knew sex like that was even possible!" Me (the Pro): "I know, right?" All weekend, we trudged through the snowbanks of Boston, ate at some great restaurants, had lots of drinks, and enjoyed massive amounts of sex. The longer we were together, the less we talked. Our communication was instinctive -- words were not important. She stayed until that Tuesday morning, when I took her back to Logan Airport.

As we waited for her plane to board, I said, "Kim, I have something to tell you, you might not believe. I was a virgin until you got here." Her face said it all. "Are you kidding me? I had no idea. Wow! For a virgin, you sure knew what you were doing!" Me: "Well, I've had a tremendous amount of practice -- with myself." She kissed me forever. "I'll come see you again soon, OK? I promise." Me: "Bye, kiddo. You're the greatest."

I watched her board. Outside the airport, I waited until her plane took off, then watched as it hurtled deep into the sky. My lover was on that plane, I thought. The one woman on the planet who really, truly, cares about me is on that plane, and now she's gone. On the subway ride home, I cried.

Kim and I spoke by phone every night from that point on. Two weeks later, she came to visit again, and during that second weekend, I took her to the top of the Prudential Building (Boston's tallest structure,) to a romantic nightclub called the "Top of the Hub." Kim and I found an intimate place to sit and ordered white Russians. A small jazz trio was playing in the corner of the club. Kim: "Aren't you going to ask me to dance?"

Holding her in my arms, I slow danced for the very first time. The band played soft, smooth music. We were, by far, the youngest couple there. Then, the trio began to play an instrumental version of "You Light Up My Life," a huge hit song at the time.

Kim and I were slow dancing. The song was romantic. She kissed me. The moonlight was shining through the oversized windows. Candles lit the inside of the club. The drinks were hitting me, hard. Everything was coming together. I became overwhelmed with emotion. This was, without question, the most joyous, romantic and miraculous moment of my life.

"Kim. I love you."

She looked into my eyes. "Really? Wow… I love you too, Dannyboy."

I began to cry. Sob, actually. I began to sob, uncontrollably. "I have to sit down." Kim walked me over to our seats. "Here, you need this?" she asked, handing me a few cocktail napkins. I was a mess. I didn't know feelings like this were possible. She gently laughed. "Looks like I fell in love with a big ole girl, huh?" she mocked, as I wiped away tears. "I think it's sweet. I think you're sweet," she added.

That night, we made the best love, ever.

In early February, Kim flew to see me a third time. Another weekend of sightseeing, walking through snowdrifts, and eating at restaurants I couldn't afford. Not to mention that we were having sex for the ages. Sex from the Gods. This was the sex I'd been in desperate need of since I first discovered my penis in 1969.

At the end of our third weekend together in Boston, I brought Kim back to the airport. We said our passionate goodbyes, professing eternal love for each other. This time we both cried when she had to board. This was a wonderfully magical time for us. She blew me another kiss goodbye, and then, once again, Kim was gone.

Kim and I continued our nightly phone calls for a few days after her third visit. And then, suddenly, nothing. Must be my imagination, I thought. But after four consecutive nights of "no Kim," I phoned her. The conversation went something like this:

Me: "Hey Kim, how are you?"

Kim: "Danny… I was just thinking of you…"

Me: "Are you OK? You stopped calling."

Kim: "Yeah, uhm, I have to be honest with you about something. Totally and completely honest."

Me: "Of course… what did you do, rob a bank?"

Kim: Silence

Me: "Kim?"

Kim: "Having sex with you these past few weeks has made me so incredibly horny, I've been going out of my mind. I never knew sex could be so intense and addicting. Not having you around whenever I need it is killing me…"

Me: (Not getting her point) "Yeah?"

Kim: "Well, I need sex, Danny, I need it badly. You've really spoiled me. So, a few

nights ago, I went to the Royal Manor, and I met a guy. Billy. You'd like him."

Me: "Huh?"

Kim: "Yeah, so, I have to be honest with you. Billy took me to his place and we banged for a few hours. He made me cum a bunch of times. But you have to know this, Danny, I want you to know this…"

Me: "Huh?"

Kim: "Every time he made me orgasm, I was thinking about YOU!"

I felt sick to my stomach. Kim was fucking ANOTHER guy? She was so horny for ME that she was fucking ANOTHER GUY? What the fuck was THAT about? I didn't understand. I couldn't comprehend this betrayal. How could she possibly do this to me? I told her I loved her. She was the first girl I ever said "I love you" to. And now she's fucking BILLY?

Kim: "Danny, are you OK? Please, please understand. It's just so hard for me to be away from you. I want to see you again in a few weeks. But, in between, I need to screw Billy, too. Please tell me that's OK? I love you, Danny."

I felt like someone just told me my family had been killed in a car crash. The room was spinning -- my stomach churning. I'd been stabbed in the back by my lover, the only woman in the universe I had ever loved.

Me: "Uhhh, Kim, I can't deal with this right now. Sorry, I have to go." I hung up.

Although I was emotionally shattered, I surprised myself by never shedding a single tear for the end of this romance. I was deeply shocked and hurt by Kim's betrayal. But instead of crying, I internalized the pain and became a techno-drone, locking the hurt deep inside my mental strongbox, and tossing away the key. I felt completely removed from reality.

I never saw or heard from her again.

Much, much later, it occurred to me that during those magical weekends in Boston, I'd simply fallen in love with the idea of love itself. The blonde girl I knew as Kim was merely a transitory figure, one whose significance in the history of my life would not be revealed to me until …

****

PART TWO (1982): I'd relocated from New Jersey to Los Angeles in October 1980, at the suggestion of my father. It took me 15 months until I secured a fulltime job within the entertainment industry.

The most famous nightclub in LA during that era (the early '80s) was "Chippendales," which featured waitresses in lingerie for the men, and half-naked, bowtie clad, beefcake-muscled waiters for the women. My new, LA-roommate, Terry, and I went there on New Year's Eve, 1982, to try to score with some babes.

After just a short time inside, an attractive black girl approached Terry and started licking his ear. I went to pee and returned. "Danny, I'm gonna take Latonya home now. I'll catch you later." It wasn't even 11 o'clock and I'd been abandoned. I recalled my friend Steve's motto at "The Manor:" "If you're thinking too much, you're not drinking enough." I drank like a fish, then danced with at least a dozen girls in a row, striking out with each.

Shortly after midnight, I vowed to myself that the VERY NEXT GIRL who walked through the front door would be mine. An adorable, curly-haired blonde, dressed head to toe in white, entered at that moment. The SECOND I first saw her, I distinctly recall thinking, "She reminds me of ME." We danced for a few songs, the first being "In the Mood."

After our last dance, she said "Thanks," and walked away. "What's your name?" I shouted. "Kim."

Kim????????!!!!!!!!!!!!!!!!!

I lunged at her and grabbed her arm. "Kim, please don't leave me," I insisted. I escorted her to a quiet place at the back of the club and we talked. The music was loud, but over the din, I was able to glean that she was a junior nurse in a hospital and had just turned 20. *Now for those of you not yet keeping score*, let me clarify this.

Here I was:

** On a New Year's Eve, just around Midnight

** In a Nightclub

** With a Girl named Kim

** Blonde Hair

** Blue Eyes

** Just turned 20

** Who Worked as a Junior Nurse in a Hospital

** Whose Last Name included the Capital Letter "W" (Van Wagner)

I'd met my "first Kim" EXACTLY FOUR YEARS EARLIER TO THE HOUR. This new Kim had EXACTLY THE SAME FIRST NAME & LAST "W" INITIAL, was the SAME AGE and had the SAME PHYSICAL APPEARANCE and JOB and had met me under EXACTLY THE SAME CIRCUMSTANCES!

Instinctively, I knew that this new Kim -- or "Kim # 2" as I called her for a time, would become the next love of my life -- this was a blatantly obvious Karmic sign that our meeting had been PREDESTINED.

I began calling her a few days into the new year -- while she was always sweet on the phone, she kept telling me she had other plans. "I'll try to squeeze you into my schedule, but I just don't know when I can see you." I was *not* going to give up.

After countless phone calls, I wore her down, and Kim finally agreed to a date (although it was iffy there for a second, when I told her I didn't have a car.) Kim gallantly offered to drive us in her old Honda station wagon. On the night of our first date, she pulled up to my apartment, and when she got out of her car, I saw "stars" swirling about her head. They looked like special effects animation from a Walt Disney movie.

We had dinner at a cool place, then attended a taping of the ABC TV series *Taxi* (1978,) which was filmed before a live studio audience on the Paramount Studios lot. A few minutes into the taping (during which time John Belushi made a surprise appearance,) we began kissing. The people behind us weren't too thrilled -- a guy back there said, "Hey buddy, could you cool it?" "First date," I snapped back. (Belushi died six weeks later.)

On our second get together, we double-dated with friends, but afterward I couldn't reach her by phone for weeks. Finally managing a third date, we went to Grauman's Chinese Theater in Hollywood to see the new Francis Ford Coppola film, *One From the Heart* (1982.) It was Valentine's Day. We held hands during the film, and, while walking back to the car, started to kiss. "Why were you avoiding me these past weeks?" I asked. "I had to get rid of all the other guys who've been chasing after me," Kim replied. "I only want to be with you now."

After hot fudge sundaes, we went back to my place and made love for a few hours. Wonderful. She spent the night with me, and the next morning, I walked her to her car and watched her drive off. I looked up at the sun. "Thank you, God," I said, wiping away a tear.

****

My first job in the entertainment industry in Los Angeles was at the American Film Institute (AFI,) a renowned filmmaking college in Hollywood, in January 1982. The job was administrative assistant to the Managing Director of the college, which allowed me access to free movie passes. This came in handy for cheap dates with Kim.

When we weren't at the movies, I'd watch Kim rollerblade at Santa Monica beach. One weekend, she insisted I try to skate. We met her best friend, Suzanne, and I rented a pair of skates. The two girls slowly held my hands, "gliding" me along. Scared to death, I imagined falling down and breaking my new jaw. I gave up moments later.

About five months into our dating, she'd come to my apartment one morning to make breakfast. While setting the table, I quickly glanced up at Kim's face. In slow motion, she turned her head:

"WIFE"

At that second, I saw, in all capital letters, the word "WIFE," inside my OWN FOREHEAD, as bright as a sign in Times Square! I swear to God, this is true. It was there for maybe five-six seconds. Kim smiled. My heart skipped a beat. Then, I looked out the window, just as two large clouds parted high above, sending a sudden, brilliant beam of sunshine directly through the glass and onto my face.

"Okay, God, well, I guess that couldn't possibly have been any more obvious," I whispered out loud, to myself. I now knew what my next step would be.

I was gonna max out my very first credit card and buy Kim a diamond ring.

****

We had a picnic up in the Hollywood Hills. I'd placed the ring (without question the smallest diamond in the history of carbon,) in its tiny little box, underneath the blanket. All through lunch, my heart was racing. Finally, I said, "Hey, Kim, what's this?" and lifted the blanket. "*What is that*?" she asked, taken aback. I displayed the ring. Trembling: "Kim, I love you. Will you marry me?" Truly shocked, she stared at the ring, then into my face, then back at the ring. "Urh, ahm, ah… I don't know," she replied. Stunned silence filled the next 15 seconds. "Yes, OK, I'll marry you. Of course, I'll marry you."

Kim # 2 was going to be my wife!

I was now spending a great deal of time at Kim's house in Santa Monica, with her incredibly non-Jewish parents. There were plenty of home-cooked dinners there, and I lived the "Good ham, Grammy" scene from Woody Allen's classic *Annie Hall* (1977,) many, many times in real life. Their house also had a terrific pool and a sculptured garden in the backyard. I was 26, dating a pretty, young blonde in Southern California, hanging out with her wealthy parents in their swimming pool, and having all the sex I wanted with a girl I loved. For me, life couldn't get much better than this.

Kim's aunt was a wealthy property owner in Santa Monica. As an engagement gift, she offered to rent us a little house she owned for a minimal sum. (Legend had it that Charlie Chaplin's servants had once lived there.) Telling Terry was tough. In the two years we'd known each other, we'd virtually become brothers. Once he accepted the fact that I was now engaged, and that he and I would be "breaking up," he was gracious enough to even help schlep Kim's possessions and mine into the new place.

That first night, Kim and I made love on the lawn in front of the "Little House," the only time in my life -- ever, to this day -- I've had sex outdoors.

Unbeknownst to Kim or her mother, however, Kim's stepfather, a noted attorney with a prestigious law firm, had recently embezzled over a million dollars. After he was caught, Kim's parents were forced to sell their home, and the resulting animosity led to their divorce. Kim and her mother were extremely close back then and were deeply distraught over this turn of events.

Kim's friend Suzanne had begun attending Bible study classes at this time and had suggested to Kim that they attend these classes together. "Maybe God can help you get through this shitty time with your parents," I advised. One night that spring, I was reading a newspaper on the couch, when Kim returned home from Bible study. She stood frozen in the living room, zombie-like. "Hey, how was class tonight?" I asked. "You're Jewish!" Me: "Huh?" Kim: "You're Jewish... you don't believe in Jesus Christ." Me: "Kim, I've been

Jewish since the day we met. What are you talking about?" Kim: "Jews don't believe in Jesus Christ. Jews don't go to Heaven, they go to Hell. I can't marry you, Danny. You're going to Hell."

I scanned the room for Allen Funt's *Candid Camera* (1960.) What on Earth was she talking about? She was JUST realizing we were of different religions? So what if I didn't believe in Jesus Christ? We were in love! Kim and I had already made extensive wedding plans at this point, and had placed deposits on the venue, the DJ, the wedding rings, and the photographer, and had even made arrangements with both a Rabbi and a Minister!

Kim: "We can't get married. I'm sorry. Plus, I can't sleep with you anymore. You'll have to stay in the other room now." She walked off into our bedroom, and gently closed the door. I remained seated, newspaper in hand. "Terrific," I thought, "My father's gonna LOVE this one."

A friend of mine from AFI with a huge apartment near Downtown LA suggested I room with him. The place was dirt cheap, probably because it was located in a drug-infested neighborhood where sleazy hookers and pathetic Vietnamese women would literally squat in the gutter, pissing and shitting. Still, to me, it was a better option than the "Bible-Belt" house in which I'd suddenly become an unexpected prisoner.

After hearing about the "Jews go to Hell" thing, my father went ballistic. "Find another girlfriend!! This girl is NOT for you! She hates Jews?? We're Jews!!! You can't possibly think you have a future with her, do you?" I was remarkably confused. A few days later, while visiting Kim at the little house, her mother, Mary, said, "Kim, did you tell him the big news?" Kim: "Danny, my mother and I are moving to Boulder, Colorado. I'm gonna go back to college to finish my degree. But we should stay in touch."

STAY IN TOUCH?? The woman I was MEANT to MARRY, who'd broken my heart, told me that I was going to go to Hell because I didn't believe in Jesus Christ, and kicked me out of our "love nest," *was now moving states away*?? How much did that suck? I went silent. "I just hope you find what you're looking for, Kim. I'll miss you," I finally replied. We hugged, and I headed back to my new shithole apartment in silence and despair.

The summer that Kim left LA, I'd gotten a new job with, ironically, The *Playboy* Channel, *Playboy* Magazine's just launched cable TV network. I became the very first publicist there. When I started, I envisioned that the employees would be walking around naked. In fact, it was just a regular, 9-6 working environment with normal people, who just happened to be focused on all things "tits" and "ass."

****

After five months away, Kim rang. "I made a terrible mistake. I never should have moved here. My mother is driving me crazy, I hate school, and I'm over the whole 'Jesus' thing. I love you, I miss you, and I want to come home. Will you take me back?" This was the call I'd been hoping for. "Of course," I said. "I love you, too. Come back. We're meant to be together. God told me you're the girl I'm supposed to marry."

Kim lined up a job as a nursing aide at a major hospital in LA, and I helped her secure a new apartment. Back in LA by that New Year's Eve, we had our first real date in a very long time. However, as we were about to eat at a nice restaurant, Kim turned ghostly white and said, "Something's wrong. I don't feel well. We need to leave… we need to leave RIGHT NOW." She ran from the restaurant. Although I was starving to death, I got up, flagged the waiter, and asked, "My fiancé's really sick… what should I do about the check?" "Forget it. It's New Year's Eve. Go be with her," he kindly answered.

I took Kim back to her place. She lay in bed, shaking and crying. "What's wrong?" I asked. "I don't know… I just don't feel well, at all. I feel really, really sick." I spent that New Year's Eve sitting on the floor in Kim's new apartment beside her bed, holding her hand, and watching her sleep. It had been exactly two years since we'd met. She was back in LA, we were reunited, and we were still in love. But something very unusual was happening. I recalled a lunch her mother and I had had the year before. "Keep an eye on Kim's health for me, Dan," Mary said. "She had a lot of strange medical problems as a child, and I'm afraid that someday all that weirdness may come back." Was Kim's New Year's Eve "mystery illness" just the tip of the iceberg her mother had warned me about? Was I in way over my head?

****

When we'd first gotten engaged, Kim and I had originally planned a fairly elaborate wedding, since, at that time, her wealthy parents were still together. Now, 18 months later, we were completely on our own, financially. We decided to have a TINY wedding, outdoors, in Santa Barbara. We'd lined up a justice of the peace to officiate in the "sunken gardens," located in the backyard of the Santa Barbara Courthouse building. We only invited our immediate blood relatives and closest friends. The body count was 16 people, total.

October 28, 1984, saw a particularly beautiful, sunny day in Santa Barbara. All our guests had arrived on time, but Kim and I were nervous wrecks. I had a 1940s style tuxedo and felt like Clark Gable. Kim had a cute, white, lacey dress with gloves and a matching hat. It had rained the night before, so the ground was rather soggy, and the high heels of the women sank into the mud. Mere moments before the ceremony, I had a panic attack and a serious talk with myself: "Are you SURE about this? Is this really the woman you're supposed to be marrying, after her whole 'Jews in Hell' routine? What if 'Jesus Freak Kim' comes back? And what's going on with her health? Do you really know what the fuck you're doing, Dan?'"

With this tumorous mass of negativity swirling through my brain, the judge began the service. A ray of bright sunlight poked through some clouds just as the ceremony began, and I took that as a positive sign.

But when Kim handed me my ring, we were both so nervous, it fell into the mud, below. I looked down -- the ring looked up. My inner-panicked voice: "Oh my God! This relationship is doomed! My wedding ring just fell into the MUD! That can't possibly be a good sign! Oh, fuck!"

Regardless, I picked up the gold band, brushed it off, and placed it onto my own finger. Bada-bing, bada-boom, we were officially married.

After a lunch reception at the romantic El Encanto Hotel (which, remarkably, and much to my utter surprise, my father paid for,) our guests left to head back to LA. Kim and I said our goodbyes, and returned, emotionally drained, to our room. She immediately took off her dress, jumped into bed, and began shaking under the covers: "I feel sick," she said, shivering, "Really, really sick." Her facial color was a cross between yellow, green, and sky blue. I stood in front of her, still in my tuxedo, thinking, "Well, this should certainly be a sex marathon of a honeymoon."

It wasn't.

We remained in Santa Barbara for three relatively calm days. During the afternoons, we walked slowly along the beach, went window shopping on main street, and ate at a variety of restaurants. But as soon as we got back to LA, Kim's "I feel sick" situation got worse. Much worse. She crawled into bed at our new apartment (now in Hollywood,) where she would remain for the next four months, even missing my best friend Terry's wedding a few weeks after ours. Kim had low grade fevers, night sweats, uncontrollable shaking and trembling, dark black rings under her eyes, and a sore throat from hell. She looked really ill, and, on many days, could hardly make it from the bed to the bathroom. I managed to locate a doctor in Century City who specialized in what seemed to be a fairly new medical phenomenon among women at that time, Chronic Fatigue Syndrome (aka Epstein-Barr Syndrome.)

He told us, "Kim, you could be the poster child for CFS."

Finally, after many months in bed, Kim eventually felt better. She'd lost a bunch of weight and was now eating only healthy foods. One night, she told me she'd decided she no longer wanted to work "with sick people" as a junior nurse, but, instead, wanted to change her career path and become a travel agent. We took out a school loan, and she attended a nearby travel college. Within a few months, she got a job as a travel agent at a popular agency in West LA. I was ecstatic -- my wife, who I loved very much, was finally healthy, happy, and gainfully employed. This was major progress.

****

I wasn't making much money at the *Playboy* Channel, so through a friend, I met with the head of publicity for Columbia Pictures Television in Burbank. He told me that he needed a "male" publicist there, since he was surrounded by too many women. Before I knew it, I had a new job at twice my *Playboy* salary.

However, just a very short time later, Kim's back went out. She was brushing her teeth one morning, while getting ready for work. Hunched over the sink, her back made a loud, "gushing" noise, and Kim was suddenly shaped like a question mark. She started to scream. I couldn't straighten her up -- she could barely move. I called 911, and two men had to lift her onto a wooden plank and into their ambulance. The doctors weren't sure what was wrong.

Over the course of the next ten years, Kim would experience many, many more bodily malfunctions and maladies. These would include: Knee Surgery, Hemorrhoid Surgery, an Impacted Colon, Carpal Tunnel Surgery, numerous Back Spasms, a "Mimicked" Stroke, various Heart Palpitations, and severe sore throats. (I'm sure I've forgotten a few.)

One night, Kim's stomach "exploded." I rushed her to Cedars Sinai Hospital. Her gall bladder had ruptured, and she was in need of emergency surgery. In the ER around 3 am, we looked up to see a surprisingly well-preserved Zsa Zsa Gabor. She held Kim's hand. "DAH-link," she said, "You are much too young to be in here! Get well soon and go home. You need to be with your handsome husband." That was kinda cool.

In between doctors' offices, emergency rooms, surgeries, and ambulances, Kim and I had decided we wanted to try to have a child. In Summer 1987, Columbia Pictures had eliminated my department, so I next scored a new job at a top entertainment public relations agency, during which time I would become Jay Leno's West Coast publicist (occasionally hanging out with him, in his underwear, backstage at *The Tonight Show.)* When Kim's health allowed, she had evolved her work skills, and became an in-house travel agent with ABC Television (booking trips for the cast members of *Dynasty* (1981.) Between us, we were finally making some decent money. After a year of trying to conceive without success, Kim had a laparoscopy, to "blow out the dust" from her fallopian tubes. It worked. She got pregnant.

Our son, Jordan Isak Harary, was born on the morning of May 10, 1988. The greatest moment of my life.

Kim and I were madly in love with Jordan -- a great little kid. We found a new apartment near Sony Studios in Culver City and fixed up his room. It was the joy that parents everywhere, since the beginning of time, have experienced. Mine brought just one other thing, however. A complete and total end to my sex life. After Kim gave birth, I no longer saw her as a sexual being and lost all interest in her -- the whole classic "Madonna/Whore" syndrome, I suppose. She quit her job to raise our son. My job was overwhelming. We were exhausted.

****

My dad came to visit his new grandson, and later, while walking together on Venice Boardwalk, he asked me if I was happy. "I'm not sure," I replied, confessing doubts about the future of my marriage. "In that case, whatever you do," he strongly advised, "do NOT have another child."

John Lennon once said, "Life's what happens to you while you're busy making other plans."

Unbeknownst to me, I'd gotten Kim pregnant a few days before my father's talk. What makes this particular "seed planting" truly extraordinary was that it happened during one of the three times we had had sex that ENTIRE YEAR. I was panicked when I realized what I'd done and became extremely depressed. (Fortunately, this would become my daughter, Anjuli, the most wonderful 'mistake' of my life!)

When my son was just under two, I was offered a higher paying job at a much bigger entertainment PR firm. Although the owner was a renowned asshole, I took it, and quickly began attracting clients of my own to his agency. During this second pregnancy, Kim once again became extremely ill, and was, once again, bedridden for many weeks.

I was doing PR for a TV show called *The New Lassie* (1987) at the time, and the star of that series, Dee Wallace (best known as the mother from *E.T. - 1982)* became a good friend. Since she, herself, had had a terrible time conceiving, Dee sympathized with my wife's plight, and, at her own expense, sent an acupuncturist to Kim's bedside for therapeutic treatments. They worked, and my wife was able to get out of bed after not too long. Dee's act would be the nicest thing any Hollywood celebrity would ever do for me.

My daughter was born on April 10, 1990. Her name, Anjuli, is a Hindu Indian word that means "to give" as in "to give an offering to God." While she was completely healthy, Anjuli decided she had no interest in sleeping a full night through for TWO YEARS. Kim and I took turns feeding, changing, and rocking her, literally every single night, for two years. We were beyond exhausted. Kim's dark rings returned under her eyes. I was incredibly irritable. We loved our two kids to death, but this extended, "no sleep" thing was torture above and beyond the call of duty.

Kim's health remained shaky at best, while my prick-head boss was constantly sending me to New York, Nashville, New Orleans, San Francisco, Houston, Las Vegas or Miami for business. He couldn't have cared less about my tenuous family situation. Kim's elderly grandmother, Nana, moved in with us to help out. It was a family team effort, and it was actually working… until Kim's back went out, again.

I don't remember the exact circumstances (this period of my life was so horrific, I've managed to black most of it out,) but Kim returned to the hospital when my kids were three and one. However, this go-round, the doctors told us she'd need a serious operation on her vertebral discs.

Kim would remain in the hospital for nearly three months.

My boss kept throwing major projects at me, while my two little kids were fighting over their toys. Nana did her best to run the household, but the stress on her was more than she could handle.

One night after work, I came home to find an 84-year-old woman sobbing uncontrollably on the couch. "I can't do it anymore, Dan," Nana managed to say, in between body-heaving wails. "It's all too much. I'm an old woman… I can't do it… I just can't do this anymore." I held her and stared out the window, trying to be as encouraging as possible. We didn't have the money to hire a nanny. Nana was the only family member we had who was willing to pitch in.

During this dark era of my life, I used to sing a Bruce Springsteen song, out loud to myself, everyday: "But Now I'm Trapped, Oh Yeah, Baby… I'm Trapped, Oh YEAH, YEAH!" I'd become a walking zombie man. Almost no sleep. Working my balls off for a total shit boss. Two babies to keep safe. An ancient woman nearing a complete nervous breakdown. And a wife in the hospital who couldn't walk. Not to mention the fact that I had NOTHING resembling romance, sex, or passion, anywhere. The only relief I had from my misery were fleeting seconds of self-pleasure inside my private little storage closet in the garage.

There had to be more to life than this. I was convinced God couldn't possibly hate me this much.

After the three longest months of my life, Kim finally returned home, her back now in rather good shape. The kids were ecstatic to see her. Unfortunately, because I'm a selfish bastard, I'd bottled up a ton of anger and frustration, silently directing that rage squarely at Kim. While her medical problems were not her fault, I couldn't help thinking I simply needed to escape from them -- from her. I couldn't keep up with this massive amount of responsibility. I needed some female attention -- a female partner.

WHAT ABOUT MY NEEDS??? WHAT ABOUT ME???

****

With Kim home, things settled down for a bit. I took Jordan to pre-school each morning, while a nice Indian family down the street babysat for Anjuli. With her intermittent CFS, Kim still needed a great deal of rest, sleeping her afternoons away. She and I were civil to each other, but we didn't speak much... our relationship had become strictly platonic. Kim suggested we see a couples' therapist, and we did, maybe three times. All I recall of those sessions is that we talked about some of the small things we each did that annoyed the other. I played the good soldier, pretending our marriage was "pretty good." My lack of sexual interest in her was never once discussed.

During one of these sessions, I decided I wanted to retain my own therapist, and without telling Kim, arranged to do so. My private therapist was an older woman -- a hard-core Freudian type. During our first session, I gave her a big picture view of my life. Predictably, she told me my mother was essentially to blame for every problem I had.

But then, she asked me the million-dollar question: "Do you want to stay married?" Me: "Huh? What do you mean?" Dr. X: "It's an easy question. Do you want to remain married to your wife?" I thought for about 10 seconds, and then said out loud, "No, I don't," truly surprising myself with that answer. I was dead set against divorce, having seen how it devastated the lives of my parents and two younger brothers.

About a month later, a miracle happened. Kim approached me: "We need to get a divorce. You don't love me anymore, and I know that you need to be with other women. It's okay. The kids and I will move away and live on our own. My back is healed now, and I feel much better. It'll all work out just fine."

I was speechless. I would NEVER, EVER, in a million years, have made this suggestion. I would have been the "brave soldier" for the rest of my life, suffering in silence -- a robotron singing Bruce Springsteen's "Trapped" song to myself, and visiting my self-pleasuring closet every night until my death.

A line from "Trapped" goes: "I know someday soon that I will find the key." Here, now, my wife was offering me the key. The enormous question was: Should I take it? I broke down, sobbing. "Kim, I am so sorry," I wailed, hugging her tightly. "I never wanted this to happen. Can you forgive me?" Kim smiled. "It's okay, really, we'll be fine. You don't need to feel guilty. Our marriage is over. The kids and I need to go in a new direction. You didn't have that much sex before we met. So, go sew your wild oats. Go get that out of your system."

The physical pain that encapsulated my body at that moment was in direct conflict with my emotional jubilation. Kim was setting me free. Free to come and go as I pleased while not constantly having to rush to and from hospitals. Free to pursue sex wherever and whenever I wanted, and to find as many young, available, beautiful women as possible, so I could bang their brains out.

Without telling me, Kim had already rented a large house in Lancaster, about a two-hour drive from where we'd been living! When I looked at a map, I freaked out. This new place was FAR away, and I was stuck driving Kim's creaky and VERY OLD Honda. We retained a mediator, and divided our meager property, such as it was. The kids would live with her, but we'd retain joint custody.

I moved Kim and my kids to the Lancaster house one September weekend in 1992. When it finally came time for me to leave that Sunday night, I fell to my knees on the kitchen floor, sobbing. My son, 4, said, "Don't cry, Daddy… we like this new house." My two-year old daughter kissed me on the cheek: "I love you, daddy. Bye." They went off to play in their new, toy-filled bedroom.

I hugged Kim. "We'll be just fine out here, I promise," she assured me. "Go live your life."

Driving my 16-year-old, shit-box car back to LA from Lancaster in the pouring rain that night was the single most difficult thing I've EVER had to do in my life, to this day. I cried so hard, I couldn't see through the windshield, and strongly considered suicide by driving off the 14 Freeway and crashing into a canyon. Yet, I somehow made it back to my barren apartment, unscathed, the remnants of my past eleven years with Kim scattered everywhere.

A major era in my life was over. I knew that I loved my children with all my heart, and that I would always be there for them, no matter what. However, as I lay alone in bed that night, I had absolutely NO idea that hundreds of future "Carrots on a Stick" lay-in-wait for me, in my not-so-distant future.

PS: In addition to some of the supernatural moments described in this chapter, I also submit these troubling tales to you, my dear jury, as further evidence of the concrete existence of my "Past Life Curse" with the opposite sex.

Chapter Sixteen

The Magical Zit, Part Two (1985)

Just preceding and following my wedding to Kim, I held, as mentioned earlier, a fun position at the *Playboy* Channel as its first publicist. The job came with an enormous office, on the top floor of the *Playboy* building in West Hollywood. The view to my right was of the gorgeous mansions of the Hollywood Hills, while the view to my left was of gorgeous *Playboy* models with "hills" of their own. The *Playboy* Modeling Agency was directly across the hall, and for a guy who'd been addicted to masturbating to the naked girls in those very magazines for the previous 16 years, I was now in a position to actually meet these same babes in real life!

I was in charge of writing up TV show "blurbs" that were listed within television program guides, and also producing photographs to illustrate each of those TV shows. My boss never asked to clear my ideas in advance, and no one was around to supervise me.

Autonomous, I reigned like Hugh Hefner, Junior.

I was also in charge of designing much of the promotional *Playboy* Channel "swag"-- T-shirts, coffee mugs, baseball caps, etc. The models who would come and go across the hall became regular visitors to my office. Wearing skimpy, mini-outfits (nipples poking through) and cowboy-boots, long blonde hair flowing everywhere, they'd saddle up to me, cooing, "Oh, these new T-shirts are so sexy, Dan… can I have a few?" And really, who was I to say no?

One day, an extra voluptuous blonde Playmate walked right up to my desk and shook my hand. "Hey, I'm Lynda Weismeier… you're Dan? The other girls say you've got the coolest stuff." I was behind my desk. She leaned ALL THE WAY OVER from the front of my desk to shake my hand, purposely smushing her big, beautiful breasts against my desktop. "I know who you are, Lynda," I said, staring into her massive cleavage. "I've studied your photos many,

many times." Giggling, she then noticed behind me on the wall a photo of Kim and I, taken from a romantic trip a year earlier to the coast of Monterey. "Who's that?" she asked. "Oh, ah, uhm, that's Kim…my fiancé." "You're gonna get married? Why?" This perfect 10, clearly annoyed, was asking me WHY I wanted to marry Kim. "Because I love her?" I answered in question form. Lynda shrugged. "Too bad… we coulda had some fun. Okay, then, ciao." She split. And while nothing would ever happen between us, Lynda would continue unabashedly flirting with me for the next year.

So now, while I was surrounded in real life by the fantasy girls I'd grown up lusting for on a daily basis, I was simply not in a position to even consider asking one for a date without breaking my commitment to Kim.

Occasionally, I would produce photo sessions with bikini models at Mr. Hefner's legendary *Playboy* Mansion, and on more than one occasion, the man, himself, would wander around and watch the proceedings. Of course, he'd be in his red silk pajamas, smoking his pipe, drinking a Pepsi, and nodding his approval. I only ever spoke to him a few times, briefly, but the fact that I was hangin' with "Hef" at the *Playboy* Mansion, surrounded by remarkably beautiful girls, was an adolescent dream come true.

I was a kid in a candy store. But, since I'd sworn to myself that I would never cheat on Kim, I was more like a "diabetic" kid in that store.

During the weekdays while I was married to a very sick wife (late '84-early '85), I was spending hours and hours with the sexiest, most beautiful women in America, quite often while they were semi-clad or fully nude. Several of them would blatantly flirt with me, winking, rubbing my shoulders and laughing. My brain would scream: "YES, YES, HOW I WANT YOU!" while my heart would counter: "TOUCH JUST ONE OF THESE ANGELS, AND GOD WILL SMITE THEE DEAD."

This was the most dramatic "Carrots/Past Life Curse with Women" dilemma imaginable.

After many months in bed during early '85, Kim eventually felt better. She then attended "Travel College," where folks were trained on early computers to learn how to book trips for customers. Thereafter, she quickly secured a job as a travel agent at a popular agency in West LA.

A few weeks into this new job, Kim had to fly to Dallas for a few days of computer training with United Airlines. Concurrently, I'd just done a photo shoot with a different Kim --actually Kym Malin -- a recent *Playboy* centerfold girl. The shoot had to illustrate a *Playboy* TV show about Halloween, so I had Kym dress up with devil's horns in the tightest red bikini on the planet. She and I had chemistry -- scary chemistry. After bonding during our photo session, Kym would swing by my office to get T-shirts for her friends. She'd sit on the couch in my office, crossing and uncrossing her legs, brushing her thick, curly blonde hair, while staring at me. I'd be engaging her in wildly flirtatious banter. Invariably, my pissed-off wife would call: "So, which Playmate is in your office with you right now, Miss May? Miss June?" Somehow my wife instinctively knew when the most intrusive times were to phone me. EVERY SINGLE TIME!

One day while my wife Kim was on a plane to Dallas, Playmate Kym came into my office to invite me to a music industry party. "Sure, sounds fun," I said. Why shouldn't I go to a party with a hot girl? I thought. She gave me her address and asked that I pick her up. I arrived at Kym's apartment on Venice Beach, trembling. "What am I doing here?" I thought to myself.

She answered the door, a vision in a tight, black, cat suit. "I've been out in the sun all day… do I look OK?" she asked. My penis smiled. Her suntan was incredible -- she was "glowing." "You look great…amazing," I managed to say. Kym finished smoking a reefer. "Wanna hit?" "No thanks, I'm cool," I said, high just from the sight of her.

We got into my WIFE's car (her mom had bought Kim a brand-new Volvo with her divorce money,) and headed off to the party.

Kym immediately opened the sun, or more appropriately now, MOON-roof, and popped a cassette tape into the stereo. As I drove, we heard Sadé sing the hit song, "Smooth Operator":

"Smooth Operator. He's a Smooth Operator…"

And, as we all know, I am truly one of life's smoothest of operators.

Kym smiled, applied some lipstick, and then started "dancing" in her seat (she refused to buckle in,) swaying gently to the music. Her hair was so long, some of it went flying out through the moon-roof. I was on a date with a vision.

Now, the conflict in my head was overwhelming: "You have GOT to have sex with this girl. You can't possibly go the rest of your life without having been with a *Playboy* Magazine Centerfold! You will NEVER EVER get a better chance than tonight. Imagine telling all your friends back East you scored a Playmate!"

Other half of brain: "Are you fucking kidding me? You're MARRIED, you stupid fuck head. You took vows to stay true to your wife, to love only her. If you even touch this chick, God will kill you… he will fucking hunt you down and slay you." This LOUD argument eclipsed all other thoughts for hours.

At the party, Kym and I danced a bit, but mostly we just talked quietly, in the corner, where she told me about problems with a recent boyfriend. I don't think she enjoyed the drooling stares she was getting from every other guy there, and, quite frankly, I was pretty uncomfortable, also. We were at the party for maybe two hours, till she said "You wanna go?"

The wild and crazy blonde bombshell I'd driven from her house to the party had become, on the drive back, serene and mellow. "You OK?" I asked. She told me she'd been drinking and smoking dope that whole day and had been lying on the beach for so many hours that her skin was now "on fire." I felt her shoulder -- it was burning hot. She was crashing from a day-long high.

We arrived back at her apartment, and she quickly hopped out of the car. WHAT the FUCK do I do NOW?? These were the thoughts racing through my pea-brain:

** Tell her you need to use her bathroom. That gets you upstairs;

** Tell her you want to get high. That also gets you into her place;

** Walk her up to her front door, spin her around, and kiss her IMMEDIATELY. Do NOT think! Just DO!

** Kiss her BEFORE you even get near the entrance to the building!

We walked in silence to her front door. She unlocked it, took one step up, turned, and looked at me with a peculiar, quizzical expression. I was completely frozen. This was far beyond simple fear. I could not move, nor could I speak. This moment, here and now, made it look like I'd been George Clooney the time I sat next to "Long Red" at my college dorm.

A remarkably loud, inner-voice screamed: "IF YOU KISS THIS GIRL, GOD WILL NEVER FORGIVE YOU, EVER. YOU CAN NOT KISS HER. IT'S THE WRONG THING TO DO. YOU'RE MARRIED. YOU KNOW IT, AND I KNOW IT."

This freeze-frame scene went on far too long, and I realized, after about 20-seconds that I'd lost any chance of having a real moment. Then, thank God, she yawned. "I am so friggin' tired," she finally said. "Guess I'm off to sleep." "Good idea," I responded, "I had a lot of fun. Let's do it again sometime." Half-heartedly, I went in for a very quick kiss on the lips but got the cheek instead. We hugged. "Later, Dan," she said, walking up the stairs.

Back in my wife's car, I felt something weird on my forehead. I looked into the rearview mirror and realized that a ZIT the size of a CALZONE had appeared from literally nowhere and was now prominently displayed in the middle of my fucking forehead -- directly in between my eyebrows! This puss-filled ZIT had NOT been there just five minutes earlier! Was this God's way of

"Cock-Blocking" me? This repulsive ZIT from Hell clearly explained the rather odd look she had given me at her doorstep!

It was then that I recalled having gotten a surprise zit just seconds before my aborted "Seven Minutes in Heaven" with Bonnie at my first "boy/girl" party when I was 14, in 1970.

I took this new zit as a very strong sign: I was ABSOLUTELY NOT to pursue this fantasy girl any further!

Kym Malin and I remained friends inside my office at the *Playboy* Building afterwards, but I left that job a few months later.

I never saw or spoke to her again.

Chapter Seventeen

The Apparition Above My Son's Face (1988)

I took my wife, Kim, to the hospital on the morning of May 10, 1988, a date we'd pre-scheduled for a caesarian section for our son's arrival, as he was expected to be large. At the time, I was taking medication that made me especially queasy. When Kim's surgeon asked if I wanted to watch the birth of my son, my nausea became so intense, the hospital began "spinning" like I was drunk, and I almost fainted.

The doctor became adamant: *"Listen, pal, if you wanna see your kid being born, you better get your ass in here right now!"*

When the doctors pulled an enormous, amorphous, white "blob" out from Kim's spread-eagle abdomen and into the air, I asked, "What the hell is THAT?"

"THAT, my friend, is your SON," came the surgeon's snarky reply.

The second I looked into Jordan's face -- the FIRST SECOND I ever saw it -- I experienced an apparition, a glowing, "ghost-like" vision of the smiling face of my late Grandpa Joe (my father's father) "superimposed" over my new son. It was like Jordan was wearing a "Dead Grandpa Joe" mask.

I swear to God this is true.

I cut my son's umbilical cord, picked him up, held him aloft, and began sobbing, uncontrollably. "Thank you, God," I said. "Thank you for my son."

The nurse standing next to me began wiping away her tears as well.

Chapter Eighteen

The Miraculous Car Accident (1992)

When Kim and I got divorced, she moved to far-away Lancaster, where she rented a house, while I moved into a small apartment in Studio City. At the time, I was working in the Mid-Wilshire district of Los Angeles. Every Friday night, I'd leave my office at 6 pm, and then drive for nearly three hours to pick up my kids. By the time I arrived back at my new Studio City apartment with Jordan and Anjuli, it was about 11 pm.

I did this every single Friday night for five years. Missing none.

The massive amount of time it took me each weekend to get and return my kids was not my biggest problem, however. In 1992, the car I owned was Kim's old, 1976, Honda Civic station wagon, which had well over 200,000 miles on it. The car's clutch was unreliable, the brakes screeched, the steering wheel shook, and much of its sky-blue colored paint had been turned to rust by the sun.

That poor car simply needed to retire.

About two months after my divorce, I was driving to work one morning (to a job I detested) and was stopped at a red light. The divorce had wiped me out financially and I had no money. While I was at the light, I started thinking to myself, "How on Earth am I going to be able to see my kids every weekend, driving this ancient, piece of shit car? It will never make it! I need to win the lottery. It will take a miracle for me to somehow get a newer, better car."

Just then, the miracle I'd asked for actually happened.

Two cars collided directly in front of me. They had been travelling in opposite directions, each doing about 40 mph. They hit each other head on, hard, and then BOTH CARS BEGAN CAREENING HORIZONTALLY, DIRECTLY TOWARDS THE FRONT OF MY CAR!

I knew the cars were going to hit me. Time itself slowed down dramatically. I braced my hands against the steering wheel to prepare for the impact. When those two cars met mine, the crash crumpled up the hood of my car, and caused my body to shoot upwards. I smacked the top of my head against the roof of my car, hard, and saw stars. Fortunately, I broke no bones and was not bleeding.

When I got out of my car, I felt light-headed and a bit dizzy. I approached the people whose cars had directly collided, and saw a woman, about 60, staggering around, babbling to herself. She'd been the driver of the vehicle to my left. When I asked her if she was alright, she started screaming nonsense at me, and I could smell liquor on her breath.

I then approached a man about 30 sitting in his car at my right. His head was bleeding. I asked him if he was OK, and he said, "that lunatic, bitch, hit me." I replied, "I know. I saw the whole thing. She's drunk!"

The police arrived, took my name and information, and arranged for all three cars to be towed away. One cop took me to Cedars Sinai Hospital, where it was determined I had sustained a nice concussion.

A lawyer friend of mine helped me sue the drunk woman for the extensive damages to my vehicle, for my hospital bill, and for my physical and emotional pain and suffering.

A few weeks later, I received a check for $20,000. I bought myself a brand new, 1993, black Honda Accord LX. The first time I sat in the driver's seat, I felt like I was inside a Space Shuttle. The dashboard was comprised of dials, lights and gizmos that felt like they were from the future.

After it was delivered to my house, I drove that car for many hours all that night, all across the San Fernando Vally, to nowhere in particular. This wondrous, brand-new car had truly been a gift to me from above -- a miracle that would allow me to see my children without endangering their lives or my own.

It was the greatest supernatural gift I could possibly have been given, at that time.

Every time I drove that new car for the first few weeks, I cried.

Chapter Nineteen

The Second UFO (1996)

I bought my son a telescope for his eighth birthday in May 1996, and drove out to Lancaster to spend the weekend with him and my daughter.

On his birthday night, May 10, Jordan and I took turns looking through the new telescope which we'd set up in Kim's backyard. We spent time trying to identify various planets and astrological star clusters. It was a lovely bonding moment for us both.

I suppose around 9 pm on his birthday night I was about to collapse the device to bring it back inside Kim's house, when suddenly my son and I noticed a very bright, off-white colored, egg-shaped object at the far-right edge of the sky -- as far to our right as we could see. I realized that the light had begun moving -- traveling quickly in a straight line across the entire sky, from far right to the very far left of the sky. I said to my son, "Jordan, look! That's a satellite!"

Then, in rather dramatic fashion, the object STOPPED MOVING and remained in place for about thirty-seconds. I said, "Oh no! That satellite is going to fall to the Earth!"

The light then reversed its course, and quickly began moving once again, but this time from left to right, returning to its original point of origin at the very far right edge of the sky!

No meteor, comet, asteroid, shooting star, airplane, helicopter, missile, rocket or satellite could possibly have undertaken such a maneuver. The object we saw had clearly traveled against the laws of physics.

That egg-shaped light was clearly, without question, something extra ordinary.

I've since discussed this story with UFO Podcasters around the world, and learned that, since Kim's house in Lancaster was located not very far from Edwards Air Force Base, the object my son and I saw that night was most likely a military craft that had incorporated reverse-engineered alien technology into its guidance system.

Chapter Twenty

The Past-Life Curse: The Middle Years (1992-1997)

For about three weeks after my divorce, I sat on the floor of my tiny new apartment in Studio City, re-reading old love letters and poems Kim and I had written each other. We really had been in love in the early days, and I fought back many a tear.

A few months later, I realized it was time for me to "get back on the horse," and start dating. In those days, long before the advent of the Internet or online dating, the *Los Angeles Times* featured a weekly section of personal ads called "Dateline." I placed an ad: "Funny, witty and warm. SWM, 36, Studio City, seeking attractive, fun, and successful woman for love and romance. I've got dark brown hair, hazel bedroom eyes and a good build. Please respond to XYZ."

Within the first weeks, I received at least 30 responses from woman as far south as San Diego and as far north as Santa Barbara. I was amazed by how impactful my stupid, free little ad had been. I dated from that ad for the next several months, but as I had my kids every single weekend, I was only available for dating during "school" nights.

Unfortunately, the women I met from my *LA Times* ad weren't exactly the most desirable of partners:

** "Tessa the Hut": A self-professed "sexy redhead" who worked as a masseuse, and "gave the best massages in town" was the very first woman to answer my ad. Intrigued, I lined up a date for Chinese food. As I stood in front of the restaurant awaiting her arrival, one incredibly good-looking couple after the next walked past me. Arriving about 15 minutes late, an ENORMOUS woman with very short, cropped red hair, waddled up to me. "Danny?" she smiled.

"I'm Tessa." I quickly glanced at my car, thinking if I ran as fast as I possibly could, it might not be too embarrassing for either of us. "Yeah, I'm Danny." "Great, I'm starving,' said a woman who appeared to have already eaten Chinatown.

Tessa and I sat, ordered, and ate. Watching her devour a plate of spareribs, smearing sauce all over her massive lips and gums, was almost intolerable. I kept glancing at the other incredibly attractive couples gracing the place that night, while I sat with "Jabba the Hut." The check arrived. Tessa: "You wanna come back to my place? We can watch that funny, new TV show, 'STEIN-FIELD.' Have you seen it?"

After a long series of hems and haws, I managed the brilliant, "Uh, gee, Tessa, that's really nice of you, but, ah, uhm, I kinda have a pretty bad headache right now. Work was really a bitch today. Can I get a raincheck?" The look of disappointment on her face was remarkable. For a split second, I felt sorry for her. She leaned closer to me: "I PROMISE that you'll leave my house with a smile on your face!" she implored.

As horny as I was, I simply couldn't make this comprise with my penis. (I'd sooner have made love to an egg roll.) "Sorry, no, I just can't." We stood, I paid, and she kissed me goodbye on my cheek. I raced back to my apartment, as quickly as the laws of physics would allow.

** The Aerobics Chick: An aerobics instructor at my local health club suggested I ask her out. The next night, I stood at her front door and heard, "Be right down." As I waited on her stoop, I noticed a prominent "humming" sound but couldn't determine what it was. Then, the noise became louder and louder, until it overtook me. A hornet's nest about the size of a large football was suspended mere inches above my head. Thousands of hornets were swirling about. Panicked, I flew off the stoop and ran into the street. My date appeared. "Sorry," she said, "Probably should have warned ya about those guys."

Aerobics Chick and I went to a classy restaurant. "Tell me about your life," I began. "Well, I make my living as an aerobics teacher now, but I used to be an actress in soft porn. You've probably seen me nude in some films, not that Glenn was too crazy about that." "Glenn?" I asked. "Yeah, we broke up about two months ago. We lived together for a while, but I told him I didn't love him anymore and made him move out. He's got a really bad temper. Sometimes he even stalks me. He sits in his car outside my place when I'm out on a date, waiting." "How does he know when you're on a date?" I inquired. "Oh, I tell him. He's gotta learn that my life goes on without him. In fact, I even told him about you tonight." I gulped. "Are you serious? Is he dangerous?" AC: "Well, he confronted one of my dates once -- punched him in the nose. They settled out of court. He's a weightlifter, but, to me, he's really just a big pussy."

During my hours with this woman, I learned that she'd: been kidnapped by a man in a leather mask off a bus in Kansas (but was spared being raped because she was on her period;) been introduced to the joys of double-dong-dildo sex with women during an orgy in Miami; and was once picked up by a gorgeous redhead model in New York. "When that redhead orgasmed all over me, I clearly remember thinking, 'If I was a guy, I'd really be enjoying this right now,'" she recounted to me.

Sensing the mood was right, I bravely offered, "I have to admit, you're really turning me on," to which this same woman responded: "Oh, I am SO SORRY! That was not my intention. I just recently decided that I've been too sexually promiscuous for far too long! I took a vow of celibacy about two weeks ago. In fact, I don't even masturbate anymore."

For cinephiles: I'd just lived – in real life - the scene from the Woody Allen film *Play It Again, Sam* (1972), when Woody is sitting on a couch next to a woman who's telling him she's an incurable nymphomaniac. Woody makes a move to kiss her, and she starts to scream: "What kind of woman do you take me for?"

Fortunately, when I dropped my date off that night, neither Glenn, nor those five gazillion hornets, chose to kill me.

** The Laxative Queen: This well-built brunette and I decided to see a movie on our first date and met in the theatre lobby. Attractive, with glasses, she had a nice smile. We each bought a bag of popcorn and took our seats.

Inside for maybe two minutes, she said, "Oh, shit. I've got a piece of popcorn stuck back here, near my molars." She opened her mouth, wide, and pointed out the criminal kernel to me. "Can you see it?" she asked. Me: "Urgh, uhm, oh yeah… looks like it's in there pretty good." "Damn," she continued, "This happened to me once before. I flossed like crazy for days, but the thing wouldn't budge. Finally, my dentist had to operate on me, sticking all kinds of tools back there -- blood squirting everywhere, puss in my gums, you name it. A real mess."

I was queasy. I just wanted the damn movie to start. Suddenly, she placed her popcorn tub on my lap and said, "Hey, can you watch this for me? I gotta hit the can! I took a laxative about an hour ago, and it just 'kicked in.'"

Laxative Queen missed the first 15 minutes of our film. When she came back to her seat, she whispered, "Got that son-of-a-bitch piece of corn outta my face AND took a major dump! I feel like a new person. What a relief." She beamed at me, elated.

I was nauseated for days.

** The Sneezer: A cute, husky lady with long, dark blonde, curly hair and big boobs, "The Sneezer" met me at a local bar for a drink. A photographer, she and I happened to have a mutual friend. During our date, she kept staring at me. "Can I tell you a secret?" she asked. "Of course." "I saw a psychic the other day, and he told me that I would soon meet the man I was going to marry. His name would be 'Daniel.' Maybe it's YOU!"

Before I could even consider being flattered, she started to sneeze. Not once.

Not twice. Not three times.

My curly-haired date sneezed at least 40 times. So many times, in fact, that all other activity at the bar and in the adjacent restaurant came to a halt. The Maitre D' came to our table offering his aid, but there was really nothing anyone could do. Waiters, cocktail waitresses, and busboys stood at the ready, in case "The Sneezer," now turning shades of purple I'd never-before seen in a human being, passed out.

"I'm so sorry about this!" she'd gasp, in between overwhelming, explosive bursts. "This hasn't happened to me since I was a child!"

** The Ketchup Mommy: A tall, lanky redhead told me she only dated guys that loved kids. I arranged a date at a nearby deli. Arriving early on a beautiful Southern California evening, I got a table on the outside patio, and was excited about this new possibility. About 20-minutes late, my date arrived, dragging her son, 5-year-old Chester, behind her. "I am SO sorry!" she announced. "My babysitter flaked at the last minute, and I really wanted to meet you. I hope you don't mind?" This woman had a very sweet smile and I could tell her story was legit. "No problem," I said, "I have small kids of my own."

The woman and her son sat opposite me. She and I tried desperately to have a normal conversation, but little Chester was impersonating "Dennis the Menace," throwing forks to the ground, spilling ice water, and pulling his mother's hair. "He's not usually quite this rambunctious," she said. "I'll bet he's just a little angel back home, eh?" I snarked.

The waiter brought our pastrami sandwiches and French fries. Chester started screaming, "Ketchup mommy! I want KETCHUP! I need KETCHUP for my French fries!" Chester reached across the table and went to grab an open ketchup bottle sitting just in front of me. It shot out of his hand, and a ton of ketchup flew all over my brand new, expensive, brown leather jacket.

Incredulous, I looked into the eyes of my date, mid-pastrami bite. "Send me the bill," she sighed.

****

** Lynda was gorgeous. Older than me (40,) she was tall, with shoulder length blonde hair, killer green eyes, and a perfect figure. We met at a Thai food restaurant near her home in Woodland Hills. I was smitten the first second I saw her. She'd been married to a wealthy lawyer named Joel for many years, but he split unexpectedly. She also had a 21-year-old daughter living somewhere in Florida.

Lynda's eyes were as sad as she was beautiful. We covered a lot of ground during that first dinner date, and I realized she was the first person I opened up to, regarding the end of my marriage. "You're so green," Lynda said. "You need time to heal. I'm not sure you're ready to be dating anyone, just yet." I responded: "I was mourning the end of my marriage even when I was still married. The fact that I'm newly divorced doesn't change my being able to start a new relationship. I'm incredibly attracted to you, and I haven't felt this way about anyone in ages." "I'm hot, and you're just horny," she chuckled. "But you are kinda cute. Maybe I'll give you a shot."

We'd met in mid-November ('92,) and for the next six weeks straight, while almost inseparable, Lynda simply would NOT let me kiss her or sleep with her. "Be patient," she'd say when I made a move. "I'm not ready, and you're not ready. Please don't rush me." We went out to dinners and movies, holding hands like teenagers. She even gave me a sexy, 8X10 photo of her from her days as a model, and actually said, "Since we're not having sex, if you wanna pleasure yourself to my picture, that's okay with me. In fact, I'd be flattered."

With the Xmas and New Year's holidays fast approaching, Lynda was particularly sad because she hated to be alone. While I was going to spend Xmas with my kids, I told her I'd love to be with her on New Year's Eve. Much to my surprise, she said, "Let's do it! I'll cook you a fantastic dinner. You bring the wine. You've been really patient with me… maybe you'll even get lucky."

New Year's Eve: I entered Lynda's magnificent condo, courtesy of her wealthy ex-husband. She'd lit perhaps 30 white candles throughout the house -- a fire was roaring in the fireplace. This scene couldn't possibly have been any more romantic. In the kitchen, I spun Lynda around and tried to kiss her. "Uh-uhn, not yet. I'm not ready, sorry," she whispered. "Time to drink, then," I said aloud.

Lynda and I had a great dinner in her upstairs kitchen with the lights off. The luminescence from the downstairs candles penetrated the room. At the end of the meal, I couldn't stand the anticipation another second. I grabbed Lynda by the waist, pulled her into me, hard, and pushed her up against the kitchen wall. We started kissing wildly, tongues everywhere. My chest was hard against her gorgeous, perfect breasts. I was in heaven. This was the moment I'd imagined for weeks.

Just then, the motherfucking telephone rang.

"Don't answer that!" I implored. "Please do NOT answer that God damn phone!" My penis was throbbing. Lynda pried herself from my death grip. "I have to… it might be my daughter." She took the call, walking the long cord into the adjoining dining room. Moments later, she returned to the kitchen. "We've been invited to my friend Robbie's house for a party. You'll like him. I've gotta go get dressed. Can you clean up?"

I didn't want to go out! I had the perfect arrangement right there. Clearly left with no choice, I drove Lynda's brand-new Jeep Cherokee to the party, about 20 minutes away. We walked in, hand in hand, to her friend's place. There were about 30 people there, a few couples, and one or two very attractive women who seemed single. Robbie grabbed Lynda almost immediately and whisked her away. "Be right back," she winked, just as a striking brunette approached me: "Can you get me some champagne?" I wasn't sure what was happening, but this woman was cute. "Sure, why not."

During the course of the party, I got so drunk, I was guzzling champagne directly from the bottle, along with beers, martinis, and random, other, lipstick-stained drinks left scattered about the place. Some of the couples were smoking pot, and a few of the men were kissing other men (something I'd never seen before.)

A sexy brunette sat next to me on the couch, as we watched a pre-stroke-victim Dick Clark broadcast live from Times Square. Robbie and Lynda returned to the living room, laughing. Lynda walked directly toward the couch, saw the brunette, and brusquely said, "Outta the way, bitch, he's MY date." Lynda collapsed onto my lap, curled up into a fetal position. "She took a few Quaaludes. Don't worry, she always gets like this," Robbie informed me. Then, he smiled, grabbed the brunette's arm, and walked away.

I had the feeling that Lynda and Robbie had been lovers, or perhaps he was merely her drug connection, but couldn't be sure of either. I was so drunk, in fact, I couldn't even remember what digits the new year was gonna be. Dick Clark did his count-down and a few folks blew noisemakers.

Perhaps around 1:30 am, the party guests began to vanish. Lynda was still curled in my lap, snoring, and drooling onto my pants. Robbie tossed me some keys. "Dude, these are Lynda's. I think you better get her home." I froze. Me, drive a car, NOW? I was so fucking wasted, I couldn't see. How in the fuck was I gonna drive Lynda's brand new, beautiful car back to her place? Everyone knows the cops are out en masse on NY Eve, just waiting to bust drunk drivers. But Robbie, holding hands with the brunette, was insistent: "Seriously, guy, I need you two to leave my house. NOW!"

Somehow, I managed to rouse Lynda, slowly steering her near-comatose body by placing her arm around my neck. Slurring her words, I'm not sure she was speaking English. As drunk as I was, I still managed to tap into my inherent sense of responsibility and drove to Lynda's place safely, without getting arrested or killed. (I literally prayed to God OUT LOUD for help.) Back at her condo, we walked in silence to her living room. She went directly to her fireplace, placed a few fresh logs in there, and lit a fire. The depth of sadness and sorrow on her face overwhelmed me. I stood a few feet behind her, just watching in silence.

Lynda stood, turned, and looked right through me. As though a scene from a movie, she effortlessly stepped out of her clothes, laid down on the thick, beautiful white carpet, spread her legs, and motioned for me to have sex with her. The moment I'd been fantasizing about every second for the past six weeks had arrived. In a flash, I removed my clothes, and positioned myself on top of her. We resumed our make-out session from hours previous. She was, without question, one of the best kissers in the history of my life. I hadn't felt this turned on in years. I sucked her perfect breasts and stroked her long hair. "Do it. Stick it in me. I want it now!" she commanded.

I had a few condoms in my pocket, but my pants were across the room. I had a panic moment: "To stick it in, or not to stick it in? That is the question." I didn't want to lose any of this spontaneity, but I also didn't want another kid walking the planet. Confused, drunk, and beyond horny, I decided NOTHING was worth interrupting this magical moment for.

Lynda spread her legs wider apart and stared into my eyes. "Fuck me, JOEL! Do it NOW!" I was stunned. JOEL??!! Hearing the name of her ex-husband at that second was equivalent to taking the ANTIDOTE to Viagra. Here was a goddess, the woman of my dreams, begging me for sex. All systems were go. She was completely nude on the floor in front of a roaring fire. It was New Year's Eve, and we were both wasted out of our minds.

Realizing my moment had arrived ("Joel/Schmoel,") I got onto my knees, and positioned myself for intercourse. Just then, the "Carrots Curse" kicked in, big time, baby. I hadn't noticed, but my penis was completely and totally limp, 100% soft, numb, and devoid of all purpose.

It was, to borrow a phrase from Howard Stern, "the size of a mushroom cap."

Lynda looked into my face. "What's happening?" She was NOT happy. "Urh, ah, uhm, there seems to be a little problem down here," I whispered. Lynda glanced at "The Incredible Mr. Limpit," and said, ANGRILY, in a sentence that's haunted me for decades: "I'm

FINALLY ready to FUCK YOU, and you CAN'T EVEN DO IT?? JESUS FUCKING CHRIST, MAN!!"

COMPLETELY DISGUSTED, Lynda got off the floor, stormed upstairs into her bedroom, and slammed the door, HARD, aurally illustrating her rage. I remained seated on the living room floor, in front of the fire, naked and dejected for the rest of the night.

I had a "Man to Dick" talk: "All the times you've made me pleasure you, and THIS IS HOW YOU REPAY ME? You are a fucking piece of SHIT, do you know that, cock? A USELESS FUCKING APPENDAGE that just happens to be attached to my body. I HATE YOU. I hate you with ALL OF MY HEART. You should only burn in Hell for eternity."

The next morning, Lynda and I had a remarkably awkward goodbye session at her front door. I never saw her again.

****

I next joined the then-popular dating service called Great Expectations -- which I would soon rename "GRAVE Expectations." That's how I met Candy, to whom I was attracted immediately. At first sight, she reminded me of a younger version of actress Mary McDonnell from *Battlestar Gallactica* (2003.) She worked in the accounting division of a leading aerospace manufacturing company. Never married, Candy had beauty, charm, grace, and a terrific sense of humor. At the end of our first date, I hugged her goodbye, and asked if I could call her again. "You better," she said.

It was easy with Candy -- she didn't sit around and brood like Lynda. No regrets about ex-spouses, starring off into space, or drowning her sorrows with Quaaludes. Candy was just a great, honest, straight-forward woman, everything I'd been seeking. Toward the end of dinner on our third date, she leaned across the table, took hold of my hands, and said, "Let's forget about that movie. Let's go to Tower Records and buy some really great 'Fuck' music!" I was amazed. Here was a woman completely in command of her own sexuality, who simply wanted to get laid. Candy was the first woman I ever knew as horny as I was, and not the least bit embarrassed to admit it.

We bought a Kenny G. CD, and went to my little apartment, where we had sex all night long. It was fantastic. We were incredibly in tune with each others' bodies, and our orgasms were truly powerful.

Candy and I were smitten with each other. Having been separated from my wife at this point for six months, I'd not yet introduced my children to any other woman. "Let's take them to the beach," she suggested. My children connected with Candy instantly. We spent a long, wonderfully sunny day at Manhattan Beach. Candy wore a tight, black and white, one-piece swimsuit. Her body turned me on like crazy, in spite of her fake boobs, which bore the scars of eight botched, plastic surgery efforts.

Candy and I continued to deepen our connection. She was, without question, the most robust sex partner I'd ever had, up until that point.

Then came a big problem. I'd asked Candy what she wanted to do for her birthday. "Bring me to the sleaziest hotel you can find. I want you to ravage me. Tie me up, blindfold me, and fuck my brains out." We found a tiny place in a beach community, and checked in as "Mr. and Mrs." We went to our room upstairs.

"Don't turn on the lights. Just fuck me hard, right now," she demanded. I pushed Candy against the wall and we had amazing sex. Her orgasm was so powerful, she began panting. Hard. Too hard.

"Oh my God," she gasped. "I can't breathe." Candy turned sheet white, and her knees buckled. She collapsed. "Oh shit. I've literally fucked this woman to death," I thought. I lifted her off the floor and carried her onto the bed. "My medicine," she whispered, "Quick! My heart medicine. It's in my bag!" Panicked, I rummaged through her purse, and found a prescription bottle. Sweat poured down poor Candy's face as she downed a few pills. Still struggling to breathe, she looked into my eyes as if to say, "I am SO, SO SORRY about this! Please forgive me!"

Unfortunately, during this episode, I began flashing back to the countless times when my wife had suddenly become ill, or had fainted, or had been in overwhelming pain. I recalled having to call 911 for an ambulance, later spending hours (or days or one time, months) at her bedside, in various ERs and hospital rooms. While Candy's medication began kicking in, I'd already begun to mentally "un-couple" myself from her. I took a few steps back, stared at her stricken condition, and flipped my mental "kill switch" to the "off" position.

About an hour later, Candy's color returned, and she appeared normal again. She confessed that she had some kind of heart condition that, only rarely, flared up. She asked that I hold her while she slept. The next morning, I awoke to the sight of Candy giving me oral sex. Then, she looked up from under the covers, laughing.

"Good morning, Mr. Sunshine!" she said. This was the Candy I knew, the happy, confident, non-deathly girlfriend I'd just spend the past five months bonding with. "Feeling better now?" I asked. "I thought I was gonna lose you last night." Candy apologized profusely: "I haven't had an attack like that in years! It must be because you're such an amazing lover."

Candy and I had breakfast that morning, but instinctively, she must have known something was wrong. She kept looking into my eyes, but an imaginary sign over my head read: "Sorry, darling, you're a great girl, but I'm so outta here." I drove her back to the parking lot where she'd left her car. "Thanks for the wonderful birthday, Dannyboy," she said, "I love you." "Me, too, kiddo," I lied. Candy must have felt like she was kissing a ghost. The look on her face said, "Oh My God! I've LOST YOU, haven't I?" That look haunts me still.

Candy and I drove off, in separate cars, in separate directions. She waved "goodbye" to me as she split -- I can't recall if I waved back or not. Because I'm the world's biggest and most insensitive shithead, I never called lovely, wonderful Candy again. Of the hundreds of times I've fucked up relationships because of self-sabotage, this one remains particularly painful.

A line from a Steely Dan song, goes: "Well, you wouldn't even know a diamond if you held it in your hand." Poor, sweet Candy was, for me, one of those diamonds.

****

This story "looms large in my legend:" A very pretty blonde had agreed to meet me for dinner. We had a great time talking. Recently divorced, she had two kids who were with their dad that weekend, and just wanted to have "fun with a new guy." Afterward holding hands, we walked past a movie theatre, located just next door. "Let's see something," she said. We checked the marquee. The ONLY film that had a starting time that made sense to us at that moment was *Schindler's List* (1994) which had debuted that day.

"I want to see *Schindler's List,*" blondie said. "Are you kidding?" I responded. "Do you know what that film is about? Jews getting cooked in ovens. That is absolutely NOT a DATE movie! I'll take you to any other movie on the planet, but NOT *Schindler's List*!" "No, no, no," she insisted, "I really want to see that. I read about it… it sounds fascinating. Take me inside." "Are you SURE?" I asked again. "Yes."

We took our seats in the theatre and held hands. The SECOND the film began, my gal pal JUMPED INTO MY LAP, and began molesting me. She was kissing me hard, rubbing my chest and my crotch, and thrusting her terrific breasts against me. I was overwhelmed with both lust and guilt: Here I was, a Jew, watching a film about the Holocaust, in a movie theatre in Southern California, with a blonde Shiksa goddess who was practically raping me with my clothes on. Compared to my poor Jewish ancestors depicted on the screen, I felt my situation was morally reprehensible. Yet, there I was, making out with this sex-starved woman for the first 10-minutes of a movie I've yet to see in full.

After the film ended, we went back to her house, and continued our kissing session. Clothes flew across the room, and just when we were about to "go all the way," she began to cry. "No, no! Please don't! PLEASE DON'T!" she insisted, sobbing. I was on my knees on her couch--she was on her back, totally nude, legs spread wide. "I haven't had sex with a man other than my husband in 14 years. I changed my mind... I can't do it. PLEASE don't stick that thing inside of me," she begged.

My next move was thoughtful, tender and loving: "Ya got any LUBE at least?" I asked in disgust. She gave me a puzzled look: "Well, there's some baby lotion in the bathroom." Completely pissed-off, I insisted that this woman pleasure me with her hands. Afterwards, I split from her house, and because I'm such a patient, kind-hearted soul, ripped her phone number into shreds, tossing them out through my car window on my drive back home.

Now: The Best Part of this Story!

About three months after this event, the TV series *Seinfeld* (1989) had an episode in which Jerry Seinfeld takes a good-looking woman on a date to see *Schindler's List* in a movie theatre. I was watching this episode from my apartment, alone. Instead of watching their film, though, Jerry and his date start making out in their seats. This was a date that had happened to me IN REAL LIFE, just a few months previous! HOW ON EARTH did the creators and writers of *Seinfeld* know to re-create an event that had happened to ME? To this day, I am convinced that someone from the show (Larry David?) was sitting behind me in that movie theatre in Marina del Rey, on that very same February night in 1994! In fact, when I met him years later, *Seinfeld* co-star Jason Alexander (who portrayed George Costanza on that show) agreed with this theory of mine!

****

A very cute, young, and just slightly "meaty" blonde, Amy (who I'd met when she briefly worked at my same PR agency -- and who told me she had a major crush on me,) had been fired by that agency, and was next employed as a secretary at a very popular, "rock and roll" hotel on Sunset Blvd. Her apartment was just blocks from mine, and after our first dinner date, she invited me there. Inside, she took me by the hand, and walked me straight into her bedroom. We sat on her bed. She lit some candles and put on some music. "I really want to kiss you," she said, and we made out for a long time. It was really, really great, passionate and romantic. Fifteen years my junior, Amy made me feel like I was in high school.

"You're turning me on so much. I think we should have sex," I suggested. "Sure… do you have protection?" she asked. And, of course, being prepared at all times, I said, "No, but I wish I did." We stopped kissing. "Well, this sucks," she said. "We could go to a drugstore," I suggested. Amy: "Wait, I might have a condom in the bathroom." We went "exploring," and found, under the sink, a condom that had likely been stuck behind a drainpipe since the Carter Administration.

Back in Amy's bedroom, clothes came off, we got under the covers, and resumed our kissing session. Naked, her body was far sexier than I'd imagined. When we were ready to go all the way, I opened the condom packet. It burst into a mushroom cloud of dust. We looked at each other, laughing. "Next time," Amy said, "We'll be much better prepared."

Amy and I dated for the next five months. At the time, I was almost 38 and she was 23. Being with her made me feel young and strong and alive.

One night, Amy insisted that I watch her "favorite movie ever," an old Nicholas Cage film called *Vampire's Kiss* (1989). We watched that film on VHS (this was the pre-DVD era,) sitting naked on my living room floor under a blanket, eating cherries and drinking wine. Amy fell asleep on my shoulder. I picked her up, carried her into my bed, tucked her in, and watched her sleep. It was one of the most romantic moments of my life.

Sex with Amy was fun, lighthearted and pressure free. She had orgasms easily, so making her cum was never a chore. One time she gave me a terrific blowjob, and I orgasmed in a matter of minutes. In a childlike voice, she innocently remarked: "Gee, guys really seem to like that, don't they?" I adored her.

My birthday was fast approaching, and we'd planned a romantic evening to mark the occasion. However, I awoke that morning and couldn't stop swallowing. I went to a doctor. He said my uvula (that little "punching bag" thing in the back of the throat,) was inflamed, infected and enormous and "should probably be removed VERY soon." He gave me two injections, which made me feel incredibly nauseous and irritable.

Back at work a few hours later, someone called out: "Hey everybody! OJ's on the run!" My 38th birthday was the day OJ Simpson decided to elude the Los Angeles police department on national television. Work stopped for us all, as we watched the proceedings with mind-numbing fascination.

That night, I picked Amy up, and we went to a candlelit restaurant. I handed her flowers, and we sat in the restaurant's backyard patio, where TV screens replayed the OJ chase scene, ad infinitum. "You brought ME flowers on YOUR birthday?" she said. "That is without a doubt the most romantic thing any guy has ever done for me." We kissed. Amy was dressed to kill in a black sexy dress that showed off her cleavage. She was all over me, and only wanted to show me a good time. But, between the shots I'd gotten that morning, and the confusion surrounding the OJ debacle, I felt so sick and confused, it was all I could do not to throw up during dinner.

I drove Amy home. We sat in the car. "Can you sleep over?" she asked in her little girl voice. As tempting as that offer was, I thought I was going to faint. "Amy, I'd love to spend the night with you, but I feel so shitty right now, I just have to go home. I'm really sorry." The look on her face was profound. "Are you sure?" she said. (All the times in my life I'd waited for moments like this one. Here it was, and I couldn't do anything about it.) "Yeah, sorry, I just don't feel well."

Home alone, I took some Motrin, and sat up in bed, watching the news. There was OJ, once again, driving the LA freeways, as people held up signs cheering on a psychotic butcher. The day had been such an extraordinarily confusing mess. The phone rang. "You okay?" Amy asked. "I feel like total shit," I said. "You want me to come over there and make you feel better? I miss you." Lost in depression, I said, "I really appreciate that. But no, not tonight. Sorry. I just can't."

At work the next day, I told my close friend Peter (a fellow publicist at my agency) about my birthday date, then confessed: "I think I'm in love with Amy." My buddy encouraged me to share that news with her as soon as possible. I drove to the hotel where she worked and called Amy from a phone in the lobby. "I need to speak with you right now. It's important. Can you come downstairs?" Amy: "I'm kinda busy... but I'll meet you in the bar in a few minutes."

"What's wrong?" Amy asked, as she sat opposite me. I held her hands and stared deep into her eyes. "I've made a lot of mistakes with other women in my life, Amy," I said slowly, "But I really don't want to make another one with you. I've fallen in love with you, Amy... I love you, and I just wanted you to know how I feel."

The look on Amy's face could only be described as abject terror. She stood so quickly her chair shot backwards behind her about four feet. "Oh, my God!" she cried. "Are you kidding me? I can't believe you just said that! What were you thinking??" I had no idea what was happening.

And then, a truly classic "Carrots" line: "If I fell in love with YOU, I wouldn't have any love left over for MY MOTHER!"

Pale and shaking, Amy turned and ran away. Literally. I sat there, looking around the room once again for Allen Funt. "Huh?" Even the bartender shot me a look of incredulity.

Anyone I've ever told the "Amy Story" to has found it simply remarkable. Common responses: "Never heard anything like it;" "Really? She's a freak," and even, "Tell her to marry her mommy."

Although we went out to a few movies "as friends" afterward, Amy and I never dated again. She tried to explain that after her father had died prematurely when she was quite young, she'd promised her mother she wouldn't fall in love with any guy until after she turned 30.

"Nothing personal, Danny," she offered. "It's just a commitment I made to my mother a long time ago. After all, a promise is a promise."

If anyone out there can figure this one out, please let me know.

****

A week before my 40th birthday, I'd had a profound session with a psychiatrist, who told me I was like "a diabetic living his whole life without insulin." He put me on Prozac, and my 25 years of undiagnosed clinical depression vanished rather quickly!

Three months later, in my new, Prozac-laced body, I was able to launch my own PR business, Asbury Communications, marking the most exciting era of my professional life. For 25 years, I'd been an employed "captive," having held a procession of demeaning jobs since the age of 15. Now, overnight, I was the owner of a corporation. I hired four fellow publicists and two assistants and also lined up an accountant, a lawyer, and a tax specialist. My company was housed inside a bungalow, just a few blocks south of the famed Hollywood Sign. My diverse range of clients created digital and special effects, animated TV shows, designed theme parks, produced music videos and TV commercials, wrote music for feature films and TV shows, designed broadcast graphics for CBS, ABC, Disney, and HBO, presented live theater shows, and were launching film festivals and various charity events.

The instant success of my new company was overwhelming. I was being pulled in three hundred different directions at once, while concurrently learning how to use a computer for the first time. I had no idea what it meant to "go online," "Google something," or how to send an "E-mail." I had to keep pinching myself to ensure I wasn't dreaming.

Shortly after hanging my own shingle, I was invited to a private party, an event marking the first social occasion I'd attended since the miracle of Prozac changed my life. I danced with a number of women, and realized I was smiling. Feeling elated after a few green apple martinis, the last woman I danced with that night was Ellen. About my age, Ellen had shoulder-length, dark brown hair, a very sensual face, and a slim figure. She told me she was a professional photographer who also had her own ceramics business. After we met, we stood outside on a fire escape, exchanging phone numbers.

Ellen and I began to date. I was in a "happy place" for the first time in my adult life and felt ready to commit to an exciting new relationship. Going out for dinners and movies, we'd return to her West Hollywood apartment, where we would tenderly make out. But we weren't having sex. At the end of our fourth date, during coffee, I asked her, "So, um, err, Ellen, do you happen to like sex, by any chance?" Deadly serious, she replied, "I LOVE sex. You have no idea how much. But, I'm almost 40. So, if I happen to get pregnant, ABORTION IS NOT AN OPTION!" She was adamant. "Well, I suppose I could use two condoms at the same time," I joked. "You don't have to over-react. But just know that if you get me pregnant, I'm gonna have your baby, and you're gonna have to deal with the consequences. Still wanna screw me?"

For the next four months, Ellen and I barely got out of bed. Our first few attempts at sex were unbelievably awkward. I would accidentally pull her hair, or elbow her in the eye, while she would pull my weiner too hard, or inadvertently knee me in the groin. "We suck at this!" I said. "I know. This is gonna take some serious practice," Ellen answered. After perhaps our fifth go-round, synchronicity kicked-in, and our love making became extraordinarily powerful, lusty, and fun.

When we had sex in her apartment, Ellen liked to keep her bedroom windows open for the breeze, since we both became overheated. Each time she would orgasm, she'd scream, "No! No! No! Oh my God, NO!" very loudly. Since this was only two years after O.J. Simpson had decapitated his wife, I often imagined that Ellen's neighbors would call 911, police would come crashing through the door, and I'd be arrested for murder.

Ellen and I developed a powerful sexual chemistry. I'd be at work, and she'd call to say, "Come home RIGHT NOW. I'm HORNY!" Only Candy, years earlier, had been as desirous of me. Ellen and I double-dated with friends, went dancing, and had quiet, candlelit evenings together. She was a classy woman, confident, talented and successful in her own right.

Unfortunately, this relationship was to be short-lived for two main reasons:

** The nightly phone calls: Each night, I would call my ex-wife to ask how the children were doing. While I was on the phone, Ellen would shoot me a look to kill. "Why don't you just get back together with HER?" she'd shout in a clearly jealous rage. She'd then storm out of the apartment, slam the door, and go for a run, returning hours later.

** The inappropriate remark: In clothes, Ellen had a fine figure. Naked, her breasts sagged against her body like flap jacks. One night after sex, I happened to lift them up. "Ever think about having a boob job?" I innocently asked. Ellen became furious. "I would NEVER butcher my body like that!" she screamed. "If you don't like my tits, you don't have to fuck me anymore!"

A few nights later after work, I was greeted by Ellen at her door: "I think we're done. We just don't have a future. We need to go our separate ways. I thought maybe I was gonna marry you. But I can see now you're not the guy I was looking for."

I was hurt, but not terribly surprised. I liked Ellen a lot and had solid feelings for her. I also knew I'd never marry her, because her rage could surge at the drop of a hat. In silence, I packed the few things of mine I kept at her place and left.

Ellen got married shortly thereafter. I never saw her again.

****

My friend Ray, a noted Hollywood journalist and author, called. "Hey Dan," he said, "I've got a girl for you." Both recently divorced men with kids, Ray and I had bonded a few years previous, discussing the hazards of dating in Hollywood. My workload was mind-boggling, but, ever on the prowl for a potential girlfriend, I said, "Okay, I've got three minutes. Tell me about her."

Sharon was a publicist for a popular children's TV series. Ray informed me she had a "killer body, nice, red hair, and a great, outgoing personality." For our first date, I met Sharon at my favorite Mexican food restaurant in Beverly Hills. She was tall and striking, had a great smile, and intrigued me immediately. We had a quiet dinner and drinks, talking mostly about the PR business in Hollywood.

After dinner, we walked a few blocks, and wound up at a coffee and pastry shop for dessert. I suddenly became overwhelmed with a desire to kiss her and did so. She responded. We kissed for a short while. "Where did that come from?" she asked. "I have no idea. I'm sorry. It was just something I *had* to do. I couldn't help it," I whispered.

("Pre-Prozac" me would never have made such a move.)

I walked Sharon back to her car, parked a few blocks away. While stopped at a cross-walk, I began shaking, almost violently, from head to toe. "What's going on?" Sharon asked. Me: "I have absolutely no idea… this has never happened to me before in my life. I think we might be onto something here."

For the next full year, exactly, Sharon and I had the most powerful, passionate, and troubled relationship I've ever had with any woman. I came to believe Sharon was the love of my life. My soulmate. The woman destined to become my second wife. Unfortunately, the circumstances of our lives never fully gelled, and, quite frankly, we just couldn't get our shit together.

The first few weeks Sharon and I dated were magical. We had so much fun cooking dinner for each other, going to the movies, drinking, partying with friends, and or just watching TV. On our fourth date, I wrote her a song (I'd bought myself a guitar) and sang it for her at her apartment:

"When I look into your eyes… Just imagine my surprise.

I have waited oh, so long… For someone to inspire a song.

Chorus: It's in your eyes. In your eyes. You're my girl. It's in your eyes."

Flattered, Sharon initiated sex for the first time. After that night, we made love fairly often, and the sex was fun, but she seemed distant and removed from the action. Eventually, she confessed that she could only orgasm if she got stoned first -- I didn't mind.

"I need your help," Sharon called one Saturday afternoon. "I'm painting my bedroom and can't do it alone." We removed the furniture from her bedroom and began painting the walls with extended roller brushes. Alanis Morrisette's CD "Jagged Little Pill" had been recently released, and Sharon was blasting it. As we painted, we accidentally splashed the blood red paint all over both the drop cloth and ourselves. We laughed so hard, we fell to the floor, and made love, rolling around in splotches of that dark liquid.

This was another of the most romantic moments of my life.

****

My mother came to LA for Thanksgiving. Sharon spent hours in the kitchen, while concurrently holding a very long conversation with my mom. My kids and I were playing board games on the living room floor, not far away. "Danny, come here a minute, I want to talk with you," my mother said. The two of us left the apartment and took a short walk outside. "This is THE girl for you!" my mother shrilled into my face. "She's beautiful, smart, and she loves you. So, I just want to say…" My mother got about two inches from my face and pointed her finger up, and almost into, my nose: "IF YOU FUCK THIS ONE UP, I'LL FUCKING KILL YOU!"

The woman had a way with words.

Sharon presented the turkey feast, then began to cry. She dashed into my bedroom and shut the door. Hours later, she emerged, after my kids and mom were gone. She told me that when she was seven, her parents had had a huge fight. Thanksgiving was the same day her father left her family behind, traumatizing her for life.

One night, Sharon invited my kids and I to her place for dinner. As a child, my son was an incredibly fussy eater, and would only eat hamburgers, ravioli, or submarine sandwiches. Sharon had prepared some kind of lamb, something he would not have eaten in two hundred years. "Daddy, what is this?" Jordan asked, with an expression of utter disgust. "It's lamb," Sharon snorted. "Eat it… it's good for you." My son: "No, I don't like this, Daddy, it smells funny." Then, looking up at her heartbroken face, he said, "Sharon, do you have any cheeseburgers?"

Holding a glass of wine, Sharon left the table, went into her bedroom, and quietly closed the door. The tug of war I would consistently experience between Sharon and my son would endure throughout the course of our relationship. She never liked him, was unable to embrace him, and found him to be little more than a complete nuisance.

Jordan became our Berlin Wall.

Sharon's parents invited us to spend Christmas weekend at their house near San Diego. After Xmas dinner, her stepfather took me aside. "She'd probably kill me if she knew I was saying this to you," he said, "but we've never seen Sharon so in love before. So, I just wanted to say, welcome to the family, Dan." His words meant a lot.

My business was booming, and I decided to throw a New Year's Eve party for my clients and friends. Sharon embraced the idea (at first,) and, together, we bought a ton of liquor and food for the big shindig. We were expecting about 40 people. Just moments before the party began, however, Sharon had another panic attack.

"I don't want to do this!" she announced. "Let's get out of here and go see a movie. Please?" Me: "What are you talking about?" I'd just spend hundreds of dollars for this event and was expecting a bunch of important clients to walk through my door at any time. I couldn't have been more confused.

The guests arrived, and everyone had a great time except Sharon, who spent the entire evening alone, on my balcony, smoking cigarettes. "What's wrong with your girlfriend?" a number of my guests asked. "She's got a migraine, that's all. She'll be fine," I meekly responded.

My father came to the La Jolla, CA, area, in search of a new home in which to retire. My kids, Sharon, her parents, and I met him for dinner at a restaurant near Sharon's parents' house in San Diego. The waitress delivered my son's hamburger. "Daddy, it's burnt," he said, "I can't eat this." Sharon (to my son): "You wanted a well-done hamburger. So now you just need to eat it. Don't complain about it." My son gave her a "Huh?" expression. "See, it's black," Jordan said in self-defense, lifting the top of the bun.

"That's OK, we'll get a new one," I said, motioning for the waitress. Steam began shooting out of Sharon's ears. She leaned into me. "You're spoiling him," she whispered. "You should just make him eat that one." "Why?" I replied. "I can afford a new one. Why should my son eat something he doesn't want?" The look of anger in Sharon's eyes was remarkable, but, to her credit, she dropped the argument when she noticed my father's concern.

After the meal, goodbyes were said, and Sharon, my children, and I got into her car for the (long) ride back to my place in Los Angeles. Hyper-ventilating the entire time, she blasted the radio LOUD, and drove at least 80 miles an hour, with the windows wide open. My poor children in the backseat were almost blown out of the car. "Daddy, can Sharon close the windows?" my seven-year-old daughter asked. I had to gently but firmly insist that she do so.

I'd arranged a surprise Valentine's Day getaway for Sharon at a beautiful Santa Monica hotel suite. She'd just come back to LA from a New York business trip. I picked her up from LAX, took her to the suite, and let her nap. While she slept, I took a shower, and much to my surprise, a naked Sharon walked in.

This was the only time I've ever had "shower sex," to this day.

The next morning, as we were about to leave the hotel to walk along the beach, the topic of my son's "burnt hamburger" unexpectedly came up in conversation. In the flash of seconds, Sharon became "Mr. Hyde." She flew into a rage.

"My father would have MADE ME eat that fucking hamburger!" she screamed. "You are spoiling that boy rotten. He needs to learn about discipline. YOU need to keep that little brat in line!" I was expecting Sharon's head to start spinning like Linda Blair's from *The Exorcist* (1973.)

"What difference does it make? Why on earth should my son, who I love, eat something he doesn't want to eat?" I argued back. For at least half an hour, Sharon and I had the worst fight of our relationship. All I was able to glean from it, when it ended, was that Sharon's biological father, a former military officer, had been a prick tyrant to his three daughters. They truly feared him during most of their early childhoods.

"I'm outta here," Sharon said. In silence, I drove her to her car. She got out, tossed her suitcase in there, and approached me. "I love you," she said, "But you and I, together, it just doesn't work. We're done. I can't see you anymore." We kissed, passionately, and then Sharon drove off. "Happy Valentines Day?" I shouted after her.

As had now become routine, Sharon called a few days later to apologize and to say she missed me. I realized that, since we'd met, we tended to have at least one major battle every four-six weeks, almost like clockwork. Sharon revealed that she was manic depressive and had been on anti-depressant medication since the age of 15. I admitted my depression to her as well and told her about my 25 years of mental illness and how Prozac had changed my life.

During this same conversation, we also discussed for the first-time previous relationships and the history of our sex lives. Sharon went to her closet and took out a notebook. Inside, she had a section chronicling the names, dates and locations, and "notes" about every man she'd ever had sex with.

"Congratulations," she told me, "You're number 50," adding my name to her list.

Sharon was only the 10th woman I'd ever slept with. The fact that she'd had so many more lovers than I'd had made me feel kinda nauseous.

For her birthday, Sharon and I spent close to a week in Santa Barbara, staying at the same romantic hotel I'd stayed at 13 years earlier with Kim during our honeymoon. We rented a large, private suite, separated from the rest of the hotel, where we drank, smoked pot, and had a tremendous amount of sex. One night we got stoned and went to Brophy's Seafood Restaurant on the pier for dinner. Before our table was ready, we sat at the bar having drinks. I looked into Sharon's eyes, and overwhelmed by emotion, began to cry. "God, I love you so fucking much," I said. "I really love you too," she replied. I came THISCLOSE to asking Sharon to marry me at that very second. But just then, our waitress called our names, and led us to our dinner table.

****

Sharon was visiting my apartment one Sunday afternoon. My kids were there as well. Lying on my couch, me at the other end, she said, "Danny... rub my feet." As I massaged her toes, my son, holding his favorite book, came up to me: "Daddy, can you please read me a story?" Never more conflicted in my life, I looked at Sharon's face, which basically screamed, "DON'T YOU EVEN THINK ABOUT LEAVING ME RIGHT NOW FOR HIM!" and my son's angelic little face, which said, "Daddy, I'm lonely for you. Please spend some time with me too." I glanced at Sharon and to Jordan, again at Sharon, again to Jordan. Finally making an executive decision, I said, "Sharon, I'm gonna read him a story. Give me 15 minutes. I'll be right back, and then I'll massage your whole body, I promise." As Jordan and I walked toward his bedroom, we heard the front door of my apartment SLAM closed. Moments later, Sharon's car burned rubber as it screeched away from my building. "I think Sharon's angry again at you again, Daddy" my son said. "Yeah, I think you're right," I replied.

For my birthday, Kim kept the kids that weekend so I could solely focus on Sharon. I stayed at her apartment. After morning sex, we walked a few blocks to a nearby cafe. During my birthday brunch, Sharon started crying. "What's wrong?" I asked, sure I'd said or done something to upset her. "I'm very sad," she said, "because, even though I really do love you, and I always will, I know, in my heart, that I'm never, ever going to marry you." This one was a heart-stopper, because I was THISCLOSE, once again, to asking Sharon to marry me. I suppose, instinctively, she knew.

"Your kids are your world, and I know how much you love them," she said, "But I really don't want to be their step-mommy. Your daughter is a love-bug, but I don't have the patience for your son. I want children of my own. If you didn't have kids, I'd marry you tomorrow. I know you're thinking about asking me, so PLEASE DON'T. It would break both of our hearts."

Sharon and I stared at each other for a while, tears rolling down both our cheeks. We finished the brunch in silence. *Happy Birthday to ME!*

I officially declared the end of our relationship the night of Halloween, '97. Sharon called me about 2 in the morning, drunk off her ass. She'd lost her house keys. "Danny," she slurred, "I'm really drunk… I can't get into my house… come save me." I hopped into my car in my PJs and drove like a madman to her apartment. There, I found Sharon, fully clothed in a witch's costume, sprawled out on the front lawn of her building, sprinklers dousing her with water. She was a complete and total disaster.

"Danny! My Danny!" she screamed like a drunken sailor. "I knew you'd rescue me!" I'd never seen Sharon so incredibly fucked up. This was a different person. I put her arm around my neck, and slowly waltzed her up the steep flight of stairs that led to her apartment. I had my own set of keys, so I unlocked her door, and walked her into her bedroom. "You're a mess," I said, truly annoyed. I dried her off, helped her into her PJs, and tucked her in.

"I'm horny!" she drunk-yelled as I was leaving the room. "Make love to me, Danny! I miss you!" I stood at her bedroom door and froze. The woman I truly loved wanted sex. But, this same woman was impossible to please, would never marry me, and, most importantly, would never, ever, open her heart to my son.

"Sorry, kiddo, I'm out… I'm done," I said, making a momentous decision on the spot. "I'm leaving your keys on your coffee table. I love you, but I can't date a Yo-Yo anymore. Starting right now, we're just friends. I'll call you tomorrow."

Shortly thereafter, Sharon attended a weekend-long seminar called "The Forum," after which she quit her job, and spent a month in Greece. Upon her return to the U.S., she bought four cats, and moved to San Francisco, where she decided to study interior design. Thereafter, she married a millionaire software computer genius and moved back to Los Angeles, many years later.

Sharon and I represent a classic line from the comedy film *Galaxy Quest* (1999) about people who "Never Give in, Never Give Up, and Never Surrender."

Past Life Curse, anyone?

Chapter Twenty-One

The Voice from the Chandelier (1996)

Backtracking a bit here: I'd been working for over seven years for a Napoleonic little prick boss at a top Hollywood PR agency. The man had once threatened to punch me in the head in the men's room because I'd neglected to mention to him that that same day was the birthday of one of his clients. I could barely stomach the thought of even looking at his heinous face any longer.

He had fired my close friend Peter over a very minor incident in the recent past, and my hatred for him began building up to a climax.

Something big needed to happen soon.

Between June and August 1996, a remarkable series of events took place that changed the course of my life forever.

My 40th birthday was fast approaching, and it was at this point in my life I realized there must be something wrong with me medically -- I was incapable of smiling. I looked in the Yellow Pages (no Internet back then) and found a psychiatrist in the San Fernando Valley.

As I mentioned earlier, I met with him, told him my life story, and he was stunned. He said, "Dan, I'm incredibly impressed with you. You've had clinical depression for most of your life and in spite of that, you've accomplished so many big things. You're like a diabetic who never took insulin!"

The man handed me a prescription for Prozac. One week later, not only was I smiling, I felt like the weight of the world had been lifted from my shoulders.

****

I asked my shit head boss for a promotion; he said, "Okay."

About two weeks later, I got my next paycheck and it was the same as it had been for the two years previous. I went into the CFO's office and asked her, "Where's my raise?" She replied, "You got your title promotion to Senior Vice President," she snarled. "That's it. Now get the fuck out of my office." I stood there stunned, staring at the woman with utter hatred. "Are you serious?" I asked.

"Yep," she replied.

While leaving her office, I vowed to myself in that moment that somehow, someday, I would get my revenge on them both.

One early evening a few days later, my prick boss and I were meeting with two executives from a local TV channel who were seeking PR representation for their nighttime newscast. For what seemed like the one-millionth time, I had to listen to my short squat boss pontificate about his life story, his years on Wall Street, how he was "discovered" by some major Hollywood big shot, etc. I could have recounted his life story myself, as every time he told it, it was the same exact verbal vomit, verbatim.

As I suffered through this meeting in my suit and neck-constraining tie, I "heard" a "heavenly voice" emanating from the long, rectangular chandelier hanging above us in the restaurant at the Beverly Hills Four Seasons Hotel. Truly, I did.

The voice spoke unto me: "DAN! START YOUR OWN BUSINESS!!"

"Huh?" I actually said out loud, staring up at the chandelier. The others at the table looked at me.

"Oh, sorry," I said, "I just remembered something."

While my boss continued his masturbatory self-aggrandizing, my heart began to race. "Holy shit," I said to myself, "I've just had a revelation from God." Pretending to take notes earlier during the meeting, I had now been "spun off" into an entirely new direction. I turned my notepad to a clean page and began writing down all of the clients I was representing, and what they were paying my shithead boss to be represented -- by ME -- through *HIS* agency.

I immediately realized if I simply represented these same clients FROM MY HOME, I could more than triple my income overnight! At this point, I stood up while my boss was still speaking, chuckled, then said, "Sorry guys, I gotta go," and dashed off without further explanation. The look on their faces was priceless.

It was, perhaps, the greatest single moment of my professional life.

That night from home, I called each client I'd been representing. Every single one of them told me they would continue to utilize my services, regardless of where I was based. Said one, "I'd follow you to Botswana."

I should also mention that that same night at home, as I was unloading my dishwasher, two, large, glass cereal bowls LITERALLY LEPT OUT FROM MY HANDS and were then THROWN violently onto the kitchen floor. As I never, ever break or drop things, I knew in that moment, this was not something "normal." I've since come to believe that when I break any kind of glass, it simply means, "change."

The next day I lined up two business partners, one who provided start-up cash, the other an office building in Hollywood, along with phone lines, a computer system, an accountant and a lawyer.

In less than 48 hours, I'd conceived and was ready to launch a brand-new company. When my partners asked what I wanted to name this new entity, I said, "I grew up in Asbury Park, New Jersey. I'm gonna call it 'Asbury Communications.'"

About to earn 100% (instead of 10%) of the same money that had been going to an asshole boss for far too many years, I now stood at the cusp of earning well over seven times the annual salary that my father, a genius who invented technology preventing World War III, ever made, even in his best year.

My company (originally Asbury Communications, and later renamed The Asbury PR Agency in 2011,) quickly became a million-dollar enterprise. As of the writing of this book, my agency has been successful for nearly 30 years.

Thank you, Mr. Voice in the Chandelier!!

Chapter Twenty-Two

The Close Call (1997)

I was invited by a friend -- the owner of an events production company -- to attend a big Hollywood party for *Vibe Magazine*, which was owned by legendary music producer Quincy Jones. The publication predominantly featured R&B, rap, and hip-hop music artists, actors, and other entertainers. My friend's company produced the event for *Vibe*.

The event was held on March 9, 1997, at the Peterson Automobile Museum in Los Angeles. I valet parked my car, and just as I entered the party, saw a heavy-set Black man, wearing lots of gold necklaces and accompanied by two much larger and taller Black men (presumably his bodyguards) walk directly past me.

He nodded at me. I nodded my head back.

Knowing absolutely nothing about R&B and rap music, I assumed this guy was a famous musical performer.

I spent about three hours at that party, which was held on multiple floors of the museum. I have to say that, without question, this party was filled with the most incredibly beautiful Black women I have ever seen in my entire life, to this day. I actually gasped out loud a few times that evening at the sight of the most stunning women I'd ever seen, period. As one of only two "White Guys" at the entire event (my friend was the other,) I must have stood out like a sore thumb.

I ate and drank a bit at this party and spoke only to my friend. Having absolutely nothing in common with any other attendee there, I felt like I was inside a mobile glass aquarium the whole time I was walking around.

At about 15 minutes past midnight, I heard a voice in my right ear. It said, "YOU NEED TO LEAVE RIGHT NOW!" Having heard this voice a few other times in my life, I heeded its advice, went outside onto the sidewalk, handed the valet parking guy my ticket, retrieved my car, and began driving back home. The time was 12:30 am.

I'll let *Wikipedia* recount the next part of this story:

"On March 9, 1997, at 12:30 am, Christopher Wallace, an American rapper known professionally as both "Biggie Smalls" and as the "Notorious B.I.G.," left with his entourage from a party for *Vibe Magazine* being thrown at the Peterson Automotive Museum in Los Angeles. When the parking valet retrieved his SUV, Wallace traveled in the front passenger seat of that vehicle, alongside his associates Damion "D-Roc" Butler, Junior M.A.F.I.A. member Lil' Cease, and driver Gregory "G-Money" Young.

By 12:45 am, the streets were crowded with people leaving the museum. Wallace's SUV stopped at a red light at the corner of Wilshire Boulevard and South Fairfax Avenue, just a few yards away. Two minutes later, a dark-colored 1994–1996 Chevrolet Impala SS pulled up alongside Wallace's Suburban. The driver of the Impala, a Black male, rolled down his window, drew a 9 mm blue-steel pistol and fired at the SUV, four bullets hitting Wallace. It was later determined that the fourth bullet was fatal, entering through Wallace's right hip and striking several vital organs, including his colon, liver, heart, and the upper lobe of his left lung, before stopping in his left shoulder area.

Wallace's entourage rushed him to Cedars-Sinai Medical Center, where doctors performed an emergency thoracotomy, but he was pronounced dead at 1:15 am. Wallace died at the age of 24 years old, his death mourned by fellow hip hop artists and fans worldwide. Rapper NAS felt at the time that Wallace's death, along with that of Tupac Shakur's on 9/13/96, "was nearly the end of rap music."

****

The heavy-set Black man I'd seen walk by me just as I had entered that party WAS BIGGIE SMALLS! When I was driving home from the party that night, I heard on my car radio that he'd just been assassinated at precisely the same spot by the Valet Stand where I had been standing just 17-minutes earlier!

Had the "Voice" NOT told me to LEAVE RIGHT NOW, odds are pretty good I would have been standing just a few feet from where the famed rap star was murdered. Once again, I have to say "Thank You" to that wondrous, protective "Voice," whoever it may belong to.

Chapter Twenty-Three

The Premonition from My Mother (1998)

Now making more money than ever before in my life, I rented, in 1998, a huge house in Encino built in the '50s. As moving men were schlepping my stuff out from my (much smaller) Studio City apartment, I spoke with my neighbor, Sarah, out walking her dog, Maestro (an ancient, one-eyed cocker spaniel.) Sarah was an attractive, African American actress who had small roles on TV shows and in movies but made her living primarily by appearing in TV commercials. (We'd only spoken a few times previously by the pool.) When the moving men were finishing up, she asked, "So, are you ever gonna ask me out on a date? Or what?"

A few nights later, Sarah and I went for sushi. We confided to each other how burnt out we were from being single and dating. She invited me back to her place, and much to my surprise, insisted we have sex on her couch. Maestro, who, with his eye patch, resembled a canine-version of Captain Hook the Pirate, watched us screw, while concurrently farting uncontrollably.

Sarah and I repeated our first date dozens of times. We'd go out to eat, then hit a liquor store and buy bottles of wine. Back at her place, we'd drink booze straight from the bottle until we were wasted, and then have hours of sex. An actress with an extensive wardrobe, Sarah would wear costumes and wigs for me in bed. She was the most creative lover I ever had.

Sex with Sarah was epic.

One night, she called me into her bathroom. She'd lit a dozen candles in the tub and was laying in a bubble bath. I joined her, and, together, we drank wine and kissed and had wild (but drunken and unprotected) sex for hours.

Thanksgiving came around, and my family convened at my new place. Sarah swung by with a pie, and joined us in the board game, Taboo. My family LOVED her. She was cute, funny, charming, and outgoing. After I walked her to her car, my mother said, "She's probably the nicest girlfriend you've ever had. Too bad she's a 'Shvartza,'" (Old school Yiddish for a Black person).

I was making breakfast the next morning, when my mother approached me: "Danny! I had a dream that Sarah was pregnant!" Taken aback for a quick second, I said, "No, mom…that's not possible. We always use protection." Mom: "I sure hope so. I don't think you want any more kids!"

New Year's Eve came around. Sarah invited me to a friend's party at a Hollywood nightclub. She was dressed in pink and reminded me of a Hostess "Snowball" dessert snack. The party was packed, and we had a bunch of drinks. After about an hour, I became quite depressed when I realized I had no real feelings for her. Although Sarah was a lot of fun, and the sex was great, I didn't see any kind of future for us together. I simply wanted to be in love.

I became silent. "What's wrong?" she kept asking. How was I supposed to tell her I'd lost interest? We left the party early and wound up back at her apartment, where we lay at opposite sides of her couch watching Dick Clark announce the start of the new year. After the Times Square ball dropped, Sarah said, "Can I interest you in some New Year's sex?" Me: "Uhm, thanks, but, ahh, I'm just not in the mood. Sorry." A short time later, I drove home, alone.

Sarah and I went out again once or twice, but I simply wasn't into the relationship anymore. After we'd seen a movie, she pulled me aside in the theatre lobby. "I've lost you, huh?" she asked. "What's going on?" Me: "You're a really great girl, and I like you very much, but I don't think this relationship is going anywhere. I'd like to get remarried someday, and unfortunately, I just know in my heart that you and I will never be that couple. I'm really sorry." Sarah's beautiful, sunshine face became dim, as though the flashlight behind her smile suddenly had a dead battery.

We drove back to her place in silence and kissed goodbye. "Friends?" I asked. "I guess so," she answered. I honestly was not expecting to ever see her again.

****

One night, about a week later, I got a phone call that *ALMOST completely changed the course of my life.*

"I'm pregnant!" Sarah announced. You know how in an Alfred Hitchcock movie, when someone learns that their child's been kidnapped, the camera rotates around them in slow motion, and their world comes to a frozen standstill? Speechless, I simply could not believe what I was hearing.

"Are you sure?" Sarah: "Yes, women tend to know these things." Me: "Is it MINE?" Sarah: "Who do you think I am, the world's biggest whore? Yes, of course it's yours. I haven't been with another man in two years." Instantaneously, a million thoughts flashed through my brain: I already have two kids! How was I going to pay for another? College? A kid out of wedlock? This would simply kill my father. What would Kim say? My friends? Mom? My children? I almost fainted.

"You'll have an abortion, right?" I asked. Sarah practically exploded: "Honey, this is MY BABY, and I'm gonna keep MY BABY! There ain't nothing YOU or ANYBODY ELSE is gonna do to take away MY BABY! The good Lord Jesus Christ is telling me to raise this child, and that's exactly what I'm gonna do."

Sarah hung up. I walked into my living room, stared at the wall, then remembered my mother's dream. "Oh my God, SHE KNEW!" I said out loud.

Every night for the next week or so, Sarah would call to discuss her pregnancy. I'd beg her to PLEASE consider an abortion, because I absolutely did not want a third child. I couldn't afford it and had NEVER planned on having another one after breaking up with Kim. Every night, I heard the same performance on the phone: "Sweet Jesus spoke to me and told me to keep this baby. This child is a gift from Lord Jesus Christ, Our Lord and Savior, and there's nothing you can do or say or do that's gonna change my mind." I implored her, "Sarah, please don't do this to me." She attacked: "You already have two kids! What if you were to lose them? I know where they live. WHAT IF THEY BOTH SOMEHOW DIED IN A MYSTERIOUS FIRE?"

Okay, so now I realized I was dealing with a psychopath. I was scared! Chills ran up my spine. I realized there was likely no way out of this mess, and that Sarah, clearly a nut job, was committed to having my third child even without my involvement.

Then, I decided I had one possible "out" -- one chance to play to her vanity. A basic Hollywood truth: Actresses love attention!

"I'll be your publicist for two years at no charge if you have an abortion," I offered. She went silent, then whispered: "I want that in writing." Me: "Are you serious?" Sarah: "Yes, and we're both gonna sign it." Incredulous, I drew up possibly the world's first, and only, "Abortion Agreement" (something I believe I may have invented?) This was a contract between Sarah and myself, that stated I would provide public relations services to her for two years, and that I would also take her to and from the abortion procedure. I'd also promised to sleep over at her apartment that night to ensure her welfare.

We signed two copies of this agreement, each keeping one.

A few days later: A nurse led us into a small operating room at the doctor's office, told Sarah to put on a blue paper gown, and lay on the table. I sat in a chair in the corner of the room. While waiting for the doctor, Sarah asked me to hold her hand. I did. Out loud, she began praying: "Sweet Lord Jesus, please forgive Daniel for making me have this, my fourth abortion."

FOURTH ABORTION? Holy Crap! This woman was an Abortion Junkie!

As I sat holding her hand, listening to her prayers, I felt about three inches tall. It was, without question, one of the worst moments of my life. I was wracked with guilt and shame and would have rather been anywhere else on the planet.

Just then a very beautiful female doctor, who resembled a young Heather Locklear, entered the operating room. She took one look at me, then at a sobbing Sarah, and shot me a look that implied: *Sir, you are an utter piece of shit!* She hooked up a vacuum cleaner-type tube, inserted it into Sarah, and sucked out the bloody fetus.

A truly horrific hour of my life. One of the worst.

****

That night, I slept on Sarah's couch, getting up every few hours to check on her. The next morning, she walked into the kitchen and seemed to be in a cheerful mood. She made me a terrific breakfast, and we talked about everything *but* the nightmare from the day before. "Listen, I've got to go to work now," I said. "You're gonna see me tonight, right?" Sarah urged, almost panicked. "Sure, okay. I'll even take you out for a nice dinner if you're up to it."

After work, I took Sarah to a fun restaurant nearby. She was laughing and happy, having returned to the "Sarah Classic" character I'd dated the four months previous. During the meal, while smiling to her face, I decided I never wanted to see her again. Yes, I'd agreed to be her publicist, but I had no real intention of keeping that promise. (What was she gonna do, sue me?)

As we walked up to her apartment, I was consumed with conflict. This woman was funny, attractive, madly in love with me, and gave me mind-boggling sex.

But she'd also threatened the lives of my children, and for that I would never be able to trust or forgive her.

We reached her door. Sarah grabbed me, and with words that resonate in my ears to this day, said, "Honey, YOU AIN'T NEVER GONNA GET SEX LIKE ME AGAIN!" "Trust me… I know that already," I responded, slowly turning and slithering away.

Miraculously, Sarah never once requested my PR services, nor ever contacted me again. Since that night, I've seen her on TV commercials a few times selling toothpaste, mouthwash, and auto insurance.

Having somehow survived this event, yet another very close call, I had a vasectomy about three weeks later.

Chapter Twenty-Four

The Dream about Julie (1999)

During my Junior and Senior years of college at Boston University's School of Public Communications, I'd befriended a short, adorable Italian girl named Julie Spatuzzi, who was in two of my same classes. A year older than me, Julie and I became the closest of friends and we also worked together on several school projects. One of these was creating an entire advertising campaign for a new product that we had to invent ourselves. (We came up with the concept of a Pocket Foreign Language Translator. a technology that would not exist in real life for another 35 years!)

Julie and I hung out together a lot, and we threw a few parties for our fellow classmates at my apartment. While she was never my "girlfriend," she WAS in fact the closest-ever girl + friend I'd ever had in my life, up until that point in time. Julie attended my college graduation (a year after hers) and met my family, including my then newly-divorced parents.

After I left Boston following my graduation, Julie moved into what had been my apartment there on Commonwealth Avenue, and even bought my furniture, my parents' original living room set of maple wood tables and chairs which I had refurbished in 1977. Today, those items would be considered "1950's Retro Classic" and probably worth a good deal of dough.

As you already know, I relocated to New Jersey for a time after college, then moved in 1980 to Los Angeles. Julie eventually moved to Connecticut, got a job at an advertising agency, got married and had a son. Over the years, and then decades, Julie and I remained in touch by phone on a fairly regular basis. I remember she was the first person I called on the evening of December 8, 1980, just after I'd seen the news on television that John Lennon had been murdered.

Cut to 1999. I was at work in my office, then inside my home in Encino, CA, when my phone rang. "Hey Julie!" I said, "How's it going?" "Uh, not very good, Danny," she replied quietly. "I've been having severe stomach pain for many months now, and I've seen a bunch of doctors, and they were all treating me with digestion medicine. Well, it turns out that that wasn't the problem. I was just diagnosed with stage 4 ovarian cancer. I don't have much longer."

I held the phone receiver to my ear but could hardly breathe. "Are you serious? Oh my God, Julie, this is horrible news," I whispered.

Julie on phone: "They say I only have another couple of weeks."

I was truly and literally stunned for a few seconds. Me: "I'm coming to see you, Julie. I'll be at your house in three days. Is that Okay?" Julie: "Really? Okay, sure. I'd love to see you." Me: "I'll ask Steve if he can come too."

Steve, Julie and I had all been friends in Boston.

A few days later, I flew to New York, met up with Steve, and he and I drove in his car up to Connecticut, surviving the most horrendous traffic I've ever experienced in my life, to this day.

When Steve and I arrived at her house, Julie met us in the driveway, resembling an Auschwitz survivor. She was walking with an IV drip medical pole attached to her arm. Steve and I gently hugged her. Then we met--for the first time--her husband, Bob, and their young son, Stephen.

Julie, Steve, and I had a wonderful reunion -- the three of us had not all been together for 21 years. We reminisced about some of the fun times we'd had together during our years in Boston, and the parties where we'd make fun of various people we knew in common.

After a few hours, Steve and I said our goodbyes, got back into Steve's car and headed back into Manhattan. "Wow, we'll never see her again," I said. "I know," added Steve. "What a shame... such a great girl."

Two weeks later, while back at my desk in LA, the phone rang. "Dan, this is Bob Dennis. Julie's gone. She passed last night. You'll never know how much your visit meant to her." I began to cry, instantly. "Wow, Bob, I'm SO, SO SORRY! God this sucks SO MUCH! She was such a special person. I'm so glad I got to see her one last time. Please give my love to your son and thanks for letting me know." We hung up.

I took a walk outside for about an hour, sobbing. This was the first loss in my life of a dear friend, and it hit me pretty hard.

When I came back into my office, I realized I couldn't possibly do any more work that day. So, I took a nap instead on my green leather couch.

As I was napping, I was dreaming. And in that dream, I clearly saw a MALE ANGEL, all in white and with large wings, SITTING ON MY BACKYARD PATIO BENCH. He looked bored, as though he was waiting for someone. Then, in the dream, I EXPERIENCED JULIE STANDING ABOUT ONE FOOT IN FRONT OF ME - TO THE IMMEDIATE RIGHT OF MY HEAD. She looked wonderful -- appearing as her normal, healthy, smiling, sharply-dressed Julie-Self!

"Danny! Please don't worry about me! It's OK! I'm doing just fine, I promise!" Dream Julie said emphatically. She was smiling broadly and clearly at peace.

This vision of Julie was SO REAL, I instantly woke, sat straight up on my couch, panting and sweating. My dead friend Julie HAD JUST VISITED ME FROM HEAVEN! This was not something imagined. This was something MORE THAN JUST A DREAM.

Julie had managed to find a way to say goodbye to me from the other side!

JULIE'S SPIRIT WAS IN MY LIVING ROOM IN ENCINO, CALIFORNIA, JUST MOMENTS AFTER HER DEATH IN CONNECTICUT! AND SHE EVEN BROUGHT ALONG AN ANGEL GUIDE WITH HER!

Today, decades later, I can still "see" in my memory banks both the Angel and the Julie Spirit that appeared to me in my dream. I hope she really is okay in Heaven, and that she knows how much I loved her, and how much Steve and I will always miss her.

Photos

Author Age 5, the Year of the Billboard Sign Fall, 1961, Neptune, New Jersey

Author and Neighbor Donna, 1959, Neptune, New Jersey

Wendy from 3rd Grade, 1965, Ocean, NJ

Author as Drummer, 1972, Ocean, NJ

Author Meets *Monkees* Hero Micky Dolenz, 2015, Hollywood, CA

Author and Parents, shortly before 1st UFO Sighting, 1969, Asbury Park, NJ

Flying "V" UFO Sighting Illustration, March 1970, West Deal, NJ

Bonnie from 8th Grade, 1970, Ocean, NJ

Laura from High School, 1973, Ocean, NJ

Long Red from Rutgers University, 1974, New Brunswick, NJ

Author During Boston University, Doppelganger Era, Boston, MA, 1977

Author with Mouth Wired Shut on Roller Coaster, Jackson, NJ, 1978

Author with Friend Steve Walter, Site of Woman's Voice, Belmar, NJ, 1979

Escorting Models for Columbia Pictures, New York City, 1980

Author Meets Hugh Hefner at *Playboy* Mansion, Beverly Hills, CA, 1984

Author with Kim # 1 in Boston, MA, 1978

Author with Kim #2 at their Wedding, Santa Barbara, CA, 1984

Author with *Playboy* Playmate Kym Malin, 1985, Hollywood, CA

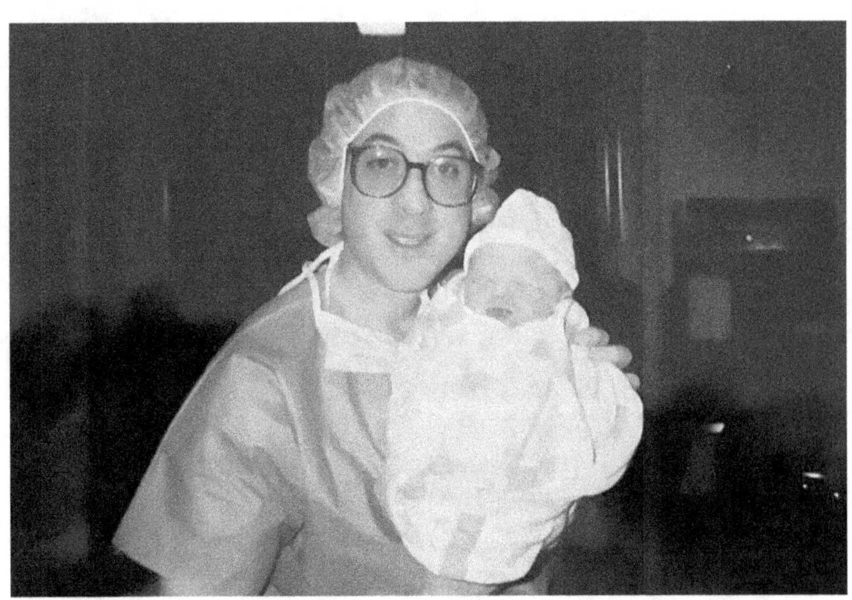

Author, Day of Son Jordan's Birth, May 10, 1988, Santa Monica, CA

Illustration of UFO #2/ Egg-Shaped Light in Sky, Lancaster, CA, 1996

Author with Candy, 1993, Manhattan Beach, CA

Author's Girlfriend Amy, 1994, Studio City, CA

Author with Sharon, 1996, Santa Barbara, CA

Life Changing Chandelier, Four Seasons Hotel, 2023, Beverly Hills, CA

Author with Asbury PR Team, 1996, Hollywood, CA

Author with Sarah, NY Eve, 1999, Studio City, CA

Author with Late College Friend Julie, 1978, Boston, MA

Author Chasing Underage Girl, 2002, Cancun, Mexico

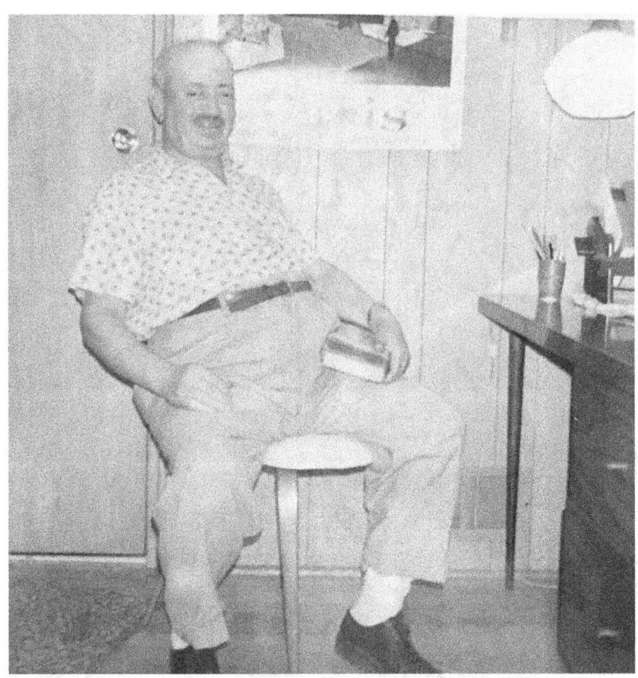

Author's Late Grandpa Joe, 1965, Brooklyn, NY

Girlfriend Barbara & Friend in Field of Orbs, 2008, Washington State

Author with Supermodel Amber Smith, 2009, Los Angeles, CA

Author with Son Jordan, 2012, Anchorage, Alaska

Author and Brother Bob, Farewell to Dad, 2016, Boca Raton, FL

With Anjuli at Musso & Frank Billboard, 2019, Hollywood, CA

Daughter Anjuli with "Ghost Chair," 2023, West LA, CA

Author with The Ten, 2015, Santa Monica, CA

Author with Natasha, July 4, 2022, Universal Studios, CA

Author with First Shipment of *After They Came*, 2023, Beverly Hills, CA

With *Ancient Aliens* TV Star Giorgio Tsoukalos, AlienCon, 2023, Pasadena, CA

With Legendary Author Erich von Daniken, AlienCon, 2023, Pasadena, CA

Presiding Over the Launch of the Hollywood Disclosure Alliance, 2023, Hollywood, CA

First Meeting of the Hollywood Disclosure Alliance Founding Members, 2023, Hollywood, CA

Promo for *Live From Hollywood...It's Paranormal Tonight!* 2024, Beverly Hills, CA

First Live Podcast with Dee Wallace, Jan 11, 2024, Beverly Hills, CA

Live From Hollywood! Podcast Interview with Movie Star Thomas Jane,
April 2024

Chapter Twenty-Five

The Disappearing Girl in Cancun (2002)

For my 46th birthday, I decided to treat myself to a real vacation, and booked a ten-day trip to Cancun, Mexico. I had three goals in mind:

1) Drink to excess
2) Sleep to excess
3) Have Sex to excess

I'd been working out with a personal trainer the two years previous, and my body was in its best shape, ever. I was feeling pretty good about myself, and I figured I'd go someplace where I'd be surrounded by women wearing minimal amounts of clothing.

I checked into Club Med's Cancun Village and hit the bar. The place was beautiful, but I noticed right away that everyone there was either much younger than me, or a couple. The girls seemed to be in their early 20s, and the couples were in their 40s or older. Instantly, I was a fish out of water. So, I did what all fish do.

I drank.

I'm pretty sure I consumed more alcohol during my time in Cancun than I'd had in my entire life, combined. Drunk from early morning till late at night, I did my best to relax and tried (in vain) to make some kind of connection with the other vacationers. I'd walk around smiling or winking at the young, hot, bikini girls walking past me, but they'd ignore me, giggle at my flirtations, or shoot me back a look that read: "Yeah, right! As if!"

These hotties wanted absolutely nothing to do with this balding, old fart.

At night, the DJ located at the bar would corral everyone together for mass dancing sessions, set to blaring "Euro-trash" techno music. There must have been at least 250 people there, but as far as I could tell, most of them were couples. One night after the dancing ended, I was walking back toward my room, when I felt a pinch on my ass. I turned to see a short, plump woman, holding her husband's hand, walk past me, smiling. She licked her lips and winked. "What the fuck?" I thought. "Why would she do that? She's clearly married." Even though I didn't find her remotely attractive, I must admit that I was oddly aroused by her actions.

Each day of my week in Cancun, I worked out, swam, played volleyball, and read a biography of comedian Jackie Gleason. I was utterly alone until the evenings, when strangers would sit together for dinners. I met some nice couples then, and even befriended a cute young blonde girl who worked there. (She moved to LA years later and we became friends again for a short while. But she soon married, and we lost contact. She appears in a Photo in this book.)

And of course, I continued to drink massive quantities of alcohol.

On my last full day at Club Med, I noticed a tall, very pretty, blonde teenage girl eating with her parents. Because I'm always the most attracted to women completely and totally out of my league – and out of my reach -- I became obsessed with her. After dinner, I walked about 30 feet behind her and her parents, as they walked along the beach, picking up seashells.

At dusk, all the young people headed to the bungalow nightclub. Like a mentally-challenged child, I followed my new "mystery girl" into the club from a distance. The place became packed quickly, the music got loud, and everyone was drinking and dancing. I inhaled three drinks in a row and forced myself to meet my new "goddess."

Melissa was a total joy -- she seemed to be instantly attracted to me. We danced and drank, drank and danced, for perhaps two hours. She pressed herself up against me and, I guess you could say, we began "dirty dancing," whatever that even is. She rubbed my bald head as we danced, and placed my hands on her ass, grinding her luscious body against me. My heart was filled with joy.

Single-handedly, this young girl was making up for the painfully long nine days I'd experienced up until that point.

About 1am, the nightclub filled with foam. If you've never experienced "foam dancing," you haven't lived. Maybe the most fun I ever had in my life. The foam, up to my neck, reminded me of the times my mother used "Mr. Bubble" in the bathtub, when I was a small child.

After a time, the club became stifling. I asked Melissa if we could take a walk outside and she agreed. Hand in hand, my blonde bombshell teenager and I were strolling along a perfect Cancun beach. The waves were still, and the full moon was so bright, it lit the entire ocean and the white sandy beach. The stars were overwhelming. The further we walked from the club, the quieter it became.

Melissa and I sat side by side on some beach rocks, still holding hands. I stroked her long blonde hair and asked if she liked sex. "Love it," she said, "Especially when a guy gives me oral… that's my favorite."

"Finally!" I thought to myself, "I'm going to make love to a beautiful girl on a perfect beach before I die." I leaned over and we kissed. It was magical. It was mind-boggling.

And, like my experience at an 8th grade boy/girl party, it only lasted about 20 seconds.

As though suddenly struck by a bolt of lightning, Melissa sprang forth from the rocks, brushed the sand from her long, beige dress, and said, "Oh my God! I'm only 17! I can't have sex with YOU! You could be my FATHER!" she shouted.

At that moment, she turned to her right, and VANISHED FROM SIGHT. And I mean that literally -- she VANISHED into thin air. Supernatural, the moment could easily have been a scene from *The X-Files* (1993.) I walked back to my hotel room in a complete daze, not once encountering her presence during that long return stroll.

****

Cancun Coda: The next morning, I awoke to find the pupils of my eyes "bright lobster red." Apparently, I was having a major allergic reaction to the nightclub foam. Back in LA many, many hours later (after my first plane caught fire,) I drove myself to St. Johns Hospital in Santa Monica. The ER was empty, and I was whisked into a patient area inside.

Without a single second of advance conversation, a doctor walked up to me, looked directly into my bright red pupils, and said, "Lemme guess… Mexico, right?"

I haven't taken another vacation since.

Chapter Twenty-Six

The Poltergeist of My Dead Grandfather (2003)

After I returned to LA from Cancun, I rejoined a "Speed Dating" organization, in my futile, yet on-going attempts to discover "The One." As I walked into a hotel lobby for yet another torturous such experience, a woman seated there said, "Hey… remember me?" I had NO idea who she was, so I sarcastically replied, "Don't tell me we already dated?" Woman: "Well, actually, YES we have."

This woman's name was Bella ("B" from here on.)

Because she was seated at the time, I did not remember her. We'd only had one date, years earlier, when we were both members of Great Expectations. But once she stood, I did recall her, because she was so tall, I'd joked to my friends at the time that I'd just had dinner with Kareem Abdul-Jabaar.

When B sat at my table during the speed dating evening, I had zero interest in her. I'd asked her out for a second date years ago, and at the time she blew me off. Now sitting opposite me, she took my hands into hers: "I am so sorry I didn't go out with you for that second date, when you called. That was stupid. I'm so incredibly attracted to you right now, I can't even believe it." Staring into my eyes, if I didn't know better, I would have said she was in love with me. "Can you forgive me? If you pick me tonight, I promise I'll make it up to you."

("Picking" someone meant that both the man and the woman each circled "Yes" on the "Yes" or "No" speed dating sheet handed out to all participants as they sat down.) Flattered, I did pick B that night, along with several other women.

A few nights later, B called, and asked me out for our "first new date." Wanting to keep it simple, we met for dinner at a deli near her apartment. Afterward, she invited me back to her place. There, I met "Lilly," her incredibly furry, bright white cat, and immediately felt my flesh crawling up my spine. Of the many, many cats I've had to endure in relationships with women during the course of my life, Lilly made me feel, by far, the most allergic.

B lit some candles, poured some wine, and kindly "whooshed" Lilly into the other room. We'd planned to watch a movie but began making out instead. After a few minutes, she pulled away. "I promised myself NO SEX tonight, but I can't help myself. I'm just VERY attracted to you." I was flattered. As I walked back to my car, I realized she was right. I couldn't wait to see her again -- soon.

The next three dates were similar, dinner, her place or mine, and making out, but no sex, yet.

After dinner at a Thai restaurant for date four, B and I were walking along the Santa Monica Promenade. "I have something important to tell you." ANYTIME a woman says that to me, I IMMEDIATELY respond with the joke, "Don't tell me you're really a MAN??" She said: "I've been dreading this since I met you. I have to tell you two things. One is that I am incredibly horny for you and I want to fuck you so badly, you have no idea. I think about it all the time. But, the second thing is that I have HERPES. And I wanted to be honest with you. I don't know how you feel about that…"

The truth is, I didn't know *how* to feel about that bombshell. I'd been with quite a few women by this point, but never had this conversation with any of them. On one hand, I was dating a woman who turned me on sexually (even though Bella was, by no means, a looker.) But on the other, I could possibly get a disease that would affect the rest of my life..

For the next two weeks, I discussed "Bella's Herpes Condition" with everyone I knew -- my friends, my doctor, my brothers and their wives. ALL of them, without exception, said "DO NOT HAVE SEX WITH THIS WOMAN! You need herpes like you need cancer." They were adamant. My (then) sister-in-law Deb yelled at me for even considering the option.

Having not seen her for two weeks, I called B: "Let's have a nice dinner and talk about this." I took her to my favorite, upscale Italian place, and we were seated in a very charming, corner booth, next to a young, very much in love couple, who couldn't keep their hands off each other.

"I'm really conflicted," I told her, having absolutely no idea what I was going to say next. "I'm attracted to you (I lied,) I enjoy being with you and talking with you. Sex is unbelievably important to me. B: "Me too. I'm a sexaholic. Sex is my favorite thing on the planet. I got herpes back in high school from some asshole guy I only dated a few times. I don't reveal this to every guy I sleep with, but I knew that I had to be honest and tell you."

We sat and looked into each others' eyes, and then glanced again at the madly-in- love couple at the next table. "They seem happy," B said. Me: "So, you really, really LOVE sex? You love it as much as I do?" B: "Probably more. I'll give you all the sex you could possibly ever want or need. That's a promise."

I was completely torn. My brain shouted: "Asshole, why even take the smallest chance of getting herpes? You'll have that for the rest of your life!" While my penis countered with: "This woman will make you cum six ways to Sunday. Look at her big boobs! What the fuck are you waiting for?"

A few more minutes of silence -- then I made my big decision. "Okay, let's do it. Let's have a sexual relationship with two conditions: You have to swear that you will always tell me when you're having a flare up. And you have to always be 100% sure that I'm wearing a condom, because sometimes when I'm drunk, I forget. Deal?" B: "Absolutely. Deal." We shook hands.

For the next dozen dates or so, B came to my place, and we had massive amounts of fun, lusty, sex, likely working off some weight in the process.

NY Eve was fast approaching. "Come away for a weekend with me," I said. "I'd like to take you to my favorite, romantic getaway." I took B up to the El Encanto Hotel in Santa Barbara (the same site where I'd had both my honeymoon with Kim, and my incredibly romantic getaway with Sharon, five years earlier). The MINUTE we got into our little bungalow room and finished putting our things away, B said, "Well, I've got a surprise for you. I JUST this SECOND got my period. Great timing, huh?"

****

During our New Year's Eve dinner, B and I had perhaps three or four drinks apiece and were laughing like idiots in the hotel restaurant. We were wearing the requisite funny pointed hats, and, at midnight, blew the requisite funny horns. On a WHIM, and DRUNK OFF MY FUCKING ASS, I leaned over the table: "I have a great idea. I want you to live with me. Your lease is almost up. My lease is almost up. Let's get a brand-new apartment together and make a life for ourselves. We have nothing to lose."

B started to cry. "Are you sure? Is this just drunk talk? Or do you mean it?" Me: "I want you to live with me. I want to do this. We're gonna do this, okay?" B: "Alright… I'll live with you." Back in LA, we took turns during our spare time to investigate potential new apartments, investigating buildings throughout the city of Los Angeles.

"You have GOT to see this incredible place in Beverly Hills I'm standing in right now," B called me at work. "I think you'll like it." Situated in a classic, LA art deco building from the 1920s, this enormous, three-bedroom place had a fireplace, hardwood floors, and arched hallways. "I love it. This is it. This is our new home," I said immediately.

An "Early Warning of Impending Doom" occurred while B and I were packing up the stuff in her existing place. (She'd been living there for more than 12 years.) We broke a big bathroom mirror, glass shattered everywhere. "Oh, fuck, that's not good," B said. Me: "The last time I broke glass, it signified 'Major Change.' I started my company that same evening. In my world, breaking glass can be a good thing."

Because our existing leases were set to expire two weeks apart, B moved into the new, Beverly Hills apartment first. The moving men set her up, and I spent my evenings there afterward, helping put her things in order. Then, it suddenly hit me like a brick pile. HOW THE FUCK WAS I GOING TO LIVE WITH LILLY THE CAT?

"Hey, B," I called out, rooms away. "We need to talk about something." I told her that I was really nervous about Lilly, and about the possibility of having future asthma attacks. "What are we going to do if I simply can't live with Lilly?" I asked. "I'll tell you what," she said. "This new place has hardwood floors, and I'll sweep up her furballs every day. And, if you still feel sick and you can't deal with it, I'll have my mother take her, okay?" Me: "Do you PROMISE?" B: "Yes, absolutely, I PROMISE."

If ever there was a "Promise" that I should have gotten in writing, it would have been that one. I moved into the Beverly Hills place on the first of April. This date is more commonly known as "April Fool's Day." Can you guess who the "April Fool" was that year?

****

B moved into the new apartment first. As she told the story, when the three moving men were outside at their truck, Bella, alone inside the hallway of the new place, heard a loud, clear, voice call out to her: "JOE?" it asked. She looked around and was surprised to find she was alone in the unit at the time. She then called me by cell phone to recount that weird event.

During our first weeks together in the new apartment, B and I experienced a series of odd things happening inside our rooms. The first: We were watching TV one night when a paper bag in the dining room, which had inside it a plastic sink drainer thing for dirty dishes, suddenly fell over. We both went to inspect. "That's odd," Bella said.

A few nights later, B and I were asleep when we heard the shattering of glass in our master bathroom. It was so loud it woke us both up. We went to investigate and saw dozens of shattered glass shards, the remains of the large glass Bella used to drink water with after brushing her teeth. "Could this have been Lily?" I asked. "No, Lily is asleep under our bed," Bella countered.

A few nights after that: Our new place had a beautiful wood-burning fireplace, and I'd just bought a new, cylindrical-shaped package of very long fireplace matches. But after I opened the seal on that package, I inadvertently pulled ALL 50 OF THE LONG MATCHES OUT OF THE BOX AT THE SAME TIME. The 50 matches ALL CAUGHT FIRE AT ONCE AND BECAME A TORCH!

Horrified, I clearly remember standing there with a LIVE TORCH OF FIRE in my hand. I was frozen and couldn't think straight about what to do next. JUST THEN, A BLUISH-WHITE COLORED WHISP OF MIST FLEW THROUGH THE LIVING ROOM FROM THE DINING ROOM, GRABBED THE TORCH OUT FROM MY HANDS AND TOSSED IT INTO THE FIREPLACE! I did not do this myself -- SOMETHING ELSE DID THIS FOR ME!! I SWEAR TO YOU THIS HAPPENED.

I stood in place for a few minutes, trying to mentally digest what had just taken place.

Our story now picks up steam: In those days, my two kids would spend weekends with me at B at our Beverly Hills apartment, each of my kids had their own room. On one of those Saturday nights, maybe 2 or 3 in the morning, I was awakened by my son Jordan, SCREAMING FROM HIS BED: DAD! DAD! THERE'S SOMETHING IN MY ROOM!

My parental radar on full alert, I instantly awoke from a dead sleep and ran into his room. I turned on the light. Jordan (age 15 at the time) was sitting up in his bed.

"Dad! There's something in my room. Or somebody! I heard knocking on the walls… and even on the glass of my TV screen." He then got out of his bed and demonstrated to me how he'd heard knocking noises on every vertical surface inside his bedroom by rapping on those surfaces with his knuckles. "It was real, Dad, honest. I'm not making this up." "I believe you," I replied. "Let's leave the hallway light on for the rest of tonight and we'll keep your bedroom door open. We'll discuss this in the morning, okay?"

That next morning, B, my daughter, Anjuli, and I woke up early and began making breakfast in the kitchen. Jordan was still sleeping in his room with his door opened. Suddenly, we three inside the kitchen HEARD JORDAN'S DOOR SLAM SHUT, HARD AND LOUD. "DAD!!" Jordan screamed from inside his room. I ran down the hallway and tried to open his door. For a second it felt as though someone on the other side of that door was preventing it from opening out in my direction. Then it opened. Jordan was again sitting upright in his bed, and now shaking.

"Dad, there's a ghost in this house," he said, almost zombie-like. "What are we going to do about it?"

It was just then that I remembered I had an old Ouija board game at the bottom of a closest. I dug it out and laid it down on the hallway floor. "Everyone, come here," I said to B and both my kids. "We need to figure this out right now!"

Each of the four of us sat on one side of the board, and we all placed our hands onto the movable piece from the game, called the planchette. I next asked the following questions and got the following responses from the game:

Q: "Who are you?" The planchette began spelling out these letters: J-O-S-E-P-H.

Q: "Is your name Joseph?" The game replied: YES

Q: "Where are you from?" The planchette then began spelling out: S-Y-R-I-A

Q: "You are from Syria?" The game replied: YES

Instantly, at that moment, I had an epiphany.

Q: "Are you my Grandpa Joe?" The planchette replied: YES

I sat back, stunned - instant tears filled my eyes. "Holy shit!" I said to my family. "Our ghost is my dead Grandfather Joseph Harary, my father's father. He was born in Syria!"

Bella was shocked to her core. Jordan was pale and Anjuli was crying.

Q: "Why are you here?" The planchette spelled out: J-O-R-D-A-N

Q: "You are here for Jordan?" The game replied: YES

Q: "What do you want with Jordan?" The planchette spelled: T-E-A-C-H

Q: "What do you want to teach Jordan?" The game then spelled out a series of words in Hebrew!

As I do not recall my childhood Hebrew, I immediately phoned my dentist. When I read the Hebrew words to him over the phone, he paused, then said to me, "That phrase means, I AM A STRANGER HERE."

Returning to the Ouija board, I next said:

Q: "Grandpa Joe! You are really scaring us here. We need you to please go away. Can you please leave us alone?" The game replied: YES.

After this, I maybe asked another question or two, but nothing happened. The planchette no longer responded.

My dead Grandpa Joe, apparently, moved along his heavenly path at that moment. I never had another poltergeist experience in that house for the remaining year I lived there.

And, hey, remember when Bella first moved into that apartment and heard someone call out the name "JOE"? Well, I'd have to say that perhaps either ANOTHER GHOST living in that apartment had recognized my grandfather and welcomed him into the building?! Or maybe my Grandpa Joe HIMSELF was announcing his presence!

****

Post-Poltergeist, I was now living with B and her cat for a few months, and my allergies were in hyper-drive. My flesh crawled when I came home, my eyes were constantly red and tearing, and my nose was dripping 24/7. I'd been getting allergy shots once a week for over 25 years, and I even asked my allergist to add some "cat dander" into my allergy serum mix, so that I would, perhaps, become immune to the presence of cat.

The new shots were killing me. I never felt sicker in my life. B and I entered a new era in our relationship. All we did now was fight, bitterly, over her promise to give Lilly away to her mom if my allergies got out of hand. "Sorry, I changed my mind," B said during these arguments. "I'll give away my cat when YOU give away your DAUGHTER." To say these fights were becoming more and more heated would be a significant understatement.

I began to daydream, almost constantly, about ways in which I could "off" Lilly:

** I could stuff her behind our washer and dryer units, then pretend she somehow had gotten stuck back there…

** I could hire a friend of mine, a security guard who'd served in the Israeli Military, to pretend to break into my apartment, ransack the place, and kill Lilly in the process…

** I could pour clear, odor-free poison into Lilly's water dish, and then feign my sympathies when she "passed"!

Of course, *this big pussy* did none of those things to Lilly, that big, white, fluffy, *actual pussy.*

****

B and I took a weekend retreat to San Diego, where we had massive amounts of sex. But when we weren't screwing, all we did was nag each other to death about the status of Lilly. Back home a few nights later, I returned from work to find B on the living room couch, sobbing. "What's wrong?" I asked. Through a barrage of tears, B whispered: "I love you so much. I thought you and I were going to get married, buy a house, and make a baby." Me: "Make a baby? You know I had a vasectomy!" B: "My father said he'd pay for you to have that reversed."

According to my surgeon, a reversal of my vasectomy would have cost over $10,000.

Me: "You know I can't live with Lilly much longer. I can't live with a cat. This experiment was a mistake. It was my mistake, and I'm really sorry." B continued to cry for hours. I went to bed.

We would sleep in separate bedrooms for the rest of our time together -- a parallel reminder of the time I did the same with my fiancé, Kim, after she discovered Jesus, exactly 20 years earlier.

****

My birthday was fast approaching, and my mother came to stay with us for a few days. She had a private talk with B. "Bella, dear," she said. "You and my son could really have a nice life together. I know you love him. You both have good jobs and the two of you are making a lot of money." (B was an accountant for a top Hollywood TV production company involved with the hit HBO series *The Sopranos*/1999.) "All you have to do is get rid of your cat, and the two of you can move forward with your lives." B: "I can't do that. I love my cat more than anything else in the world. I'd sooner cut off my hand than give away my cat." My mother: "Well, then, I'm afraid the two of you are doomed to fail as a couple."

My family and friends threw me a small birthday gathering at a steak joint in Beverly Hills. As my kids, my mother, and I were getting dressed for the event, I saw that B was sitting in our bed, wearing pajamas, and reading. "You gonna get ready?" I asked. Calmly, B said, "No, I'm not going. I've decided not to celebrate your birthday with you. In fact, I've found a new apartment for myself and Lilly. We'll be moving out next weekend. And, by the way, I got a gift for your birthday. But I've decided I'm going to return it tomorrow."

I stood a bit stunned, frozen in my own (former) bedroom. I wasn't completely surprised by this news, but I was taken aback by the calm, almost robotic manner in which she delivered it.

Dinner sucked. B and I were breaking up, and it was announced to me on my fucking birthday. My mother took me aside. "Let's be honest," she said. "You don't really love this girl. You only THINK you love her, because she's SO IN LOVE WITH YOU!" The woman's insight was dead-on. She was absolutely right.

When my kids, my mother, and I returned to my apartment, I entered our bedroom. "Quick, close the door," B said. "Why? What's wrong?" I panicked. "I want you to screw my brains our RIGHT NOW!" B pulled aside the covers, showed me her naked body, and spread her legs wide apart. "Bang me as hard as you can, birthday boy," she demanded. Ever the horny bastard, I fulfilled her request, albeit reluctantly.

It was by far the best sex we ever had.

****

That weekend, I watched with mixed feelings as moving men removed Bella's possessions. I would now be fully responsible for the lease agreement on this very expensive place. I also had to fork over to Bella 50% of her share of the security deposit, the washer and dryer, the draperies, and the custom closets we'd jointly purchased.

This, my "second divorce," would cost me many thousands of dollars.

****

On that last day together, I walked Bella to her car. She placed Lilly inside, hugged me, and whispered, "I'm sorry this didn't work out." "A noble effort," I replied. Moments after she drove off, I found a broom, and swept every fucking square inch of that enormous apartment. It took me over two hours, and I was sweating like a pig. When I was done, I scooped up a Volkswagen-sized ball of errant cat fur and tossed it into the trash can behind the garage.

I came back inside, opened every window in the place, took in a long, deep inhale, and then slowly and gently exhaled.

And at that moment, while I had lived through, yet again, another truly disastrous relationship with a woman, and added, yet again, another painful chapter of proof to my Past Life Carrots Curse theory, I never felt happier, healthier, or freer, in my entire life.

Chapter Twenty-Seven

The Third UFO & The Field of Orbs (2008)

I was in a bookstore sometime in 2007 and stumbled into the "Paranormal Books" aisle. Having never-before seen books like these, I left that store with an armful of them, and began to study the history of "UFOlogy." I was fascinated by legendary UFO sightings that took place in Washington State, Mexico City, Florida, Texas, Phoenix, Washington, D.C., the Bermuda Triangle, the UK, and above New York State; UFO saucer crashes covered up by the government, including those in Roswell; Aurora, Texas; Kecksburg, PA; and elsewhere; the abductions of Betty and Barney Hill, Travis Walton, and Whitely Streiber; Hitler's flying saucer research and "flying disc" program, and the various theories behind the "Truth Embargo" and the international and intentional governmental cover-up of visitors from Outer Space.

After extensive study, I came to realize that extraterrestrial biological entities (EBEs) have been visiting Earth for tens of thousands of years. I joined MUFON (the Mutual UFO Network) in Los Angeles and began attending that organization's monthly meetings. I also attended various lectures across Southern California on this topic, one that had become unexpectedly important to me.

I got really lucky with MUFON -- the very first meeting I attended in 2007 featured a guest speaker named Giorgio Tsoukalos. Giorgio, who had been mentored by Erich von Daniken, the author of *Chariots of the Gods* and the creator of the "Ancient Astronaut Theory," presented a 90-minute lecture about that theory and showed films and slides of ancient architectural sites from around the world. Giorgio proposed the idea that extraterrestrials have been visiting planet Earth for a very long time and have interacted with human beings since the inception of mankind. Two years later, Giorgio would go on to create, produce, and star in the hit TV series on the History Channel called *Ancient Aliens* (2009).

I was absolutely awed by Giorgio's talk, realizing instantly that here was the "hidden history of mankind" – facts that were never presented to me by my parents, my Rabbi, or my grade school/high school/college teachers. At the end of Giorgio's presentation, I shook his hand, tears in my eyes, and said, "Giorgio, thanks so much for sharing your wisdom with us tonight! You've just changed my entire world view." To which he replied, "Cool, thanks man. I'm glad you're one of us now!"

Concurrent with my newfound UFO fascination, I got a call from a woman I'd paid $1500 to for matchmaking services a year earlier. I'd forgotten that she even existed. "I've found the perfect woman for you," she said. "An Emmy Award-winning writer for television. She's smart, funny, Jewish and has a great sense of humor." Me: "Is she attractive?" Lisa: "Well, *I think so.*"

Bethany became my next "Carrot."

Our first date was very pleasant. She and I went to an Indian food restaurant near her apartment in Studio City. We talked and joked and laughed for a long while. I learned that her father was also a brilliant scientist who'd invented technology for the government (we had that in common,) and her mother was a retired schoolteacher. She also had a sister who was a schoolteacher in Massachusetts, but one who'd never married. "She's the oddball in the family," Bethany revealed of her sibling, "she's got a touch of Asperger's."

For our second date, we had Chinese food, and I drank two martinis. We saw a movie, and afterward, (as she'd say later) I "kidnapped her" into having an ice cream sundae for dessert. I walked her to her apartment door and tried to kiss her goodnight. As Bethany later told it, my mouth was open as "wide as a lion's. I thought you were going to eat my face off! You scared me away."

That Christmas Day, I spent time with my children, when I got a call from my matchmaker. "What did you do to poor Bethany?" she asked. "She wants nothing to do with you." I was taken aback. First of all, I barely remembered even trying to kiss her, and secondly, I thought she kissed me back. "I tried to kiss her goodnight, that's all. I didn't jump on her, rape her, or grab her boobs. What is she telling you?" The woman explained that I'd been "much too aggressive" with Bethany, and that, "unless you do some serious apologizing, you'll never see her again."

The rest of that holiday weekend, I was so annoyed, I cleaned my enormous apartment from top to bottom. I scrubbed every hardwood floor in the place, on my hands and knees, with a bucket, Playtex gloves and a scrub brush. I could not believe that I'd scared this new woman away so quickly.

Finally, I got up the nerve to call Bethany. "Listen, I hear that I mauled you last week. I'm sorry. I didn't mean to do that. I would never hurt you, ever, in any way. I'd like to see you again, but if you don't want to, I understand. I just wanted you to know that I am truly sorry." She admitted that she was attracted to me, and that I was a "great guy," but she was NOT seeking a highly physical or sexual relationship "just yet." "If we have chemistry together," she explained, "then I'm certainly open to sleeping with you. But that's not what I'm looking for right away."

Bethany gave me a shot at a third date. A total gentleman, I never once touched her. Dates 4, 5, and 6 were similar, and, by date seven, she agreed to come to my apartment for dinner by my fireplace. I cooked the one and only dish I knew (lemon chicken). We ate, drank wine and watched TV. After we cleaned up, we curled up next to each other on my couch, the fireplace roaring, and we kissed.

The first second I kissed Bethany, I had the utterly odd feeling that she and I were RELATED. Kissing her felt like I was kissing my Aunt Edie (my mother's sister) back in Brooklyn. The feeling wasn't sexy or intriguing or romantic. It felt like I was literally kissing my SISTER, if, in fact, *I actually had a sister.*

After just a short time we both stopped kissing each other. "Well, that was interesting," she said. "Interesting… yes, I think that *is* the right word for it," I added.

For the next ten months, B and I became inseparable. She met all of my friends, my children, my parents, my brothers, and was well-liked by all. Even Kim, my ex-wife, said, "Bethany is the one you should marry, Dan."

Bethany made dinners for me at her apartment at least once or twice a week, and we'd take turns renting old, classic movies, that one, or the other of us, had never seen before. After the movies, we'd kiss for a while, hop into bed and have unbelievably awkward sex. This lasted for three months or so.

We then had a talk: "Bethany, I love you. You're the nicest, smartest, best woman I've ever known. But our physical connection just doesn't work -- I think you know that already." Bethany: "Yes, of course I do. I'm not stupid." Me: "The only way I can explain it, is that it feels to me like we're related somehow. When I'm with you in bed or kissing you, I feel like I'm having sex with one of my aunts from back East. It's the strangest thing… I've never had this experience before with any other woman. I'm really, really sorry, but I just can't be sexual with you any longer."

Bethany nodded. "I absolutely agree. I really wish we had that physical chemistry thing, because I love you very much also. I think we're probably doomed to just being friends, I guess." "Best friends," I added.

Both of our mothers thought we were nuts. "So, what's holding you up in marrying my Bethany?" her mother once asked me, point blank, during a deli lunch also attended by Bethany and her father. Me: "Well, urh, ah, uhmmm, I love her, I really do love her, but I don't think we're 'IN LOVE' with each other." B's Mom: "Well GET IN LOVE!" Her father was awash in embarrassment.

After my mother met Bethany, she said: "So what's wrong with THIS ONE? This girl is PERFECT for you. You should marry her tomorrow!" Me: "Ah, mom, our sex life is terrible. It doesn't work.

Screwing her is like screwing Aunt Edie." My mother: "That's ridiculous. You could find a pimple on Jesus' ass. You're obviously a moron."

For the next eight months, Bethany and I did, in fact become BEST FRIENDS. Together, we went everywhere, did everything, helped each other with every problem, on a virtual 24/7 basis. She helped my daughter write a major essay for college, helped me identify the fact that my son also had Asperger's Syndrome, and took my daughter to her first, ever ballet.

I gave Bethany feedback on the book she was writing, advice on how to get payments from her freelance writing clients who were in arrears, and even attended her parents' 50th wedding anniversary dinner as her boyfriend.

I was also able to interest Bethany in my UFO studies. She and I would attend MUFON meetings together, fascinated by the speakers and their flying saucer-filled movies. We'd laugh hysterically at the questions asked by some of the whack-o attendees. ("Do you think that Mr. Spock and Darth Vadar were related?" asked an enormous man, of a world-renowned UFO investigator. Bethany and I nicknamed this huge guy, "Tiny.")

One such MUFON seminar featured a cleric named James Gilliland, who owned a ranch in upstate Washington called ECETI. His property was a world-famous UFO hot spot, as the skies above it offered spectacular UFO shows almost nightly. The site had been researched by hundreds of authors, scientists, and professors, as well as by the U.S. Air Force, NASA, and the FBI. Gilliland held an annual 4th of July gathering at his ranch every year, attracting UFO buffs from around the world. I asked Bethany if she'd go with me. "Are we gonna sleep in the same bed?" Me: "Yes, of course." Bethany: "Let me think about it."

After a couple of weeks of my hounding her, Bethany finally relented. "OK, I'll go to the UFO ranch with you, but you have to promise me that you'll bring your CPAP machine. You snore like a wild boar." (I'd invested in a machine that alleviated my snoring the year before. It was heavy and clumsy and had to be filled with water, but my gal-pal insisted I schlep it to upstate Washington.)

We flew first into Portland, then drove through the magnificent mountains and forests of upstate Washington, until we finally arrived at a cozy little bed and breakfast place. That week, Bethany and I attended several seminars about UFO sightings, heard theories about ancient aliens (those who helped construct the pyramids in Egypt and Central and South America,) and watched an interesting documentary film about "Orbs," something I'd never heard of before. Orbs are bright, usually round-shaped lights that appear only in digital photos or on film. They often appear floating about a person or group of people. Theories about orbs vary. Some believe they are physical manifestations of the dead, either human or animal. Some people think they're visitors from other dimensions.

That first night, dozens of people set up lawn chairs on Gilliland's ranch property, and shot hundreds of digital photographs of themselves, dancing and singing. Bethany and another woman joined in the activities, as I took photos. When we reviewed those digital pictures moments later, there were HUNDREDS of very prominent ORBS appearing all around her! These same orbs could not be seen by the naked eye.

While sitting in the field of "Orbs" each night of that three-day weekend, we'd see bright lights, moving in all directions across the sky, every few hours. However, I was skeptical, since these lights could have been meteors, or comets, or shooting stars, or satellites.

During our third and final night in the field, we were looking up at the sky and nothing was happening. I took my car keys out of my pocket. "Barbara, if we leave right now, we can beat the traffic," I stated to her.

Seconds later, a fairly large, jet-black craft appeared directly above our heads, perhaps 200 feet in the sky. Materializing out of nowhere, it was impossible to make out the shape of the craft. On its bottom was a large, clear dome which began to beam down upon us a very bright, emerald-green-colored light you'd never find in nature.

(The same color as the Land of Oz in *The Wizard of Oz*/1939.) This intense, emerald-green light then BLINKED ON AND OFF ABOUT A DOZEN TIMES (Morse code?) During these light flashes, I received these messages: "Hello, sorry we kept you waiting so long. We were in the neighborhood and wanted to say hi. We love you and we wish you the best, always. Be kind to one another. We'll see you again, one day." The craft then SIMPLY VANISHED. Everyone in the field applauded.

This vehicle was NOT a meteor, comet, shooting star or satellite. It was not a plane, helicopter, missile, drone, or Chinese weather balloon.

I realized I was crying… so touched by this extraordinary moment in my life. My heart was beating fast. This was, without question, a bona fide, 100% UFO sighting! I am convinced that whoever, or whatever, the "pilots" of this craft were, they did not belong to the human race.

****

For the next five months, Bethany and I continued our "best buddies" routine without interruption. We'd become family to each other and did everything possible together under the sun EXCEPT have sex. Then, one day just before the holidays in December, she called me. "I need to talk with you about something. It's important. Can I come over now?" I knew this wasn't gonna be pretty.

I was cleaning out my car, which was parked in my garage, when Bethany pulled her car up in the alley where I was standing. I could tell immediately she'd been crying. "We need to talk," she said. We sat on the ground between our two cars. "I love you very, very much, and I know that you love me, too. And I just have to tell you that it's killing me that we're never gonna marry each other. I decided I can't just be friends with you any longer, Danny. I love you too much."

She began sobbing. I felt like a total piece of crap. "I am so, so sorry," I offered. "I really wish things were different between us. I don't understand why 'karma' or 'fate' or 'destiny' would play this cruel trick on us." I held her in my arms as she cried.

"We can still be friends, though, right?" I asked. "No, I'm sorry. You don't understand. I CAN'T SEE YOU ANYMORE AT ALL. It's too painful," she said. At that moment it really hit me. I was about to lose my very best friend. A few tears filled my eyes, and I realized she wasn't joking around. "Fuck!" I said. "I don't think I can live without you. What am I supposed to do now?" Sobbing again, Bethany waved goodbye, and drove away.

It took me many months to "de-Bethany-ize" my head, my heart, and my life.

While we emailed each other a few times afterward, I saw her just once more (for a quick lunch) many years later. Last I heard, she was now happily married.

PS: Past Life Curse, anyone?

Chapter Twenty-Eight

The Voice and the Supermodel (2009)

One night in early 2009, I stood in my living room, channel surfing on my large, hi-definition TV, when I came upon a program featuring an incredibly beautiful blonde woman sitting on the floor, vomiting into a trash can. Fascinated, I stood watching the rest of the show, *Celebrity Rehab Presents Sober House* (2009,) which aired on VH-1.

I'd never heard of the series, which presented eight "celebrities" (most of whom a far stretch from that word) going through withdrawal from their addictions to drugs and alcohol, on national television. There was a marathon of *Celebrity Rehab* episodes that day, so I sat watching half a dozen in a row. Quite simply, I was mesmerized by this blonde woman, who was coming off a 20-year addiction to painkillers.

As I watched her puking, sobbing, and wiping tears from her Goddess-like face, I HEARD A VOICE that whispered into my right ear: "SHE NEEDS YOUR HELP!"

I swear to God, I really did!

Her name was Amber Smith. Go ahead, Google her photos. I'll wait.

I'd never heard of Amber before, so I looked her up on the Internet, and found her website. There, I saw photographs of perhaps the most stunning, blonde, sex-bomb model ever. I discovered she'd appeared on the cover of more than 300 magazines around the world, including a 1985 issue of *Playboy* that had been published during the time I worked there. Amber was a tall, extremely attractive blonde from Florida who, in the *Playboy* layout, had posed with large yellow feather-fans, and very dark red lipstick.

At the bottom of Amber's website was a phone number as a contact. I called and left the following message: "Hello, Amber, my name is Dan. I'm a publicist in Beverly Hills. I've been watching your show, and I simply have to say that it's breaking my heart. Your story has touched me, deeply. If you need some help re-starting your career, I'd be glad to try to help you. I know this sounds kind of crazy, but I simply felt compelled to call and reach out to you. If you'd like to have lunch with me sometime to meet, please let me know. My phone number is XYZ. Either way, I wish you the best of luck with your sobriety and I hope you're able to stay away from drugs in the future. Clearly, they're NOT your friends. Take care."

A few days later, I got a call. "Dan? This is Carol Smith. I'm Amber's mother. We were very touched by your message, and we'd like to meet with you."

I was taken aback. I'd actually gotten a response!

Over the course of the next few days, I researched everything I could find on the Internet about Amber Smith. I also developed a list of possible publicity, promotional, and marketing ideas for her, such as potential product endorsements, public appearances, speakers' bureaus, talent agents to meet with, etc. I wanted to be prepared for this meeting with my "Damsel in Distress."

I'd chosen my favorite Hollywood restaurant, Musso & Frank, for our lunch meeting. Arriving in an old, loud, junk-heap of a car, Amber and Carol got out. We sat at a plush red leather booth (Amber in the middle) and for the next two hours, I told them about myself, my career, and my ideas for Amber to pursue, now that she was sober. She revealed a good deal to me about her struggles with drugs -- an addiction she shared WITH HER MOTHER -- for over 20 years! Carol had become clean, also, but now the two women faced an even more prominent problem: poverty.

"I'm broke," Amber told me. "I had everything, a house, cars, clothes, money in the bank. It's all gone. My problem got really bad about five years ago, and my mother and I were almost homeless. We were living in a tiny Hollywood hotel room, and I didn't know where my next rent check was gonna come from. Then, I heard about the *Celebrity Rehab* TV show, and I called the producers, begging them to help me. I didn't do that show for the fame or the publicity. I did it because without it, I knew I was gonna die."

Amber's ability to articulate her struggles with drug addiction and the devastation it left behind in her personal life, were extremely powerful. I sat on the edge of my seat. I'd never, in my life, met a hardcore drug addict before.

I told Amber that "a voice" told me to help her, and that I'd like to be both her personal publicist and her manager, for free. "I'm not here for money," I told the women. "I'm here because I'm supposed to help you." I picked up the check for lunch and walked the two back to their shitty car.

Later that week, I invited Amber to have dinner with me. I wanted to discuss our new relationship and have her sign a management contract. I picked her up and drove her to a Mexican place in Beverly Hills. She looked stunning. As we entered the restaurant, I noticed that the head of EVERY SINGLE PERSON (both men AND women) turned, to watch her simply walk across the room. When we sat at the booth, I said, "Wow. Everyone stared at you walking in here. What's that like?"

She replied, "It's been happening to me since I was 15. I don't even notice it anymore."

Amber and I had a fun meal. Our "relationship" was fresh and brand new. We talked about our childhoods, our careers, and our lives, in broad strokes. The fact that she had been a true supermodel in the 1990s (*Maxim* Magazine once voted her "One of the Sexiest Women Alive"), never entered into the conversation. We were just "a guy and a girl" having dinner and bonding as friends.

During dinner, Amber told me she'd been invited to participate in another VH-1 TV show, this one called *Sex Rehab with Dr. Drew* (2009).

"Are you a sex addict?" I asked.

"Oh God, no, not at all," Amber told me. "I'm not even a big fan of sex, at all. Actually, I'm a LOVE ADDICT. It's something entirely different."

She went on to explain that during the course of her life, she'd had "a lot of sex with a lot of men," but other than the "15 seconds of cumming and then, so what?" she never enjoyed it. She confessed she'd never had a "real" boyfriend, had never been married, and had never experienced "true love." The concept seemed alien to her.

Her affliction in this area was a mental, romantic "disconnect." She'd meet an extremely good-looking man at a party or a nightclub, speak with him briefly, and then become completely and totally smitten with him, beyond anything resembling normalcy. She would start stalking these men, finding out where they'd be and when, and show up, unannounced, just to stare at them from a distance. Amber told me the "high" she felt from doing this was even more powerful than the high she got from drugs.

"Wow," I said. "I did that with a girl I couldn't talk to in college. I called her 'Long Red.' I never knew there was a name for that condition."

Amber replied, "Most people don't know anything about love addiction. It's not been discussed within popular culture. I'm hoping that my appearance on the new show will help spread the word about this disease to others."

For the *Sex Rehab* TV program, Amber, along with seven actual sex addicts comprised of rock stars, porn stars, models, and filmmakers, would be confined to the Pasadena Recovery Center for three weeks. She would have limited access to a telephone, and none to the Internet. During those weeks, I began reaching out to a variety of potential business partners for us, including talent agents, modeling agents, nightclub promoters, marketers of new products, ad agencies representing iconic brands, etc.

However, I quickly came to learn that because of her recent national "celebrity" on the TV shows that had aired the year previous (*Celebrity Rehab* and *Sober House*), Amber had earned a reputation for herself as, perhaps, the country's most beautiful drug addict. One noted, female talent agent actually told me, "She's probably the most stunning woman I've ever seen in my life. Unfortunately, she has the 'stink' of drug addict on her. I don't think that's something she'll ever be able to shake off, certainly not in Hollywood."

During her second week at the rehab center, Amber called and invited me to come for a "family and friends" BBQ visit, asking if I wouldn't mind picking up her mother along the way. During that car ride, Carol told me how sad it was that Amber just couldn't find the "right guy," had never been in love, and had never even had a real boyfriend. When we arrived at the clinic, Amber (and a TV crew) approached us. She looked especially sad.

"What's wrong?" I asked.

Amber replied, "The therapy here has been really tough. This is so much harder than even drug withdrawal." She explained that since she was now drug-free for the first time in 20 years, she was beginning to "feel again," and was delving into long-hidden feelings about her father's abandonment and guilt over his death. (Amber's dad, who left when she was five, drank himself to death. His body, along with hundreds of empty alcohol bottles, was found aboard a boat he owned. Amber, who was on the set of a low-budget movie at the time, blamed herself for not being there for him the day he passed away.)

After Amber was done with the three-week stint filming the new TV series, she and I, for the next four months, took meetings all over town with agents. Amber once turned down an offer for her own reality TV show (much to my dismay) because the powers that be wouldn't name her an executive producer! We also met for lunches at least a few times a week, visited each other at our respective apartments and spoke by phone at least four times a day.

I threw a birthday party for myself that June; my closest friends attended. About an hour late, Amber walked in, bringing all conversation to a screeching halt.

My friend, Jamie, pulled me aside. "Danny, I'm so NOT a lesbian, but for HER I'd make an exception!"

Jamie's husband, Andy, added, "God, she's so good-looking, it's off-putting."

Amber instantly eclipsed the attention of my gang, but it meant a lot to me that she showed up at all. When she left, she handed me an oversized birthday card. It read: "I know the going hasn't been easy so far, but I really appreciate all you have done to help me, and all of your selfless sacrifices. I honor our friendship and have had a lot of fun! You have quickly become a great friend and confidant to me. Here's to a wonderful, prosperous future. Happy birthday, and may this year be unforgettable for us both. Love, Amber."

Amber was invited to sign autographs at a booth at "Comic Con" (the biggest science fiction and comic book show in the world) that summer in San Diego. I suggested that she and I drive down together and stay at a (cheap) area motel. I'd help her set up her station at the booth. "Sounds like fun," she said.

From that Friday morning until that Sunday evening, Amber and I were inseparable, although I'd injured my right ankle dancing at my niece's wedding the weekend prior and was forced to walk with a cane the whole time! We drove down to San Diego together, picking up a wacky, model girlfriend of hers along the way, checked into our little motel rooms (side-by-side), and set up shop at the booth of her sponsor, a top comic book company. Amber was among at least eight other "Booth Babes" sitting there, including several former *Playboy* bunnies, rock stars' wives, indie film "scream queens," and one red-haired, WWF wrestler to whom I said, "You RE-INVENT the word HOT!" The woman replied, "I know!"

While the attendance for the show was record-breaking, guys who wanted to shell out good money for photos of pretty girls weren't amongst the crowd. (These geeky guys wanted autographs from "Mr. Spock" from *Star Trek*, (1966) and "Captain Adama" from *Battlestar Gallactica* (2004,) not from half-naked babes.) Amber and I lost money that weekend when we factored in gas, motel rooms, food, and "bike taxis." After parking the car incredibly far from the convention hall, we would sit very closely together in little bike taxis, pedaled by incredibly muscular men and women. Laughing and talking incessantly, we had tremendous fun during those trips, with fees of $25 in each direction. Those costs quickly mounted.

One night after her appearance, Amber and I shared some fast food in her hotel room. I chomped down fries, as I watched her remove her makeup, kick off her high heels, and change into her casual clothing (averting my eyes on purpose).

"I wish I didn't have to do these appearances anymore," she lamented. "I've been doing them forever. Girls my age don't make much money from autograph shows these days."

I said, "I only wish I was still making the income I made up until last year. We could start a business together."

Amber: "What happened?"

Me: "Wonderful George W. Bush fucked the world and killed the economy. I'm only making about 12-grand a month now, down from 32-grand a month, which I made for years."

Amber stopped eating, rolled her eyes, said, "32-grand a month?" and pretended to faint, actually dropping to the floor. We laughed. "God, I wish I was making that kind of money."

Me: "Didn't you make millions in your heyday?"

Amber: "A lot of people made a lot of money from me for a very long time, but during my very best year ever, I only made about $250,000. I was making good money for a while, but never 'Gisele Bündchen' money, even though I was her body double a few times."

Back in Hollywood, I helped Amber schlep her unbelievably heavy suitcases up to her apartment door. We hugged and then, as I turned to walk away, she said out loud, but perhaps more to herself, "I love you, Dan."

I froze in time. Did I just hear correctly? I turned around. Amber stood about 15 feet from me, staring. The moment was suspended.

Me: "Amber, I love you, too. You know that, right? You KNOW I love you, RIGHT?"

She smiled. "Yeah, yeah, I know. Thanks for everything. Good night."

We stared at each other for a few seconds more. Then I split. I didn't know what else to do.

For months that summer, I arranged public appearances for Amber around the U.S. at nightclubs, parties, autograph shows, and even at a college campus, where she spoke about overcoming drug and love addiction. While I was helping her generate a few thousand dollars a month (and constantly driving her to and from airports for those appearances), she hit a snag financially.

"Dan, I can't pay my rent. What am I gonna do?" she asked.

Deeply touched and completely smitten with her, I handed her $2,000. "You'll pay me back someday when you're making the big bucks again," I said.

Hugging me, she said, "You're the only man on the planet I can count on and completely trust. What would I do without you? You are truly my hero."

I arranged a meeting for Amber and myself with a multi-bestselling author who I was able to contact, as he was friends with my cousin Franz, an internationally acclaimed magician. This author (whose book about picking up women was an international bestseller) was instantly smitten with Amber and agreed to help us pursue a book deal with a major, New York-based publishing company for rights to her autobiography. Then things took a strange turn. This author hired a nobody, young, potential hot new author he discovered from Toronto to write up a few sample chapters of Amber's life after having spent just a few days with her, one-on-one. When this famous author presented us with those sample chapters, Amber and I were shocked and disgusted. "These chapters are not remotely in "Amber's voice," we told the famed writer and rejected them.

Once that happened the whole thing fell apart, plus the publishing house this author was associated with decided that, while Amber's life story would "certainly make for compelling reading," they just didn't feel there would be "enough of an audience to actually buy such a product." Amber and I, who'd literally performed a dance for joy in the street after our first meeting with that best-selling author, were crushed when the deal, which seemed like a sure thing, eventually fell through.

We decided to drown our sorrows over our lost book fortune at a killer Indian food restaurant in Beverly Hills. As I slathered up a big piece of naan with raita, and was about to inhale it, she said something like, "Yada, yada, yada, blah, blah, blah, AND IF WE EVER END UP HAVING SEX TOGETHER, etc., etc., etc., yada, yada."

I almost choked on my naan. I wished at that moment that the previous two sentences had been videotaped, so I could have played them back. I wasn't paying close attention to her preceding thoughts, so I wasn't 100% sure if her "having sex together" phrase was in reference to *me* or to one of the "love addiction" guys she was obsessed with from afar. (I didn't ask, so I'll never know.)

Amber and I went to see the incredibly scary horror film *Paranormal Activity* (2009) together. We were so frightened during the course of that film, we took turns grabbing each other's legs, and turning to each other with fear. (She was so scared she had her eyes covered at the very end of the movie, the most unsettling moment of all.) After the film ended, we were so rattled, we remained in our seats for quite a while, until the feeling subsided.

Leaving the theater, we went to a nearby nightclub, where we watched one of her best friends perform stand-up comedy. I hadn't felt this close to any woman in years. A Martian observing the two of us together would have said that Amber and I were on a date. (In heels, Amber was *very tall,* I think 6'3". I used to insert "lifts" into my shoes to add some inches to my 5'8" height when we were together!)

Amber was invited to tape an appearance on *The Oprah Winfrey Show* (1986,) along with Dr. Drew Pinsky, and two of her cast mates (sex addicts) from the VH-1 program. I worked with Oprah's team to make Amber's arrangements (the show taped in Chicago.) Weeks later, when that episode of Oprah's show aired, my daughter was home from college and Amber came to my apartment to watch.

There I was, sitting on the couch with my beautiful daughter to my left and my beautiful best friend, the supermodel, on my right, as the three of us watched Amber chatting with Oprah about the differences between sex and love addiction. It was truly a surreal moment in my life. (Oprah really seemed to "spark" to Amber's plight, even confessing a case of "love addiction" that Oprah, herself, had experienced decades earlier.)

****

"I got a great booking in Vegas," Amber called. "Fifteen hundred bucks to show up at a club and sign some autographs."

"Sounds like fun," I replied. I then realized I had both a brand-new Mercedes Benz, and absolutely nothing to do with myself that weekend. "Let's go together. I'll drive," I said.

"Great," she replied, "Should we stay there overnight? The gig will end around 2 am."

Thinking quickly, I offered, "Why don't I get us a room with two beds?"

Amber: "Perfect, thanks. Sounds like a plan."

I went online and arranged for a fairly inexpensive room with two beds, within walking distance of the nightclub in which she was to appear.

For the next four days, I was a nervous wreck. I was going to be sleeping in the same room with my best friend, Amber Smith, the supermodel. I wrote down a little speech I planned to deliver during that weekend. "Amber, I think I'm starting to have feelings for you, and I just felt the time has come for me to let you know."

I picked Amber up from her tiny dive apartment in Hollywood at 2 pm that Saturday afternoon and for the next six hours straight, we drove through a good deal of traffic to Las Vegas. We never once played the radio or the "positive thinking" CD she brought along for the road. We talked about everything under the sun, neither repeating a stream of conversation nor ever running out of stories to recount.

We arrived at the front desk of the Vegas hotel. I gave the female clerk my info and credit card, and she pulled me up on her computer. "Here you are," she said.

"The room's got two beds, right?" I asked in full sincerity.

The woman slowly looked at me, then the blonde goddess standing beside me, then looked back at me. She said, "Yeah, sure, right." (Only in retrospect did I realize she was being sarcastic.)

Amber and I got upstairs and, you guessed it, there was only ONE BED in the room. We both stood, frozen. "Amber, there's only one bed in here."

Amber: "Yeah, I see that."

Me: "You KNOW I ordered two beds, right? I just want you to be sure that you KNOW I did that, okay?"

Amber: "Yes, I know. Don't worry, I believe you. What should we do? Should we go back down and switch rooms?"

Realizing she only had about two hours to eat dinner, get dressed, and walk over to the nightclub, I said, "You know what? I'll sleep on the floor. Don't worry about it, it's not a big deal. I really don't care."

Amber: "Thanks, Dan. I appreciate that."

For the next 90 minutes, Amber and I sat side-by-side on the bed, ate a really shitty room service meal (ice cold French fries and greasy burgers), and watched an old comedy movie.

"God, I have NO INTEREST in doing this appearance tonight," she said.

Me: "I know. I would do ANYTHING if you and I could just stay here on this bed all night and watch movies."

Amber: "Me too! That sounds like heaven! I WISH we could do that and nothing else!"

The time came for Amber to prepare for her appearance. Watching her stand in the bathroom in just bra and panties, putting on her makeup, installing her hair extensions, and slinking into her skintight sexy costume, I was greatly surprised to find myself *not* turned on! In all honesty, I actually felt like Amber was my wife and we were simply a married couple getting ready for a night out on the town.

We arrived at the club and Amber was asked to pose for some photographs with the owner in front of the entryway signage. The promoter handed me Amber's check for $1,500, which I pocketed, then led us inside. The place was packed, and the DJ's music was deafening. (I have custom-made ear plugs for such occasions.) The club owner then brought us to the VIP table, sat down with Amber and me, and had two very sexy waitresses bring us round after round of Petron tequila. Amber, a recovering alcoholic, said, "I SO shouldn't be drinking tonight."

"I know," I answered, "but I don't think there's much of anything else to do here right now."

Amber: "You're right. A little tequila won't kill me."

The club owner split, and Amber and I sat on our big fat asses for the next four hours, drinking. Occasionally, a club patron or two would approach her for an autograph or a photo but, by and large, we were on an incredibly loud "date," for which she was being paid solely for her wondrously luminous presence.

A club photographer came by at one point and snapped a Polaroid picture of Amber and me hugging. The SECOND I saw that photo I said to myself, "Oh My God! I'm IN LOVE with AMBER SMITH! What the fuck am I gonna do now?" (Stupidly, I let Amber keep that photo – something I tremendously regret today.)

Not to be gross, but almost every rap music song the DJ played that night had lyrics revolving around the singer's demand for anal sex.

Amber and I, now both drunk, were laughing hysterically, taking turns reciting the unbelievably nonsensical words to these horrific rap songs. "John Lennon must be spinning in his grave right now," I screamed into Amber's ears. She fell against me, laughing, her lovely breasts pressed against my shoulder and her long blonde hair spilling over my face.

Finally, 2 am arrived, and the promoter "sprung" us from this hellhole. He walked us back to our room, shook my hand, hugged Amber goodbye, then split. We entered the room, drunk, and were both instantly reminded that there was just one bed.

Not wanting to let the tension last too long, I simply said, "Amber, I need to ask you a HUGE FAVOR right now."

Amber: "What's that?"

Me: "I really don't want to sleep on the floor tonight. Can I share the bed with you?"

"Yeah, sure, of course, that's fine," she said.

I popped on my PJs and slid under the covers, while Amber entered the bathroom to "de-supermodel" herself. She returned in sweatpants and a loose-fitting T-shirt with no bra.

Amber got under the covers and turned off the lights. I was now lying in bed with one of the most beautiful women on Earth, at 3 in the morning, drunk. Just inches apart, I realized if I didn't do SOMETHING just then, I'd regret it for the rest of my life.

I next did something so spontaneously stupid, I truly surprised even myself. I got onto my hands and knees, straddled Amber, and positioned myself directly over her face. "Amber, I need to kiss you right now," I declared. I stared into her eyes with love.

Her eyes were those of a deer caught in the headlights. She was horrified!

I slowly leaned my mouth down to press my lips against hers. She quickly turned her face. I got "the cheek." Truly surprised, I lifted my head back up, looked again into her shocked face, then went back down for a second try, this time kissing the other cheek. I lifted my head, looked directly into her face for a few seconds, then said, in hasty retreat, "Well, goodnight then." I got off my hands and knees, crawled under the covers, and instantly passed out, snoring just seconds later.

For all these years since, I've questions myself a thousand times: "Why didn't I tell her I was in love with her?" or even, "Why didn't I just gently suggest the possibility of sex to her?" The truth is, I knew instinctively that Amber simply had ZERO physical attraction toward me before I even went in for that first kiss. No amount of friendship-style love was ever going to change that, and it was just a fact of reality I was going to have to accept.

The next morning, my gal pal and I awoke about the same time. "Hey Amber, I just realized I can tell all of my friends I SLEPT WITH A SUPERMODEL!"

"Yeah, I guess that's true," she chuckled sincerely, and I knew she was not the least bit offended by my reprehensible actions the night before.

We drove back to L.A., and again chatted non-stop for six consecutive hours. Amber brought up the "I've never had a real boyfriend, never been in love" theme she mentioned the day before, and I replied, "You know what? I actually find that hard to believe. Take me through the history of your love life, and let's be honest."

Hours later, Amber realized that there were a number of men she'd known in her past that truly DID love her. While most of them dumped her for becoming too clingy and needy, she did admit that she even dumped a few of them herself, when THEY became too clingy to HER.

"Wow," she said, "I never realized that before. I *have loved* some men, and some men have loved me."

"Of course," I said, "who could possibly date you and NOT fall in love with you?"

Then, the killer part came up. She said, "These days, it's so hard for me to find someone to date, because I'll only go out with extremely good-looking men, over six feet tall, who remind me of my father. My dad resembled Superman. I can't possibly be attracted to anyone else, for some reason." I believe this was Amber's cryptic way of telling ME that *I* simply would never make the "cut" within her stringent dating criteria.

I'd pre-written (prior to our drive to Vegas) my little "Amber, I think I'm starting to have feelings for you" speech on a yellow sticky post-it note, which was pasted to the left side of my steering wheel.

I promised myself that at some point during our time in Sin City I was going to spill my guts, and let her know how I really felt. After the "I only date extremely good-looking, tall men who look like Superman" speech, we stopped off for gas. I surreptitiously tore off the yellow sticker from the dashboard and tossed it in the trash. "It's just NEVER GONNA HAPPEN," I said out loud to myself, as I filled the tank, preparing for our long drive back home to L.A.

A few weeks later, Amber met a multi-multi-millionaire at one of the Texas nightclub appearances I booked for her. This recently-divorced guy made his fortune by inventing some kind of unique dental implants. Soon thereafter, he bought a mansion in the Hollywood Hills solely to allow Amber to live there so she would be available to him at his beck and call. At this point, my relationship with her quickly faded into history. My family and friends said to me, "God, she used you SO BAD," to which I, unfortunately, have no defense.

I became extremely disappointed that the minute Amber got involved with a mega-wealthy man, she was unable to find the time to maintain our friendship, dropping me like a hot potato. I honestly and sincerely believed that we'd become REAL honest-to-God friends, having shared so many intimate moments during our 10 months together.

With regard to our short relationship, I feel Amber's biggest flaw was simply her extraordinary inability to appreciate and nurture the love of a true friend. Her TV mentor, Dr. Drew Pinsky, once said of her, "Amber Smith is an empty person and she's struggling. She has a lot of emptiness and she doesn't even know sometimes what she's feeling." For me, those sentiments sum it up best.

Now, 15 years later, I reflect back on Amber as my penultimate "Carrot on a Stick"—a woman with brains, beauty, honesty, sexuality, and mystery—whom I truly loved, or thought I loved, but could never quite "attain."

Today, she will no longer return my phone calls, emails, or texts. So close and yet so far!

My relationship with Amber Smith the Supermodel did, however, provide me with something tangible and everlasting…the material you just read in this chapter.

Chapter Twenty-Nine

The Alaskan Psychic (2012)

When my son, Jordan, was 14, he'd been taken on a cruise to Alaska by his grandmother—Kim's mom. When he returned to LA, he said, "Dad, when I'm an adult, I'm moving to Alaska. While I was there, I never felt better or happier in my life." My response was to chuckle and say, "yeah, sure kid. That'll happen."

Jordan attended college at Cal State Long Beach and during that time was diagnosed with "the worst allergies I've ever seen in my 40-year career," according to Dr. Robert Eitches, LA's leading allergist. Jordan felt so sick during his freshman and sophomore years at Cal State, he was barely able to attend classes. We thought he had narcolepsy.

I took him out to dinner for his 20th birthday (May 10, 2008.) There, he said, "Dad, I'm dropping out of school and I'm leaving California. I'm moving to Alaska. Will you help me?" Now, I was stunned. "Are you SURE you want to go there, son?" I asked. "It's VERY FAR AWAY and it's VERY COLD."

"I AM moving to Alaska, Dad, with or without your help. But I'd prefer it if you could help me," he whispered.

Realizing that my son had a calling, that his allergies in California were literally killing him, and that he was now an adult, I agreed. In quick succession, I helped him get a job in Anchorage at a Best Buy store (Jordan is a true computer genius -- all I had to do was phone that store's manager, who told me, "I need your son and 20 more just like him ASAP"); I found him a one-bedroom apartment in Anchorage via an online realty website; and I arranged for his car to be shipped to Anchorage from Seattle, as well.

By September 2008, Jordan was living, working -- and doing well! -- in Anchorage, Alaska.

My son was also pursuing a spiritual path… he'd visited Peru on a class trip in high school, during which he'd taken the drug *ayahuasca* and had had astounding visions and revelations. Now up in Anchorage, he discovered a group of like-minded individuals who'd meet regularly to discuss spirituality, religion, the supernatural, and other mind-altering doctrines and philosophies.

I regularly visited my son up in Alaska once a year religiously. And while I'm not a big fan of freezing my balls off, I grew to understand his fascination with a state that offered "Air as God intended it to be," as he'd say.

During one of my visits to the Last Frontier, Jordan told me about a remarkable event that had taken place during one of his spirituality group's regular gatherings just a few weeks previous. I'll let him relay it:

"Dad, we were meditating in Patti's (his group's leader and a psychic) office, when suddenly the lights went out and everything became completely silent. There was a static electricity-type feel in the air. Then, a Being resembling a man, walked out of the closet in the office. He was glowing—he spoke no words. We all think he was Jesus, but I'm not 100% sure. This Being then opened his mouth, and jewelry and coins began pouring out. I have some of the coins as proof! We were all amazed. The Being smiled at us after he spat out those items, then silently glided backwards into the closest from which he came. I looked inside the closest afterwards, but no one was in there."

Of course, I was HIGHLY skeptical of this story. But my son SWORE TO ME that it had indeed really happened!

During that same trip, I mentioned to Jordan that I'd like to meet his psychic friend, Patti, to get a reading for myself. He phoned her and we set up a reading for the next day.

I'd only been to one "fortune teller" previously -- the one in Long Branch, New Jersey, back in '79 who told me, "Many women are attracted to you, but something goes wrong with each one you meet." Given that her pronouncement was spot-on, I had an open mind about those who worked within the psychic profession.

I met Patti at her office while Jordan remained in the waiting area. We sat, she lit a candle and we were silent. She closed her eyes for a while, then opened them and held my hand.

"Your Guardian Angel is standing behind you, right now," she whispered. "He's a tall man... funny, great sense of humor. He watches out for you and protects you. Died prematurely. Hot dogs... apparently, he loves hot dogs? He tells me that you were his favorite friend. His name starts with a capital P."

Silence for a few minutes. Then...

"His name is Paul. He encouraged you to move to California. He's very proud of all that you've accomplished."

I was truly amazed. My late friend Paul Dorfman -- my childhood friend Steve's cousin, and the man who gave me my first job post-college -- had died back in the '90s. A carpet salesman, he was showing customers a variety of rugs in the store where he worked when he suddenly collapsed and died in front of them, without warning, right there on the floor.

And yes, Paul was tall, extremely funny and LOVED hot dogs!

I never got a chance to tell Paul how much our friendship (1979-80) meant to me -- never was able to say goodbye and was unable to attend his funeral.

I do believe that Patti the Alaskan Psychic DID ACTUALLY SEE PAUL! And I'd like to also believe that perhaps it was Paul's Voice that I heard calling out to me from that "Chandelier"— the one that changed my life back in 1996.

Paul was a cross between Howard Stern and Jerry Lewis -- the funniest man I ever knew in real life.

I hope he's resting in peace and that I'm not causing him too much stress with the ongoing madness that is my personal life.

Chapter Thirty

The Death of My Father, Including the Lucid Face in the Men's Room, the Voice in the Florida Parking Lot, the Stopping of Time, the Voice from Under the Hotel Room Bed, the Bedroom Visits, the Dead Dad Dreams, and the Spiritual Chills (2016 – 2018)

As I'd mentioned previously, my father, Jack Harary, worked for the U.S. Department of the Army as an Electronics Engineer and Physicist for 45 years in New Jersey. Retiring in 1996, he and his second wife, Jean, relocated to Boca Raton, Florida, where he would live for the rest of his life.

From 1996 until 2012, my dad would fly out to Los Angeles once a year to visit with me and my kids; my brother Bob and his kids; and my brother Michael and his kids. He loved California very much -- in fact, he'd planned to retire to La Jolla, CA, in 1996, but Jean simply would not hear of it. So, instead, he was forced by marriage to make a compromise and move to Boca Raton, Florida -- something he decisively did NOT want to do.

The last time my father ever came to California was in May 2012 -- not to Los Angeles, but to San Francisco, to attend the college graduation of my daughter, Anjuli. At that time, he told me and my younger brother, Bob, that he was being treated for prostate cancer. He'd had "golden seeds" placed inside his prostate... the seeds attracted the radiation from the therapy he was undergoing, in hopes of eradicating the cancer cells.

Bob and I were greatly disturbed by this news, but our Dad seemed optimistic. After all, he'd just flown 3,000 miles by himself, at the age of 82, to attend his granddaughter's college graduation. We very much hoped and assumed that his radiation therapy would "do the trick," and knock the crap out of that disease.

In early 2013, Jean called to tell me that my father would no longer be able to fly to California to visit us. "If you want to see him, you and your brothers will have to come to Boca," she instructed. "No problem," I said.

My brother Bob and I flew out to visit Dad for his subsequent birthdays, during November 2013 and November 2014. He seemed to be doing fine and we had great dinners and talks with him. (Our youngest brother, Michael, had his own relationship with our Dad, and he and his family would go visit him in Boca, but far less often than did Bob or I.)

During our visit in November 2015, for his 85th birthday, Bob and I were eating with Dad and Jean at a great Italian restaurant. At one point, Dad got up to use the bathroom, and while he was away from the table, Jean dropped the bombshell. "Boys, your father has Stage 4 Prostate Cancer," she stated matter-of-factly. "It's incurable. He's decided not to prolong the radiation therapy. So now, it's only a matter of time until the end."

Trying to digest this surprising information, with tears in our eyes, Bob and I looked at each other in horror, as our beloved Dad came back to the table from his bathroom visit. "What did I miss?" he said. "Nothing, Dad, we were just telling Jean about our jobs," I lied.

A few months later, back in Los Angeles, I got a call from Jean. "Danny, your Dad's starting to have some really bad days. He's forgetting things and sometimes doesn't make it to the bathroom. I just want to put you and your brothers on alert that I might have to do something drastic with him in the near future." To which I replied, "Jean, Dad trusts you. Please do whatever YOU think is the right thing to do, and Bob and I will back you 100%."

Cut to: November 2016. Bob and I made our annual trek to Boca Raton to visit Dad for his 86th birthday. We'd been warned by Jean a few weeks prior that "Your Dad's memory is failing rapidly, so don't be surprised when you get here. It's been diagnosed as 'Mild Cognitive Disorder.' He's not the man you know anymore..."

Bob and I rented a car and made our way to Dad and Jean's new condo apartment. We met the two of them in the parking lot outside the building. We jogged up to Dad, and Bob and I took turns hugging him and kissing him on the cheek. "Hey Dad! So great to see you again!" Bob said. The man's reply: "Dad? Am I someone's father?" Me: "Yes, Dad. We are your sons – Danny and Bob." Dad: "Sons? I have sons? Isn't that nice! Jeannie, I have sons!"

It was a remarkable and heartbreaking moment. Bob and I were standing with our greatly beloved father -- a man who no longer had any idea who we were. My brother and I also realized this was NOT 'Mild Cognitive Disorder.'

Our Dad had severe, overwhelming Alzheimer's!

Bob and I spent that three-day weekend with Dad and Jean. We went out to breakfasts, lunches and dinners, walked through some shopping malls, and strolled along the beachfront. That Saturday night was Dad's 86th birthday – we were eating at a restaurant and the waitress brought over to our table a cake with some lit candles. Everyone in the place sang "Happy Birthday." At the end of the song, Dad looked at me and Bob and said, "Is it someone's birthday?" He had no clue that HE was the birthday-boy.

The next morning, a Sunday, the four of us went to have breakfast at a great pancake house. During the meal, Jean said, "Danny, your Dad needs to go to the bathroom. Can you take him?" "Of course," I replied. I took my Dad by the arm and we slowly but steadily made our way into the men's room. We peed together, standing at side-by-side urinals. He then washed his hands.

As I began washing my hands, he said, "Danny? Is that you?" I turned around instantly. My father's face looked different. He was smiling! And for about 30 seconds, HE HAD BECOME LUCID!

HE HAD BECOME HIS TRUE SELF AGAIN AND KNEW WHO I WAS!" I said, "Dad!! Is that YOU?" "Of course!" he responded confidently. "Dad, I love you SO, SO MUCH," I said, instantly bursting into tears. We hugged. "I love you too, Danny," he replied. I looked deeply into the face of perhaps the person I'd most loved on Earth and saw the beloved man I'd known for 60 years, one last time. However, mere seconds later, his smiling face changed and quickly morphed back to its clueless, Alzheimer's-ridden, expressionless state.

My Dad -- the man who knew me so well for six decades -- had made an ever, oh-so-brief, final appearance inside a pancake house men's room. Then his true persona evaporated once more, reverting into the face of a seriously ill man who needed my help to make pee-pee.

That same Sunday evening dinner was to be the last meal Bob and I had scheduled with Dad, as we had to return to California the next morning. We had a fine meal at a seafood restaurant, during which time my brother and I noticed that Dad could no longer order from the menu. Jean had to order for him. She'd inadvertently ordered more food than he could finish, so when he became full, there was still a good amount of salmon left on his plate, along with half a baked potato.

Our father was a child of the Depression. My brother and I never, once, in our lives, ever saw him NOT FINISH the full meal on his plate.

Dad turned to his wife. "Jeannie, can we take this fish home?" "No, Jackie, we don't 'do' leftovers," Jean replied, harshly. Bob and I looked at each other, thinking this was a rather uncalled-for response.

My Dad then continued asking Jean that same question OVER AND OVER AND OVER AGAIN -- at least a dozen more times! "Jeannie, can we take this fish home?" "No Jackie, I told you, no. The sauce will spill in my car." "Jeannie, can we take this fish home?" "No Jackie, I don't want fish smell in my house." "Jeannie, can we take this fish home?" "I told you already! We're not poor! We don't eat leftovers!"

Bob and I looked down at the floor while this exchange continued without end. Had it not been so remarkably and painfully sad, I suppose it might have been quite funny.

Finally deciding to placate her husband, Jean told the waiter to put the leftover fish and baked potato into a "to-go" box. My father was thrilled, expressing glee like a little boy.

As the four of us left the restaurant, Jean, behind my father's back, tossed the "to-go" box into a trash can on the sidewalk. Our father did not notice this act.

Now standing at the side of Jean's car, Bob and I took turns hugging our dear father goodbye. "I love you, Dad," I said, fighting back tears and kissing him on the cheek. "Thank you for being my father," to which the old man, who once again had no idea who I was, replied, "You're welcome!" Bob also kissed Dad on the cheek, and they embraced.

We did not hug Jean goodbye.

Dad then got into the passenger seat of Jean's car, while Jean got into the driver's seat. The vehicle slowly pulled away from Bob and I, and we watched as Dad waved "bye-bye" to us through his window, in the manner of a young child. When the car left the parking lot, Bob began walking over to our rental car. I stood in place, though, watching the red taillights of Jean's car vanish into the mist of a pitch-black, Boca Raton highway.

Just then, a VOICE SAID MATTER-OF-FACTLY AND QUITE AUDIBLY INTO MY RIGHT EAR: "YOU'LL NEVER SEE YOUR FATHER ALIVE AGAIN!"

I instantly turned around to see if Bob was behind me. NO ONE ELSE was anywhere near me in any direction.

Once I grasped the meaning of the Message from the Voice, I fell to my knees in that Florida parking lot and began sobbing uncontrollably. Bob, who was already inside our rental car, came back out to see what was delaying me.

"Bob! A voice just told me we'll never see Dad alive again!" I was crying so hard, I could barely talk. I hugged my brother, who was now also in something of a state of shock. "Danny, I can't handle this," he admitted. "I can't watch you cry this hard. I'll wait for you in the car." Bob returned to the driver's seat of our rental, while I remained on my knees, for several minutes, balling my eyes out.

It was the hardest I'd cried in 25 years -- since the time I had to say goodbye to my children on the very first night I had become divorced.

****

Back in LA… I got a call from Jean on a Sunday morning, April 9, 2017. "Danny, they just brought your Dad from the hospice into the hospital. They say he has maybe a day or two left. Thought you should know."

I called both of my brothers, putting them both on alert. I begged Bob to hop on a plane with me the next day to go see him once more. "We already said goodbye, Dan," Bob said, much to my surprise. "He wouldn't know us even if we showed up tomorrow." My brother Michael, who had already made plans to visit Dad THE FOLLOWING WEEKEND, also did not feel compelled to change those plans, even in this emergency setting.

That same evening, I arranged for my two brothers and I to have a "conference" call with Jean at Dad's bedside at the hospital. With Jean holding her cell phone up to our Dad's ear, me, Bob and Mike were each able to say a few words of farewell to our wonderful father, who was unable to respond in any way.

I have never forgiven myself for NOT jumping on a plane and racing to his side to say a final goodbye in person. The truth is that without the support of my brother Bob by my side, I knew I would never have been able to handle that experience by myself.

Jean called me the next morning, Monday, April 17, 2017, to say that "Dad has a few minutes left." I asked her to once again hold her cell phone up to his ear for me. "Dad, I love you so, so much," I said. "I was so lucky to be your son. It's time to go now, Dad. You have to go meet God now. Go meet God, okay? I love you, Dad. Thank you for being MY father. Goodbye."

Jean called me back ten minutes later. "Well, your phone call did the trick, Danny," she sobbed through the phone. "He's gone."

I was sitting at my computer at my work desk at the time. I called my two brothers, pulling each one out of a meeting at their respective jobs. I then sat at my desk, unable to move, for the next eight hours. I did not stir. I did not eat or drink. I did not go to the bathroom.

I'm sure this phenomenon is experienced by countless others in times of grief, but TIME STOOD STILL FOR ME THAT DAY. That night, when speaking with Bob and Mike, they both told me that they left their offices, went outside to sit on benches, and realized that TIME HAD STOPPED for both of them, as well.

****

My Dad died on a Monday. The Friday of that same week, I had to fly up to Silicon Valley for a meeting with my biggest clients -- the producers of a huge, annual computer graphics convention. I'd told my clients about my loss, and they told me I didn't have to attend. I responded that I wanted to… that that meeting would help me to try to move ahead from my grief.

I was staying for the weekend in a Hotel in the Silicon Valley, as there were several more meetings that weekend for me to attend. That same Friday night, as I was asleep, I was SUDDENLY AWAKENED by VIBRATIONS IN MY MATTRESS. MY FATHER'S VOICE BEGAN EMANATING DIRECTLY UP FROM UNDERNEATH THE BOXSPRING OF MY BED!

The Voice said, "Danny! Jeannie CHANGED MY WILL!"

My Dad's voice was loud, clear and decisive. It was as obvious and prominent as if my normal, "living" father had been standing two feet away. And only my father called his wife, Jean, "Jeannie"!

Once my trip to Silicon Valley had finished, I returned to LA. I called Jean a few nights later, asking her if I could get a copy of my dad's will. I also asked if she could tell me about any life insurance policies that he had for me and my two younger brothers.

"Whatever your father told you in the past, that's what exists," she said coldly. When I pressed her about a specific $250,000 life insurance police that I knew he had, she replied, "I have nothing more to tell you, Danny." Then she hung up on me.

Now fully suspicious, I contacted my two brothers, told them about my "Dead Dad Voice" and about Jean's distant responses. "Let's hire a lawyer to look into this," my brother Bob suggested.

We retained a lawyer. He was able to send my brothers and I copies of my father's final will. It was created three months before he died, at a time when he was suffering from full-blown dementia and didn't know his own name. There, on the bottom line, was *his* signature -- yet it clearly looked as though someone (Jean!?) had been holding his hand while he signed… the lines of his name were shaky and noticeably more "troubled"-looking than his normal signature.

Bottom line here is that Jean had indeed changed my father's will, along with two of his life insurance policies. My father had intended for my brothers and I to receive about $80,000 each -- instead, we only got $ 9,000 apiece. By the time we discovered these misdeeds, we assumed Jean had already squirrelled away her dough by giving it to her two daughters. We discussed with our attorney a possible course of action, but after further investigation he told my brothers and I there was "almost quite literally zero chance of recouping any of those funds." So, we let the matter drop.

****

About three weeks after my father's death, two events took place in my bedroom in the middle of the night. Event One: A few years before he died, my dad had gifted me with a miniature toy drum set, which resembled the real drum kit he'd bought me back in 1968. I kept those little toy drums atop my dresser in my bedroom.

On the night in question, I was sound asleep, it must have been about 3 or 4 in the morning. Suddenly, I was awakened by the clanging sound of the CYMBALS FROM THAT LITTLE DRUM SET BEING PLAYED, as though someone was "flicking" them with their fingers! I woke up abruptly from my deep sleep and shouted, "WHAT THE FUCK?" The cymbals noise continued for another few seconds, then stopped.

My heart was racing and my palms got sweaty. I had no idea what had just happened. Shortly thereafter, I fell back to sleep.

Event Two: A few nights after the cymbals were "played" in my bedroom, I was once again abruptly awakened when the LAMP ON MY DRESSER TURNED ON AND OFF SEVERAL TIMES IN A ROW! The interesting thing about that is, that particular lamp could ONLY GO ON AND OFF IF TOUCHED BY A HUMAN HAND!!

This time I was so scared, I shouted, "DAD, IS THAT YOU? IF THAT'S YOU, PLEASE STOP! YOU'RE SCARING THE SHIT OUT OF ME!"

The lamp went back off, and that was that. Neither the cymbals nor the lamp were ever again touched or fussed with during a night of my sleep.

It's quite obvious to me that after I yelled STOP at my Father's Ghost, he ended those phenomena from ever again taking place. Today I feel guilty. Had I not been so terrified in the moment, I could have tried to coax a dialogue with my beloved Dad, knowing that it was, absolutely for sure, *his spirit* visiting me in my bedroom those two times.

****

Perhaps three months after his death, I began having a series of incredibly vivid dreams about my late father. In each of these dreams, I saw a much younger and healthier "version" of him, and we had conversations. The three most memorable of these dreams were:

Dream 1: I hear a knock on my living room door and open it. There, standing naked but for a white towel wrapped around his bottom half, is my father, about 40 years old, with a very prominent, dark black moustache (something he never had in real life.)

"Dad?" I said in this dream, amazed at the sight. "You look Great!" At this, my dead Dad in the dream said, "Why, thank you very much!" My dream self then said, "What are you doing here?" to which he replied, "I wanted to play with Jordan."

I then watched as my Dad walked into the living room and sat on the floor. My son, Jordan, about age 7 in this dream (and 29 in real life at the time,) was playing with his trains. My Dad and Jordan played with those trains together (something they'd done together in real life 25 years previous,) while I stood nearby and watched, dumbfounded.

Dream 2: In this simple dream, my late father, my brother, Bob, and I were seated at a rectangular table. There was total blackness behind us. Again, my Dad was perhaps in his 40's and looked great. I said to him, "Dad! What are you doing here? You're dead!" to which the dear man quietly replied, "yes, I know that… but I really wish I wasn't."

I then turned to my brother Bob and said, "Bob! We are ACTUALLY TALKING TO DEAD DAD IN A DREAM!" At this, my brilliant sibling replied, "Duh, really? Don't you think I know that already?"

Dream 3: In this dream, I'm walking side by side with my late father on a San Francisco sidewalk. It's a beautiful day. His wife, Jean, is walking about ten feet ahead of us -- she is arm in arm with another man.

"Why isn't Jeannie walking with me?" my father asked, mournfully. "Did I do something wrong?" To which my dream-self replied, "I'm not sure, Dad. Looks like she's found another man. Maybe it's because you're dead?"

At this my father simply sighed in defeat. "Yeah," he said, "you're probably right. But I really wish I wasn't…"

****

During the very last week of 2018, my daughter, Anjuli, and I went back East, both to visit my mother and to attend the wedding of one of her best friends.

While we were back in New Jersey, I drove my mother and daughter around my old "stomping grounds" in Asbury Park and Ocean Township, as well as in Neptune, where my family and I first lived from 1956-1962. As we were driving past my first house -- the "Pink House," which is, today, green, we noticed a young couple in their 20's standing on the front lawn of that house.

I parked the car and told my mom and daughter that I wanted to go talk to those people and possibly go inside that first house of mine. I'd not been inside there since the summer of 1962.

My mother wanted nothing to do with this idea (it would bring back too many memories of her life with my dad,) so Anjuli and I hopped out of the car, approached the couple, and asked if we could go inside. They agreed.

The first second I walked inside this living room, a truly remarkable thing happened to me. Instead of seeing what was really there -- the furniture, artworks hanging on the walls, knickknacks, etc., I, INSTEAD, SAW WHAT THE HOUSE LOOKED LIKE IN 1962! I have dozens of old home movies that my father shot of me and my mom (and later brother Bob) taken during that house from '56-62. Those were the images I was now seeing in real-life, in real-time, here in 2018, 56 years later!

It was a mind-boggling experience. But the best was yet to come…

As Anjuli and I left the living room to walk into the dining room, A SUDDEN, OVERWHELMING, REMARKABLY COLD BLAST OF ICY WIND SHOT DOWN THE BACK OF MY COAT AND SHIRT, AGAINST MY BARE SKIN. IT WAS SO COLD, I FELT

LIKE SOMEONE HAD POURED ICE CUBES DOWN MY BACK!

I looked all around—I was not under an AC vent (this was in December in New Jersey, after all), nor was there a fan or any other source of cool air around.

Concurrent with this cold blast, I INSTANTLY FELT THE PRESENCE OF "SOMEONE"! I ASSUMED IT WAS MY DEAD FATHER!

I fell to my knees, "Dad! Is that you?" I shouted. Then, I began sobbing. I didn't just get a bit teary-eyed. I cried harder than I did the day my father actually died. (Note: I also felt a burst of adrenaline -- like I'd just downed six cups of coffee!)

The young couple (owners of the house) and the owner's mother were all standing directly behind me while this took place. They were so touched by my experience that THEY ALSO BEGAN TO CRY! The mom hugged me! Complete and total strangers!

At this point, the young couple told me and Anjuli that the man's grandfather – the guy who had owned the house since 1962 – was in fact, the same man WHO HAD PURCHASED IT FROM MY PARENTS THAT YEAR! And that he had just died inside the building a few days previous!

When I got back to my mom's house that evening, I did some research. Here's what I found online:

"Spiritual chills feel like random energetic downloads—they almost always feel like a current of electricity flowing through the physical body and it always ends with a shake. You will intuitively know when you are experiencing spiritual chills. It is up to you to connect to your intuition and know that there is a deeper meaning behind it all. Spiritual chills are not random cold chills, in fact, they are random chills that give you a shuddering feeling and mostly even goosebumps. These spiritual chills can be known as psychic chills as well, and you should pay close attention to your surroundings when this happens. It is a sign from the angels of a message that needs to be conveyed. Spiritual chills are mostly a sign from the

angels regarding assistance or guidance that you require in your life. They are designed more to give you a feeling of bursts of energy, rather than to shock you."

So now in retrospect, I have to wonder if the Spiritual Chills I experienced that day were a message from my LATE FATHER? Or were they, perhaps, instead, a shout-out from the RECENTLY DEAD OWNER OF MY OLD HOUSE, knowing that I was the son of the previous couple from whom he bought the property 56 years earlier? And that I had lived in that same house from 1956-1962, as a very young boy?

Either way, I am convinced it had to be one of those two men who tried, quite successfully, to get my attention that day!

Chapter Thirty-One

The Home Movie Download, The Pastrami Sandwich, and the Birth of *After They Came* (2017)

A few days after my Dad died, I was sitting alone in a West Los Angeles deli, where I'd gone to get a pastrami sandwich and think about my father. I ordered my sandwich, and then, suddenly a powerful bolt of "light" or "energy" or something supernatural (perhaps from Heaven?) beamed into my brain from above. This power source thrust into my mind incredibly vivid imagery -- what I can only describe as like a digital download -- of "the home movie" from the 1970, silver V, UFO sighting I'd had with my father – an event I'd completely forgotten about for 47 years! It made me gasp. I recalled every moment – how my Dad and I stood in front of his car as I was pointing to the sky and jumping up and down with excitement. I also watched in amazement as my Dad, standing right next to me, appeared completely nonplussed and seemingly bored by the extraordinary sight.

As I continued to watch this home movie from Heaven, I then saw that my Dad had winked at me, said "Come on, kid, let's go home," and ordered me back into his car.

The home movie stopped. While still waiting for my sandwich to arrive at my table, I asked my waiter for a pen. On the paper placemat before me, my right hand began to perform what's called "automatic writing." My hand recorded these three phrases: "Write a book about benevolent Aliens." Then, "Lead character's father knew about UFOs." And finally, my hand wrote down the capital letters "A", "T" and "C."

My hand stopped moving, and I stared at what I'd just written. At first, I had no idea what ATC meant. A few minutes later, it dawned on me -- the universe had just given me the title of a new science fiction book I was destined to write. *After They Came.*

I spent the rest of 2017 and early 2018 writing that book. Concurrently, I read Richard M. Dolan's 2002 book, *UFOs and the National Security State,* and was thrilled to discover, toward the back of the book, Dolan's chronological "Table of Military UFO Encounters." Listed there were two entries that blew my mind: The first on September 10, 1951, being a radar and visually confirmed sighting of a metallic, disc-shaped object flying at 900 mph over the skies of Fort Monmouth, New Jersey. My Dad had begun working at that site as a civilian Electronics Engineer just a few months earlier! Another UFO sighting over Fort Monmouth is also listed in Dolan's book: July 1, 1952. On that date, Dolan notes that radar and visual contact occurred of two unidentified flying objects which hovered over the base, then sped away.

I now believe that my father may very well have witnessed one, if not both, of those events -- UFO sightings that took place directly overhead his then very new place of employment!

As I was writing *After They Came*, I phoned my mother, Joan, (83 at the time and my father's first wife), to ask if my father had ever spoken to her about UFOs. She told me a story I'd never heard before: "Very early on in your father's career at Fort Monmouth, in the early 1950's, they took him down deep into the vaults, and spoke to him, and showed him something down there that they said was highly top secret. He was not to ever share what he saw down there with anyone. I remember he was really frightened when he came home. In fact, he was pale and shaky and scared shitless. When I asked him what was wrong, your father said, 'I saw something today I can never tell you, or anyone, about, as long as I live.' He was never the same after that."

Also, while working on my book, I reviewed dozens of my family history scrapbooks, where, much to my surprise, I discovered a newsletter from my father's workplace that profiled him in 1985. The document was one my Dad had given me decades previous – an orange sheet of paper I'd never previously read. Here's what I learned:

"Jack Harary worked as a Civilian Electronics Engineer and Physicist for the U.S. Army from 1951 -1996 at Fort Monmouth, New Jersey, within the Radar Branch of the Camp Evans Signal Laboratory Installation. There, he designed and invented missiles and radar systems, and was involved in the design and production of the earliest days of drone technology. He had top secret security clearance; gave talks at the Pentagon; and wrote reports read by at least four U.S. Presidents."

I read that my father had worked on a variety of airborne electronics systems for air navigation, position location, missile guidance and drone control. He supervised the Surveillance Drone Data Base Program which expanded the base of unmanned aerial surveillance and target acquisition.

He also directed the Remotely Piloted Aerial Observer System program, which resulted in the first successful laser designation of a tank target from a mini-Remotely-Piloted-Vehicle (RPV), resulting in a direct hit by a laser-guided artillery round at White Sands Missile Range in 1975.

According to this newsletter, over the years, my dad received many awards, commendations, and certificates. I never knew my dad won any awards at all! That's how secretive he was about his work!

I next did some research into the history of Fort Monmouth, my dad's longtime workplace, for the first time in my life, and discovered: Fort Monmouth was the site of some of the most significant communications and electronics breakthroughs in military history, and was known as America's Home of the Signal Corps. During the 20th Century, over 4,000 patents were issued to the scientists and engineers who invented new technologies at Ft. Monmouth.

The forerunner of the Army Air Corps and the U.S. Air Force had its roots in Ft. Monmouth!

During his life, my father had only ever told me two things about his career: He once told me he'd invented a drone that looked like a flying garbage can that shot film, then parachuted the rolls of film—which emitted electronic beeping signals—down to the ground, so our troops could find them and retrieve them.

And each time I asked my dad what he did for a living, he would always (and only) reply, "I helped America win the Cold War."

More recently, I discovered documented evidence that Ft. Monmouth, NJ, was one of 150 U.S. military bases that had its scientists working on the reverse-engineering of extraterrestrial technology gleaned from crashed UFO crafts retrieved from around the world.

Now, after having put all of the clues together about my father's mysterious work for the U.S. Army, I have become convinced that he knew what the giant, silver V, UFO was that we saw together in 1970! Today, I honestly believe that it was a manmade, American military drone that had incorporated recovered Alien technology from crashed UFOs. And since my Dad invented missiles, drones and radar systems -- all things that had to do with flying in the sky -- for 45 years, he may even have been involved in the design of that giant silver V. I am convinced that my Dad must have been aware of whatever futuristic technology existed within America's military-industrial complex that had allowed the giant V, UFO craft to glide so silently and effortlessly above our heads, nearly 50 years previous.

After all, my father began working for the U.S. Army just four years after the infamous UFO crash at Roswell in 1947! And it marries perfectly with WHERE he worked and the kinds of work that he and the other scientists performed at Ft. Monmouth for so many years.

I only wish he was still alive, so I could ask him!

And what if that big, giant, Silver V was *not man-made*? Well, then I would have to tell you, my dear reader, that what my father and I experienced that day was a truly remarkable spacecraft from another planet, star system, time, or dimension. But whatever it was, my brilliant father seemed to find it commonplace and utterly non-threatening.

If my Dad knew that extraterrestrial life did, indeed, exist on Planet Earth, between 1951 and his death in 2017, he, unfortunately, took that history-altering information with him to his grave. However, I strongly believe that it was my father, from Heaven, who sent me that magical movie download, just days after his death. I think it was his way of saying, "Danny, I couldn't share with you the details about my work with UFOs while I was alive! But now that I'm dead, I want you to know that I WAS familiar with that giant V spacecraft we saw back in 1970 -- after all, it was one of my top-secret projects!"

I finished writing *After They Came* in 2018 but could not find a publisher. My novel sat in a drawer until 2022, when it was accepted by Genius Book Publishing. In March of '23, the book was finally released.

Its popularity would quickly alter the course of my life.

Chapter Thirty-Two

The Message from the Billboard Sign (2018)

I was on a date (from Match.com) one night in November 2018, at the famous Musso & Frank Grill on Hollywood Boulevard. It was a great date (or so I thought at the time), and it turned out my female companion was the ex-wife of a famous TV sitcom star. (FYI, she claimed that that star happened to owe her over $1-million in back alimony.)

I walked my date to her car when our meal was done, then walked back toward mine, which was parked in Musso's lot behind the building. Just before I unlocked my car, I glanced up and saw the enormous green Musso & Frank sign that proudly proclaimed the restaurant's prominence in Hollywood "Since 1919."

At that moment, the Universe spoke unto me: Here I was in November 2018, and in just two months, Hollywood's most iconic venue was going to turn 100! I believe an actual LIGHT BULB may have lit up over my head. I actually glanced around to see if any other Hollywood publicists were standing behind me!

The next Monday, I called the restaurant, but could not reach the owner. I was, however, given his name. Unable to secure his email address, I sat down and wrote him an old-fashioned letter and sent it to him, care of the restaurant's address, via snail mail. I never thought in a million years he'd read it.

Four months later, Mark Echeverria, the CFO/COO and a fourth-generation member of the family that owns Musso & Frank, called me! He enjoyed my letter, told me he wasn't happy with his existing PR team, and asked if I could come in to meet with him? I set up a date and time for that meeting, then immediately reached out to my longtime friend and fellow publicist Peter, who had much more experience in handling restaurants, hotels, and resorts than I did.

Peter and I met with Mark, his lovely wife, Tina, and Andrea Scuto, the General Manager of Musso's, for lunch. That lunch was a hit -- not only did we talk about our dozens of PR ideas for the site, but Peter and I also regaled the assembled with very funny stories culled from our previous years together.

We were hired on the spot! This was mid-March, 2019.

Mark told us he was planning a number of special projects to commemorate the historic restaurant's 100th Anniversary milestone. These included: securing a Star on the Hollywood Walk of Fame for Musso's (they would become the only restaurant ever so honored); publishing a book about the history of Musso's; releasing a brand-new wine label; hosting a VIP dinner on September 27, 2019, the exact 100th anniversary date, that would include various celebrities and notables; and producing a charitable, fund-raising event with the Motion Picture and Television Home for aging Hollywood employees.

Between March and September 2019, Peter and I generated countless newspaper, magazine, radio, television and online articles and stories about the history of Musso & Frank. (Charlie Chaplin originally put the place "on the map" back in the venue's earliest days. He used to ride his horse to the restaurant -- on the dirt road that was Hollywood Blvd. at the time -- from his Chaplin Movie Studio Lot on La Brea Ave., just a short distance away. During those lunches, he would sit in the only booth inside the restaurant that had a window, to keep an eye on his horse!)

Peter and I spent countless hours at Musso's during 2019, including lunches and dinners with media members, photographers, TV crews, and various journalists from around the world.

On the 100th Anniversary date itself, September 27, 2019, I produced the ceremony we held on Hollywood Boulevard, just in front of Musso's front doors, to unveil the Star on the Walk of Fame. (We had fans and media lining the entire sidewalk.) For this event, my friend Marc Summers (longtime host of legendary children's TV series *Double Dare*/1986) appeared as MC (as a favor to me,) with actor Danny Trejo of *Machete* (2010) fame serving as our keynote speaker. Danny talked about how, when he first came to Hollywood, he'd spend days at Musso's trying to make connections with Hollywood agents and casting directors, to help launch him into the acting field. He'd been to "University" (prison) before then and wanted nothing more than to break into showbiz, which he felt was his means by which to steer away from a life of crime.

His talk was rather fascinating–and heartfelt.

That night, the VIP dinner at Musso's was truly wonderful. I brought my beautiful daughter, Anjuli, with me as my "plus one." Together, we spent time talking with such celebrities as: Director David Lynch of *Blue Velvet* (1986) and *Twin Peaks (1990)*; Marion Ross of *Happy Days* (1974); Danny Trejo (he asked me if he could ask my daughter out on a date! I told him he was much too old!); Composer Randy Newman; Comic Actor Fred Willard – the man's skin was yellow and he clearly was ill. He died shortly thereafter); Richard Benjamin and Paul Prentiss -- I told the couple I used to enjoy their '60's TV show, *He and She* (1967) and they were amazed that I remembered it; Donal Logue, co-star of the TV series, *Gotham* (2014); Jeffrey Katzenberg, co-founder of the movie studio DreamWorks SKG along with Steven Spielberg; and actress Jeanne Tripplehorn, whom I told about the time I was planning my escape from my last employer, and was nervously copying documents like Holly Hunter did in Jeanne's movie, *The Firm* (1993.) She seemed rather intrigued by my story.

The evening was magical. Everyone had a great time.

During the past few years while working at Musso's, I've also met: Lucy Lawless, star of *Xena: Warrior Princess* (1995); T.J. Miller, co-star of the sitcom, *Silicon Valley* (2014); actor Giovanni Ribisi of *Saving Private Ryan* (1998) and *Ted* (2012); comedian Drew Carey; and Beach Boys founder/genius Brian Wilson, with whom I was invited to have dinner!

Handling the PR for the Musso & Frank Restaurant (from 2019 – present) has been, without question, one of the highlights of my 40-plus-years as a Hollywood publicist. The owners and staff are the nicest people in the world, the food and martinis are amazing, and the prestige factor of the site's more than 100 years as a true Hollywood icon has rubbed off on me in countless -- and highly beneficial -- ways.

As a result of my success in the new field of "Restaurant PR" that accompanied my representation of Musso's, I was later hired to help promote several other prominent venues in Los Angeles, including the 100-year anniversaries of: Barney's Beanery in 2020 - an iconic, LA venue famous for hosting major '60s rock stars including Janis Joplin and The Doors - (in fact, Janis ate at Barney's the night she died); and El Cholo from 2022-2023, LA's oldest and most famous Mexican restaurant. That venue was Jack Nicholson's favorite nightspot during the '50s, '60s and '70s, during which time he was a struggling actor.

I even became friends with Michelle Phillips, the singer from The Mama's and the Papa's, while repping El Cholo!

Chapter Thirty-Three

The Ghosts Inside My Daughter's Three Apartments (2010, 2018, 2022)

My daughter went off to San Francisco State University in Fall 2008, and at first lived in a dorm room, until one night her roommate became insane and threatened her life. She then moved into an apartment with some other girlfriends, where she lived during her Freshman and Sophomore years.

Just before the start of her Junior year, Anjuli found an apartment for rent so she could live alone. It was the bottom floor of a three-story house owned by a rather intense woman named Sharon, and her husband. Sharon's mother had lived in that bottom floor apartment for the last years of her life -- the elderly woman had also died there.

According to Anjuli, "I had just moved in and set up my bedroom, it was Fall 2010. I had my bed directly in the middle of the room. But when I slept there that whole first week, I kept noticing that something was making me feel unsettled and uncomfortable. I ended up sleeping on the couch. Over the course of time, the overhead light in that bedroom kept flickering on and off, and I just knew something was wrong."

"I remember one day, I ran into my landlady, Sharon, and I said, 'I know your mom passed away recently inside the apartment -- can I ask where?' to which Sharon replied, 'in her bed -- the same bed you are now sleeping on.'"

"Shortly afterwards, as I was going through my possessions inside various boxes, I felt so uncomfortable in that bedroom, I stopped what I was doing and said out loud, 'You need to fucking leave! You need to go, you're scaring the shit out of me! In Jesus' name you need to leave, now!' With this, the room shook -- I swear to God, Dad -- the walls made a loud 'bang' noise. I knew right then that whatever I had said in that second worked! Although after that moment, I still felt uncomfortable every so often, I never looked at the room the same way again. I never felt that same presence there again."

(Author's Note: One day while I was in that bedroom visiting Anjuli, I said out loud, "Is Sharon's mother here?" The response I received came from the overhead bedroom light, which flickered on and off just once.)

****

Anjuli graduated from college in May 2012, then moved back into my apartment in Beverly Hills for a few years. She left in Spring 2017 to live with a boyfriend for a year and a half in North Hollywood, CA.

Says Anjuli: "One day in 2018, I was coming into the bedroom, out from the adjoining bathroom, at the North Hollywood place. My dog, Brownie, was in the bedroom. I came out and walked past the king bed and realized my dog was scared shitless. She was shaking. She was looking intensely into the sliding glass mirror doors from the closet. The doors were shut, but she was staring at the mirror. Her back was up against the bottom foot of the bed -- she was facing the mirror and was basically sitting up on her ass with her feet out. I'd never seen her in that position before. She was scooting herself backwards into the bed, clearly trying to escape from whatever terrifying thing she was seeing in the mirror."

"I was so startled, I said, 'Brownie, what's wrong?' My dog then started convulsing… for the very first time! I'd had her for five years at that time… this had never happened before. She was seizing incredibly badly… I thought she was possessed. I started crying and screaming. I grabbed her and together we dashed into my car. We flew to a nearby emergency animal hospital. They checked her out, scanned her brain, and told me that she'd just had a seizure, and that she had epilepsy. I still have no idea how that happened."

****

Anjuli broke up with that No. Hollywood boyfriend, then moved back into my Beverly Hills place again for a while. Then on her birthday in April 2021, she had the funds to move into her own apartment, a huge, one-bedroom, newly refurbished, place located in West Los Angeles.

There are several stories regarding this apartment. Says Anjuli, "I felt weird in this apartment as soon as I moved in. I felt great there during the day, but it had a different, weird vibe at night. I was only there for a few months when a new boyfriend moved in with me. I wasn't scared there at that point, because he was a big strong guy. Unfortunately, our relationship didn't work out -- right after he left a few months later, I had an invasion of enormous rats in my kitchen. They were in the cupboards, in the drawers, and behind my refrigerator. Large, girthy rats… mine was the only unit in the entire complex of 56 apartments that they seemed to want to occupy."

"After he moved out, I gave him his stuff back, but I kept a few items that he'd given me as personal souvenirs. It was at this point that the overhead light in my dining room would go on and off for no reason -- but, Dad, this only happened when YOU were here! The light didn't flicker… it would just go on and off by itself."

"In my living room, I know for a fact that my dog saw something sitting in the decorative chair in the corner of that room. For about 10 minutes late one evening in Fall 2022, Brownie was staring at the chair as though someone was sitting in it. I kept trying to distract her and moved her away, but she kept going back to the same spot to stare at that chair. Before she started staring at the chair, she was looking around the room as though she was following the path of maybe a flying orb or something -- it wasn't a fly, because she chases those. She was watching something trail through the air."

"I was so scared I called my mother to come over. She told me to pray in Jesus' name -- like I did in the San Francisco apartment. I did that out loud, but this time it wasn't working. I was so uncomfortable. Brownie kept staring at the decorative chair and the vibe was different in the living room. I knew something was wrong.

I kept asking Brownie, 'Is it bad people?' -- she understands my words. My mom came over and said prayers in every room. Then, she sat on the couch with me, and we slept that way that night. Once Mom came over, Brownie stopped looking at the chair."

"Even today, there are times when Brownie's sleeping on my armchair, and she'll suddenly pop-up from sleep as though she just saw or heard something. She will watch invisible objects flying through the air, until the object trails off, then she'll go back to sleep. Sometimes, also, she'll pop-up from sleep and start smelling all around the armchair -- she's obviously smelling something really weird."

"Also, right after that boyfriend left, I began to notice strange things happening in my bedroom. My mom had given me a very pretty glass lamp that was passed down from my great-grandmother to my grandmother then to my Mom, then on to me. It sat upon my nightstand. I never really used it as a lamp – it was just a decorative piece. Shortly after I got the lamp, there were times when Brownie would wake up in the middle of the night -- the TV was not on, and she would wake me up on purpose. She would then sit and stare at the lamp, even though it wasn't on. I stared at the lamp, too, but didn't see anything. I tried to distract her and move her away, but she just kept staring at it. She was so scared, she started shaking. We had to go into the living room to sleep on the couch."

"I realized at that point I needed to get rid of this lamp. So, I placed it atop my dining room table. That's when the overhead dining room light started turning on by itself once again. Clearly, the lamp was haunted, so I finally took it to Goodwill."

"Twice after I got rid of the lamp -- both times around 3:33 am -- I was awakened by Brownie coming toward me. She woke me up. I was startled because both times she was shaking like a leaf and so uncomfortable. She was looking into the corner of my bedroom where the mirrored-door closets are, and she was obviously seeing something there. I looked at the same spot and I felt as though there was an actual person standing there. Brownie was looking at the

'Being' at eye level. It felt, to me, like a man was standing there. I got a very strong vibe that whatever this thing was had a masculine presence. It was profound… like looking at something you can't see but you KNOW is there. Because of all this, I still sleep with the lights dimmed in my bedroom and not pitch black, so that it's less scary when I feel someone is watching me."

"Before he moved to Alaska, I once told my brother, Jordan, that Brownie could 'see things.' He told me that he believed I was the one that was making those things happen! I was once watching Brownie from across the room, when I saw her ass being lifted 4-5 inches into the air, then slightly moved 20 degrees to the right! Then, she was set back down again. Brownie looked at her ass, then looked to me as if to say, 'Mommy? Did you just do that?'"

****

Side Note # 1: One Saturday afternoon around 1994, Kim drove my kids to my Studio City apartment for the weekend "hand-off." Kim had parked her car across the street from my building. My son and his little suitcase were standing on the sidewalk just in front of my place. I was with Kim across the street, helping her unload some kid stuff.

Very suddenly, little Anjuli, perhaps 4 years old, ran out of Kim's car and directly into the middle of the street. There, she stopped and stood. I turned to my right to see a large, black SUV, speeding down my street, coming from the top of the hill and heading directly towards Anjuli's position.

I saw the driver of the SUV. He saw my daughter, and then he looked at me with utter horror. We both knew he was ABOUT TO HIT HER!

Instantly becoming Superman, I bolted to my daughter, scooped her up in my arms, and flew the two of us horizontally onto the opposite sidewalk, all in very slow motion. Time changed. As I was still airborne, I glanced behind me to see that the SUV just missed hitting my legs and feet.

I'd literally flown across the street, Anjuli in my arms, as though I'd become a superhero.

Side Note # 2: Anjuli and I were once at The Grove -- LA's most popular, outdoor shopping mall. The occasion was a Christmas Show for the general public, at which my famous magician cousin, Franz Harary, was doing magic tricks along with TV host Jimmy Kimmel, on a large stage within the main courtyard.

Anjuli and I were watching the show from a bit of a distance -- the crowd there that night was huge – many hundreds. In order to see the stage, Anjuli had been standing on a folding metal chair, right next to me, and her Aunt Melanie.

Suddenly, Anjuli, from a height of well over seven feet, fell backwards, flew off the chair, and landed HARD – the back of her head slamming loudly onto the pavement. She instantly got up, unfazed.

At this, Aunt Melanie said, "OMG Anjuli, are you alright? I thought you were going to die! How are you NOT HURT RIGHT NOW?"

To which my remarkably lucky daughter replied, "Pillows, Aunt Mel. When I fell to the sidewalk just then, it felt like I'd landed on a huge pile of fluffy, soft pillows!"

Chapter Thirty-Four

The Past-Life Curse: The Latter Years (2012 - 2022)

After graduating from college and returning to LA, my daughter encouraged me to "get back out there" and start going to bars, clubs and social gatherings to meet someone. During the course of those next ten years, I met a wide assortment of women, each of whom ultimately became a "Carrot":

** Willow was a very attractive redhead who worked as a hairdresser in the San Fernando Valley. On and off for the next few years, I would retrieve Willow from her small apartment deep in the valley, go out for nice dinners with LOTS of alcohol involved, then return to her place and have literally mind-blowing sex. I was so incredibly attracted to her, it was unreal. Along the years, she introduced me to doing cocaine before sex -- I only did it three times, because the following mornings I would invariably end up with the worst headaches of my life.

Willow turned me on a great deal, and even, on a few occasions, invited some of her attractive girlfriends, and female neighbors, to come over and join us in our sexual acrobatics! But over the course of years, I realized that her behavior was becoming erratic, and she had developed a severe case of ADHD. She could NOT STOP TALKING, ever, even during sex, and would dance around the apartment, trying on different outfits, changing channels on the TV, calling her sister, playing with her cat and dog, and fidgeting with her hair and makeup, all while sweeping her floors, ironing her clothes, and rearranging her furniture.

I finally realized that, due to her cocaine addiction, Willow simply was not someone I had the patience to be around. We broke up on a New Year's Eve, after I'd watched her prance around her apartment for four straight hours, never once stopping to ask me how I was doing. Simply being in her presence was exhausting.

** Zappy: I met Zappy at a party in a popular sushi restaurant. She had long, straight blonde hair, green eyes, a very good figure, and reminded me a bit of Meryl Streep. A divorced accountant with two kids in college, she told me over drinks that she was there simply to "meet a new guy and have a good time." I walked her to her car, and we kissed briefly. "Call me anytime," she said, handing me her card. "You're cute. I'm sure we could have some fun."

For the next several months, Zappy and I lived for sex. The routine was always the same: She'd come to my place, we'd go to a local restaurant for dinner and drinks, and return to my place, wasted. Having just discovered the joys of Viagra, I would surreptitiously pop a little blue pill into my mouth before each meal. Without question, this lady was one of the better-looking women I'd ever dated. Our sexual chemistry was powerful, but, every time we were in bed, we didn't really "make love." We had porn star sex.

During our months together, we managed only one daytime date. Walking along the Santa Monica Promenade, we held hands, ate pizza slices, and bought each other cheap sunglasses. It was the one time I considered her a "girlfriend." That night, we had sex three times in a row. Sweating and exhausted, we finally fell asleep.

About 4 am, I was awakened by a tug at my arm. Me: "Huh? What's wrong?" "Danny, you're a great guy, really. I'm attracted to you, and I like you a lot. But you and I don't have any 'Zap.' I'm so sorry." Dreaming at the time, I had no idea what was happening, or if this conversation was even real. "Oh, no problem," I replied in my sleep.

Later that morning, I awoke to find Zappy staring at me. "How about one last screw for the road?" she suggested. After we finished, she hopped off my bed, showered, dressed, then said, "Walk me to my car?"

We kissed. "Thanks… I had a nice time," she said, and drove off. I went to work. About three hours later, the word "Zap" popped into my head. "Did this same woman actually tell me we had no "Zap?"" Confident it had been a dream, I called my lady friend at her office: "Did you tell me last night we had no 'Zap?' Or was that my imagination?" "No, it wasn't a dream," she said. "I think you're a really sweet, funny guy, and I like you very much, but we have no future. We just don't have any 'Zap' other than when we're in bed. I'm sorry. I'm not trying to hurt your feelings. I just wanted to be honest."

More than slightly dumbfounded, I replied, "Didn't we just have sex four times in the past 12 hours? Isn't THAT 'ZAP?' What is 'ZAP?' exactly… I don't understand." Without hesitation, she said: "Zap—either you have it, or you don't. We have sex, we have fucking, we have orgasms. But, I'm sorry to say, we just don't have 'Zap.' Goodbye."

So now you know how this particular "Carrot" earned her nickname.

** Chubsy-Ubsy: During yet another torturous "Rapid Dating" event, I met Chubs, a hefty blonde woman who had, quite possibly, the most beautiful, angelic face, I'd ever seen. I'd noticed her when I first walked in the room. She stared at me from afar and never stopped. I approached her: "Clearly, you're attracted to me, huh?" "Yes, I am. Very much so," she replied. "How could you tell?"

On our third date, Chubs and I wound up on her living room couch, making out. But with two cats nearby, I could feel my allergies acting up, so I stood to leave. "Wait a minute," she said, "Let me put them in the other room. I need to talk with you." Chuby-Ubsy then regaled me with her tale: She'd been married for 12 years, divorced for eight, and had two small kids. She hadn't had sex since her divorce, when her husband left her for his secretary.

"Eight years… really? God, you must be the queen of masturbation," I joked. "Would you like to see my vibrator collection?" she replied. Large Marge looked me in the eyes: "I'm ready to be with a man again. And, if you're interested, I'm inviting you to have sex with me tonight." This woman's face was as beautiful as her body was large. I must admit I was scared at the prospect of having sex with such a heavy partner, but I knew this woman was truly attracted to me, and who was I to turn down her offer?

After we had sex, she said, "Thank you so much… that was wonderful. Can you please sleep with me tonight? I don't want to be alone." I reminded her about my cat allergies. "Don't worry about that," she said. "I'll keep them locked in another room for the night."

Moments later, the Chubster was out cold. And then she started snoring. And I mean SNORING. I have never, ever, in my life, heard a louder sound coming from another person's mouth that wasn't a scream. I lay next to her for hours, wide awake, cringing at the inhuman (and inhumane) sounds emanating from her enormous gullet.

Every time I was THISCLOSE to sneaking out of bed, getting dressed, and heading back to my place for peace and quiet, pangs of guilt overwhelmed me: "This woman hasn't had sex, or trusted another man, in eight years, and YOU'RE going to run away in the middle of the night? She'll be devastated. You can't do that to her -- she's too nice of a person. You just have to eat shit tonight and wait for daybreak."

Morning finally arrived. I was unbelievably irritable, having been subjected to her interminably long, God-awful, snort-and-gasp session. When she walked me to her front door, she smiled. "Sleep OK?" No longer able to hold my anger, I replied, "Yeah, terrific. I especially enjoyed listening to your unbelievably loud snoring for nine hours. Gee, I wonder why your husband left."

I apologized immediately.

Chubs and I had several more dates after the "snoring fiasco," but as she was also one of the world's most boring conversationalists, I simply had zero interest in her. Trying to be especially nice, she took me to see a live band for my birthday that year. I should have told her in advance I have a hearing condition called hyperacusis. To me, a survivor of incredibly loud rock music from The Sunshine Inn and countless rock concerts during the '70s, listening to loud music, live, for me today is comparable to someone sticking a nail file deep into my ear drums.

After just minutes, I insisted she drive me back home. "I'm really sorry I fucked up your birthday." The look of disappointment on her face was sincere. I felt like the biggest asshole in town. "Not your fault," I said. "Besides, I hate my own birthdays with all my heart. They don't interest me." I got out of her car, watched her drive away, walked inside my apartment and KISSED MY LIVING ROOM FLOOR. I looked skyward, and said, out loud, "Thank you God."

My phone rang about five days later. Chubsy: "Hi, there, listen, I don't think it's gonna work out between us. So, I just wanted to say I enjoyed meeting you, and I hope you find what you're looking for. So long." Me: "Oh, really? Oh, okay, I understand. Thanks for the call."

I'd rarely been more elated.

** Ten: While attending another singles event, I bumped into Ten, by far the most attractive "Carrot" I ever pursued. I'd spent the last two hours striking out, left and right, with every other woman at this nightclub, and was just about to walk out the door when our paths crossed. A stunning blonde along the lines of a young Christie Brinkley, Ten and I sat for a time and talked.

Hand in hand, Ten and I then ran three blocks to her car in the pouring rain, laughing. Inside the car, we kissed briefly, before exchanging phone numbers.

I wined and dined the Ten for several months, taking her to very expensive sushi, steak, and seafood restaurants. I once bought her a bottle of pricey, perfume, "because I really dig you." "Obviously," she replied.

Ten and I spent a good deal of time together, with only brief smatterings of kissing involved. One night at a club with her best friends, we had a few drinks, and danced for a while. Like magnets, we kissed passionately for the first time, and, again, in the parking lot afterward.

Ten was my date for a client Christmas party that year. Every guy's head turned as we walked into the restaurant. She was the most attractive woman in the room. My male clients were "high fiving" me during the night, assuming that I was sleeping with this raging beauty. I wasn't.

During dinner at that party, I realized I needed to have a "Come to Jesus" talk with my stunning "Carrot." "So, listen, we've been dating for a while, now. Can I ask you why we aren't having sex?" Without missing a second, my Ten replied, "Are you gonna marry me and give me two babies? Because if you'll commit to me, right now, I'll give you all the sex you could ever want in your life. And trust me, I'm good."

I was dumbfounded--Ten was so extraordinarily attractive, I thought I would have said or done anything to sleep with her. However, since I already had two children and a vasectomy, I knew that her request was simply not something I could have fulfilled without lying. "Uh, err, ahm," I stammered. My penis was livid: "Tell her you'll do it, schmuck! Tell her ANYTHING! Just get me inside those pants!" My good guy/angel voice quietly whispered: "I'm afraid you'll need to let this lovely woman go. You're not going to have more children with her or anyone else, ever. Continuing this will only frustrate both of you. You have no future here."

"I adore you and I'm incredibly attracted to you," I finally answered. "But I already have two kids, and I had a vasectomy years ago. I can't give you what you're asking. God knows, I really wish I could, because I could so very easily fall in love with you. I'm really, really sorry."

Ten made a sad face. I never saw her again after that evening.

** "Manny:" I'd joined an expensive dating service called "It's Just Lunch," which, oddly enough, only arranged dinner dates for its clients. I got fixed up with a real estate developer, 20 years younger. She had a nice figure and a pleasant face, but I found her extremely short, wavy, blonde hair distracting. Her haircut reminded me of the hair of a man ("Manny"—get it?)

Manny was really a great lady, but I was truly conflicted about dating her. Of course, I knew how shallow I was being. She really liked me, but I was just unable to overcome my ambivalence.

Manny and I had numerous dinners and saw a bunch of movies, usually making out briefly at the end of those dates. Shortly after we'd first met, she called me about 2 AM one night from Las Vegas: "I'm in love with you. I thought you should know that." "You're just drunk," I groggily replied. "I know," she replied, "but that's still the way I feel."

My physical reticence toward Manny remained a problem during our many months together. We had sex several times, and while it wasn't bad, it wasn't quite "right," either. Realizing it was time for some honesty, I said, "I think I'm being a bit put-off by your hair. I'm attracted to women with long straight hair, and, for whatever reason, I'm not getting turned on by yours. I feel terrible about this, but I realized I can't disguise these thoughts any longer."

A few days later, I was at an amusement park with my kids, when I got a cell phone call. Manny was at an expensive, Beverly Hills hair salon: "I'm about to get long, blonde hair extensions," she informed me, "And they're thirteen-hundred dollars. I need you to split the cost, okay?" I was on the spot. "Six-fifty?" I replied in disbelief. "Is this really necessary?" Manny: "I need you to be attracted to me. So, this is how we're gonna do it. Are you IN?" Me: "Yeah, sure, I guess so."

A few days later, Manny arrived, unannounced, at my office in Beverly Hills, sporting her new, long blonde locks. I was stunned… they looked so incredibly phony, I was aghast. She had tried so hard to please me, yet I felt her extraordinary efforts were in vain. During lunch that afternoon, she asked, "So, what do you think?" Me: "Urgh, ah, uhm, it looks great... very sexy… really nice job," I lied, while writing her a check for six hundred and fifty smackers. Because I'm the world's most shallow man, I didn't see, or call, Manny again. Like the little boy that used to ring neighbors' doorbells, I was, once again, simply running away.

A few years later, I happened to bump into Manny at a grocery store. Her hair had returned to its normal state, and she honestly looked much better that way. She told me she was dating someone new, and, much to my surprise, I felt a bit jealous. As I walked her to her car, I leaned in, and we kissed for a quick moment. Then she pulled away.

"Oh, no, get lost, buster" she said, half-kidding. "I gave myself to you a long time ago and you blew it. I'm not going to be your 'I don't have any other woman in my life right now' sex friend. Good luck finding another great chick like me!"

I was sad to see her drive away.

****

In 2016 (the year of my 60th birthday,) I attended a singles party and met a remarkably beautiful brunette from Poland who was an actress on TV shows, films and even starred in a popular videogame. "A" was quite simply stunning, and we dated for many, many months, but, for some reason, without having sex. I asked her a number of times why we weren't having sex, and she told me that she had never been a fan of it, that she'd made her (now ex) husband sleep in another room from hers all during her marriage, and that, as she was raised a hardcore Catholic, she felt sex was dirty, sinful and wrong.

Finally, at the very tale end of that year, she came to my place and had dinner. She then asked me if I had any pot? My daughter had left some in the house, so we got high, then drank champagne. We began to kiss for the first time and she said, "Do you think I'm a bad girl?" I replied, "A, of course not! I am SO INTO YOU, I have been waiting for this moment for SUCH a long time. Do you think we can finally have sex tonight?" She replied: "No oral and no intercourse. But otherwise, yes, we can fool around."

I led her onto my bed and we "fooled around" for about an hour before falling asleep. (I must say that she had the most beautiful naked breasts I've ever seen in my life.) Then, perhaps at 3 or 4 in the morning, she woke me up and said, "I need to go home now." I walked her to her car and hugged her goodnight.

The look on her face just before she drove off clearly indicated to me that she'd been traumatized by our sexcapades. While I have seen her a number of times since that night, we never had "sexual activity" again. My gut is that something terrible happened to her in childhood and there was no amount of future "begging" from me that was ever going to change her inherent feelings about sexual intimacy with me, or any man, at any point in the near future.

****

The following year, I was hired to do the PR for a funny, all-female play in West LA about five housewives who were going through menopause and having to deal with their daily life problems. The writer and creator and star of that show was an attractive singer/ actress named Tina. In a short period of time, we developed crushes on each other, and dated a few times, going out for dinners or movies, or both. After one of those dates, we got into my car and fooled around in the backseat. I then told her how badly I wanted to have sex with her.

"Oh, for that, I'd have to charge you money," she responded, deadly serious. "You don't think I make enough money to survive just from my plays, do you?"

Quite literally shocked, I drove home, alone, my balloon deflated that such an attractive and talented woman, who'd seemed to really like me, *had to be paid for her sexual affection!*

****

I met a terrific woman named Kayla, a fiery redhead with a feisty personality, during an event I was producing at The Grammy Museum near downtown LA. We quickly became very close, albeit short-lived, friends. During our first date together, she and I were at an art walk event downtown where thousands of people had congregated. As we were leaving a private party, two perfect, stunning blondes, both of whom resembled the beautiful singer

Agnetha Faltskog from ABBA, approached me. They said, "Ve are from Sveden. Vhere should ve go now?" Since I'd never had two "10's" stop me on the street before in the history of my life, I froze in my tracks, unprepared for the experience.

Kayla, standing just a few feet away from me, was furious-- steam shooting out of her ears. She stormed off. I curtailed my conversation with the Swedes, ran after her, and asked what was wrong. "If you ever stood a chance of sleeping with me before, forget it, buddy. It's gone forever. You're like a 12-year-old boy with his tongue hanging out when you see a pretty girl. You're so immature. I was hoping you were a man."

After apologizing profusely, Kayla gave me a second chance, and we wound up having dinners and seeing movies together for the next several months. (She even attended a mini-family reunion of mine and spent one of my birthdays sightseeing with me in Santa Barbara.) While we were certainly bonding as friends, we rarely kissed, and we weren't having sex.

One night along the way, Kayla told me that she was very attracted to me, but she would become my lover ONLY if I promised to give her a baby. (Shades of The Ten!) She realized I was much older than her (20 years), but she thought, perhaps, I might consider the possibility, regardless.

I really enjoyed my time with Kayla and could easily have developed feelings for her. I did give the baby idea some thought, then asked my daughter her opinion. "Dad," she said, "do you REALLY WANT another KID?" Without hesitation, I answered, "No, of course not." "Then, that's your answer," Anjuli replied. "It's a no brainer."

After a long talk with myself, I realized that since I'd already had a vasectomy and two adult children, I simply did not have the wherewithal to grant Kayla her wish. In spite of the fact that I was truly smitten with this woman at the time, and even in spite of the possibility that, perhaps, she was "The One," there just ain't no way this guy's gonna make any woman "Baby Number Three" anytime soon.

****

I was having dinner with my dear, close friend, Shauna, at a restaurant in Beverly Hills, when our very attractive, brunette waitress came to our table. I quickly flirted with Penny, got her number, and began pursuing her. While she was a waitress in real life, she was also an aspiring actress and wanna-be TV producer. She was hoping to sell a TV series about restaurants and bars in Los Angeles in which she would also star.

I quickly came to learn that Penny had a serious boyfriend and that there was no chance she'd end up with me. However, I was so enticed by her that I did try to help her sell that TV show idea to a network (no luck.) I also wined and dined her at the top restaurants in town. During those meals, we each revealed to the other some very interesting (and hot) sex life details, which made me want her even more. (At the end of one of those dates, I kissed her in her car. That didn't go over too well.)

A week later, Penny invited me to her birthday party in West Hollywood. I got very drunk there, and flirted (obnoxiously, I might add) with several of her girlfriends. At the end of the night, when I went to leave and hug her goodbye, she said, "Hey, you were a real shithead tonight to my friends. And, by the way, I haven't forgiven you for trying to kiss me the other day. Please don't call me again."

****

** I heard from a very long-lost female friend, Tracy, a photographer I knew back in the mid/late '80's. We found each other on Facebook and decided to meet up for lunch. On our phone call prior to that lunch, she told me she was no longer married, and that she'd had a crush on me back during the years we were friends, 35 years earlier.

Tracy showed up two hours for our reunion lunch, and when she arrived, I was pretty shocked by her appearance. She was almost bald and walked in a halting and staggering-type manner. It reminded me of Frankenstein's movements.

She sat at the table and told me that she'd had a massive brain tumor removed a few years earlier. It was obvious she no longer had the same "presence" that she'd enjoyed during the old days.

I was heartsick and deeply saddened by her appearance and manner. Of course, completely not her fault, but the fact that such an adorable girl had become such a remnant of her past glory was very upsetting. Even our waitress at the restaurant looked at me as if to say, "Oh, I'm sorry. Your girlfriend looks like she's had a rough time of it."

When I walked Tracy back to her car, she kissed me goodbye and told me she'd very much like to date me. When I got home, I actually blocked her number on my cellphone. It was one of the toughest decisions I ever had to make about a woman, but it was easier for me just to block her than to tell her that I simply was not attracted to her "new self" at this stage in our lives.

****

** I was attending a Monster convention in Pasadena on behalf of a longtime special effects client of mine, when I met Natasha, a remarkably beautiful, black-haired woman. An actress, Natasha had developed a horror genre-type character based on the idea of a female vampire. When dressed in her character's attire, she wore all black and showcased remarkably alluring cleavage.

The SECOND Natasha and I met each other, we both felt a powerful spark. We actually discussed it in the moment. I told her, "I think we were meant to meet and become friends for life," to which she instantly replied, "Yeah, I know! I agree."

For our first date, I took Natasha to Musso and Frank's restaurant, where we mostly gazed into each other's eyes for several hours. I could not recall another dinner in my entire life when I was more mesmerized by the beauty of my female companion.

A few days later was July 4th. Natasha and I had another fun dinner (this one at Barney's Beanery, a fun, very casual place,) and then drove up to Universal Studios City Walk to watch the fireworks display.

Natasha and I were kissing and hugging for hours that evening, and when we stood directly underneath those fireworks, I felt a swelling of emotion I hadn't felt in 25 years. This was one of the most romantic moments of my life.

I was falling in love with her.

Of course, in a normal world, Natasha and I would have continued dating, having incredibly romantic moments together, falling in love and possibly getting married.

However, given the FACT that I am the victim of a Past Life Curse, the exact opposite happened. These are the events that took place starting just a few days after our magical Fourth of July date:

** I was producing a Hollywood party for a very famous make-up special FX artist's 100th birthday. Natasha was going to be my date. That morning she called me to say she had an incredible sore throat, so she couldn't attend.

** Two weeks later, I was booked to appear at the Barnes & Noble store located inside LA's "The Grove" shopping mall, to promote my book, *Flirting With Fame*. Natasha had promised to be my date that day and evening at both the book signing and the after-party.

The night before, she called me, sobbing. She told me that her father had just

contracted Covid 19 in Florida and that she was worried sick that he might die. We spoke for a long time that night, I reassured her the best I could while continuing to implore her to please show up at my event, even if for a short time. I'd already bragged to all my family and friends about her, and I wanted to show off this new prize in my life to all assembled. She told me she would come for a little while.

My book event and party came and went -- no Natasha. Everyone asked me where she was, and I had to reveal that she was so upset by her sick father that she couldn't make it.

**The next time I heard from Natasha, a few days later, she called to tell me that her 13-year-old dog had bitten her finger, and that she was now the victim of a "full-body bacterial infection." She laid out for me, in graphic detail, stories about all of the doctors and emergency rooms she'd been to, both for herself, and her elderly dog, who apparently was dying and had suddenly become frightened and violent.

I wished her well and told her that as soon as she felt better, we'd get together again!

** Natasha was sick from that dog bite for three weeks. When she finally sounded like her normal self on the phone, I invited her to a romantic dinner at Dan Tana's, a famous, West Hollywood Italian restaurant that is regularly frequented by celebrities. She told me she loved that place, and that she would arrive at my house the next night at 7:30 pm.

I was showered, dressed, and, at the ready that next night -- dinner reservations had been made. Natasha called around 6 pm. "Uh, sorry, Dan, I'm really sorry about this, but, uh, my house just flooded! All of my papers and clothes are soaking wet and I can't leave. I have so much work to do now. Sorry... another time, okay?"

"Sure," I said. "Please keep me posted."

** Two weeks later: I called Natasha. "Hey, how's it going, kid?" Her response? The most remarkable BARKING-TYPE HACKING COUGH imaginable. "Covid!" she gasped. "I've got unbelievable Covid. Sicker than I've ever been in my entire life." "Wow!" I responded. "Why didn't you tell me? I could have brought you medicine and soup?" She paused, then came back with, "Well, I never told you this, but I'm kinda seeing this guy. He's married, but he's trying to get divorced. He's been coming by and bringing me things I need, and he took me to the doctor." Me: "How come you never told me about him before?" Natasha: "Well, I was trying to break up with him, after I met you, but he wouldn't let me. He wouldn't hear of it. He's the head of one of the biggest Hollywood studios, so he's a powerful guy, not to mention very rich. I tried, Dan to break up with him for you, really. But he just wouldn't let me."

At this point in the phone conversation, I realized that Natasha had firmly secured her place within the Pantheon of Women who existed solely to provide further, concrete proof of my Past Life Curse.

"Can we have dinner together again, once you're feeling better?" I asked. "Of course," she said. "I'll keep you posted."

I didn't hear from Natasha again for about six weeks. A friend of mine told me to give it one last chance, so I called her again. She was no longer sick from Covid and sounded happy and fine. We made a dinner date for right after Halloween, and she seemed eager to see me again.

The afternoon of THAT date, she called to tell me her house had flooded AGAIN! And that she was so sick and tired of Los Angeles, she decided she was going to move back to her home-city of Miami, Florida. I wished her well, hung up, then deleted her name and phone number from my cell phone.

If the story of Natasha ALONE does not convince you, my dear reader, that I am TRULY LIVING OUT A PAST LIFE CURSE WITH WOMEN, I don't know of any other means by which to do so!

Chapter Thirty-Five

The Coincidence of Leon Harary (2022)

My first book, which chronicled the history of my career within the entertainment industry, was called *Flirting With Fame: A Hollywood Publicist Recalls 50 Years of Celebrity Close Encounters.* Upon its release in 2022 by Bear Manor Media, I made a number of appearances at prominent LA bookstores to discuss it, and to sign copies for those who made purchases.

My final book promotion for *Flirting With Fame* took place in October 2022 – just a few days after my mother's 88th birthday. I was visiting her in New Jersey, and had arranged for that book signing event to take place at the Asbury Book Coop, located on Cookman Avenue in downtown Asbury Park -- my original hometown -- so she could attend.

About 25 friends of mine from high school, two of whom I'd not seen for close to 50 years, attended that book talk on October 12, 2022. It was great fun… we took lots of photos, I sold 20 copies of *Flirting* and was even reunited with a long-lost ex-girlfriend from 1977.

At the end of the three hours we'd been there, the manager of the Asbury Coop told me that we had to leave RIGHT NOW! She needed to lock up and go home. It was 9 pm.

My friends, along with my mom in her wheelchair and Tina, her aide, left the book store's front door to enter onto the sidewalk. Concurrently, a young couple approached one of my friends, Sandy. The man from that couple saw that my name, DAN HARARY, appeared on the front cover of the book Sandy was holding in her hands. The man said a few words to Sandy, who then called to me, "Danny, come over here. You won't believe this."

I walked up to Sandy and the couple. The man said to me, "Are you Dan Harary?" I replied, "Yes." He then said, "I'm Leon Harary."

I immediately countered with, "Harar-Y? or Harar-I?" (I've seen both variations during my lifetime.) "Harar-Y – same spelling as yours," Leon replied.

I was stunned. It turns out that this guy was a distant, distant cousin of mine. My late Grandpa Joe was one of nine brothers, so apparently there were countless other Harary's I'd never met or heard of who existed beyond the realm of my knowledge.

The reason I consider this story supernatural? What are the chances that Leon Harary and his wife would be walking directly past the front of that Asbury bookstore at precisely the same exact moment in time that my friends and I were leaving the store?

If he and his wife had walked past just 10-seconds earlier, he and I would never have coincided, and we never would have known of each other's existence.

Plus, I'd not been on Cookman Ave. in Asbury Park for over 40 years.

Leon and I were equally surprised by this coincidence. And while I did hand him my business card that night and told him to contact me, as of the writing of these words, he has not yet done so.

Chapter Thirty-Six

The Dreams (1973 – 2023)

I go "elsewhere" when I dream. I know I do. I'm not sure they're even dreams. I believe I either hallucinate, or travel to another dimension. As far back as high school, I began to realize that I was having extraordinary dreams. Of course, it's hard to say if my dreams have been, and remain, any more vivid or realistic or fantastical than anyone else's. But they are so powerful that when I wake up every morning, I have to sit still on the edge of the bed for at least two-three minutes, until I can come back to "reality."

Convinced that when I dream, I am truly "leaving my body," I did some research on Astral Projection. Here's what I found:

"Have you ever seen yourself outside your body? Have you ever had lucid dreams, those dreams with the sensation of falling-down or flying? Very real dreams where your senses and even your lucidity were much more exacerbated? Do you admit the possibility that these experiences happened outside your physical body?

You may have gone through an Astral Projection, the phenomenon of consciousness coming out of the physical body.

Astral Projection is a popular name for this phenomenon in which some people perceive themselves outside their body, experiencing the reality around them, and even being able to visualize their sleeping physical body. This phenomenon is also known as an out-of-body experience -- Astral Travel.

All human beings dream every night, yet most people don't usually remember very much of these experiences. In the same way, it is assumed that everyone also goes through out-of-body experiences during sleep, even though we have no memories of it. Reports of people leaving their bodies during dreams have existed since ancient times, in different cultures and lines of knowledge all over the planet, and have been experienced by people of every age, gender and race.

Some researchers believe that these dream experiences occur in extra-physical dimensions, far from the place where the projected person's sleeping body was physically located. These researchers feel that dreams are a means by which to "get out of yourself -- out of your own body," and are a way by which to carry out self-research and qualify one's own personal evolution.

Dreamers 'project themselves' as they undergo these dream experiences. This is a means by which dreamers can acquire more information about themselves and their lives (past and present,) as well as the universe that surrounds them."

****

Amazing, right? So having said all that above, here is a selection of eight especially vivid dreams I've had during the course of the past 50 years:

** I'm an Astronaut walking on the Moon. I can see the landscape before me—the craters, a NASA Lunar Lander, the stars in the sky. Everything I see has an orange "tint"—I'm looking through the clear plastic orange-colored sun visor that is attached to my helmet.

** In this dream, I awake to see Jesus Christ protruding from the ceiling above my bed! He has an important message for me. Alas, I simply cannot remember what it was.

** I'm Ringo Starr, actually playing the drums with The Beatles, live on a huge stage before a massive audience! I can see John, Paul and George standing in front of me playing guitars, while I'm high up behind them on a drum riser. This dream, notably, was in black and white and is the ONLY DREAM I can recall that I ever had not in color. We are playing a song called "Yes, I Do," which DOES NOT EXIST IN REAL LIFE. I was living a scene from *A Hard Day's Night* (1964).

** I'm the personal Press Agent for President Donald Trump. We are flying together in his helicopter high above the buildings of Manhattan. He is dictating to me what he wants to accomplish in an upcoming meeting. The scene then "cuts" to that meeting: We are inside a NYC skyscraper and numerous men are approaching me, asking if I can help schedule some private time for them with the president. (Note: Since I loathe Donald Trump, I found this dream to be particularly strange.)

** I'm a passenger in Mick Jagger's car, a gold colored Porsche, and he and I are driving around London, together. (I've never been to the UK in real life.) Mick is smoking a cigarette in a long holder and is wearing a peach, red and gold colored scarf. He tells me that he's thinking about breaking up The Rolling Stones and asks me for my advice!

** I'm onboard a large military ship, an intense thunder and lightning storm is all around us as we bob up and down on a very turbulent Pacific Ocean. As I am standing on the deck, I can see incredible things crashing into the sea all around me -- other ships, airplanes, helicopters, car tires, massive chains, buses, etc. At the same time, enormous items are also bobbing up onto the surface of the water from the depths, whales, dinosaurs, and an assortment of other large and colorful sea monsters.

** I'm walking with Walt Disney and his wife, Lillian, on a boardwalk. I know that the year is 1933. Walt is asking for my help in erecting a massive, 20-story high neon sign of Mickey Mouse. Then, suddenly, that neon sign exists and is lit, its sky-blue glow lights up the entire boardwalk. Lillian Disney asks me how I might suggest promoting the new attraction to the general public, to which I reply, "Gee, Mrs. Disney, I'm not sure. Television won't be invented until 1943. That's not for another ten years!"

** This final dream is a great example of how my Past Life Curse has even permeated my sleep: I'm a doctor in a modern-day hospital, wearing a white uniform. I see ahead of me in the hallway a beautiful, red-headed nurse, also wearing a white uniform. I approach her, and silently take her hand. Together, we stroll down the hallway, back in the same direction that I (the doctor) just came from. I find a door and open it, revealing a janitorial closest with shelves of cleaning supplies, mops, brooms, buckets, shovels, etc.

I lead my pretty nurse over to a worktable and there we begin to kiss passionately. This evolves to the start of intense, passionate lovemaking… WHICH IS THEN SUDDENLY INTERRUPTED when a squad of POLICEMEN (think the Keystone Kops) in uniforms bursts into the closet, blowing their whistles and raising their billy clubs in the air! "This must stop IMMEDIATELY!" screams the Police Chief to me. Sullen, the nurse is led away by the chief, who turns and shoots me an angry snarl. Then he and all of the other policemen leave the closet, slamming the door behind them.

Does my subconscious mind know more about the "Carrots Curse" than I do?

Chapter Thirty-Seven

The Past-Life Curse: The Proof
(2013 – 2023)

Several years after Bethany and I broke up, I began thinking that, perhaps, since she seemed so very "familial" to me that I'd known her from a previous lifetime. I sought out a "Psychic to the Stars," and arranged a meeting. Tom, an elderly, deaf medium, lived on a farm about 20 minutes north of LA, with his wife, Janet, another psychic. Tom was renowned for sending himself into a trance during a reading, and then, while talking to the ceiling, would reveal very specific details about each client's past, present, and future.

I was fairly apprehensive as I entered Tom's little office shack in his backyard. I sat in silence before the great man. He studied my face, then asked me to toss some coins onto his desk. I did. Tom then began chanting, softly, to himself, before entering a trance. When his eyes returned to normal, he again looked at me. In rapid succession, he said:

"Your ex-wife has a new boyfriend… he's a much older man"

"Your son's name is Isaac" and then…

"A woman writer, capital letter 'B', was very close to you A dear friend… a colleague… but not a lover. A distant relative to your mother."

I digested all of the above: My ex-wife, Kim, had just recently met Hank, a much older man whom she was now dating. My son's middle name is Isak. And the capital letter "B" thing I had to assume referred to Bethany.

Tom's eyes rolled back into his head. He continued: "Yours is an old soul. You were a star in the Hungarian theatre in the late 1880's. In the 1930s, you were a comedy writer for the 'Fred Allen Radio

Show,' but you died of a heart attack. Your name then was Larry Marks."

He went quiet for a long time. Assuming he was finished, I stood. Then, his eyes shot open: "You were a sin-eater, a beggar, in Scotland…1820s. Families hired you to absolve the sins of the dying by consuming food and drink. You sat beside their deathbeds, so the souls of the dying could rest in peace. Religious magic."

What the fuck??

Driving home from Tom's place, I was now more convinced than ever that past lives did, indeed, truly exist. And that my CURRENT life has been deeply affected by my past ones!

****

"You should see my friend Brianne," my friend Heather (a former employee of my company) advised. "She's an 'Aura Healer.' Perhaps she can help cleanse you."

I met Brianne at her office in Beverly Hills. "Nice to meet you," she said, "Let's get started." She led me into a small room, closed the lights, and said, "I need you to completely relax and clear your thoughts. Do I have your permission to touch you?" Me: "Yes, sure." As I got comfortable in my chair and closed my eyes, Brianne gently ran her hands over my head, neck, shoulders, back and arms. She inhaled and exhaled deeply, and I felt a sense of sinking into my seat. After about 20 minutes, Brianne turned on the lights. "Wow," she said, "I have a lot to tell you." Me: "Great. Go for it."

Brianne said that there was an extremely dark presence that surrounded me and had been following me during the course of many past lives. "If that's true," I said, "Why?" She continued to say she "saw" that I'd been a murderer of two young women in the 1880s. "You raped and strangled two teenage girls in a forest," she said, "And then you went home and stabbed your mother to death. You were a psychopath! You terrorized your community. A hunter tracked you down and shot you to death in a field. Those terrible deeds from that life created powerful dark energy. It remains with you… it's something you continue to carry forward today."

"Can I fix this?" I asked. Brianne said she would try to remove this energy, and once again ran her hands over me in the dark. She did. I paid her and left. While I don't believe a single thing changed as a result of this visit, I did find her story rather compelling.

****

I attended a seminar at the "Whole Life" Expo near LAX led by a nationally renowned hypnotist (and former dentist) whom I will call Dr. Bruce. This guy had been profiled on dozens of television shows and in magazine articles during the course of the past 25 years. He was considered an "authority" on past life regression hypnosis. During the seminar, he presented videotaped sessions with several of his patients, each of whom described the facts of their lives during previous incarnations, while they were under a hypnotic spell.

Most impressive about these hypnotic sessions was the research that followed. Dr. Bruce investigated tidbits revealed by many of his patients during these trances, unearthing factual evidence of names and circumstances from past lives. One guy apparently had been a Civil War soldier, another a pilot from the 1920s. A woman turned out to be a Spanish Queen, while another had been a slave in the Deep South.

Whether or not these researched facts *proved* that these past lives existed remains open to personal belief. However, I was completely convinced that all of this stuff was 100% for real.

I contacted Dr. Bruce shortly thereafter and had a private session in his office. In a darkened room, I sat in a recliner, as he set up his audio recording equipment. He instructed me to relax, taking deep breaths. Counting backwards out loud, the guy managed to lure me into an extraordinarily deep state of tranquility.

After about 10 minutes in this bliss, he began to instruct me. "I want you to open your mind to what came before," Dr. Bruce said, "Remember who you were and where you lived, what you saw and how you felt." I saw a kind of swirling blackness during this hypnosis, flashes of colors and images sparking through my brain like a Tesla experiment. Then, a scene popped into view that was crystal clear:

"I'm in Egypt," I said, "I'm performing a burial service for a queen. I'm a priest in white robes. Her coffin is on a raised platform inside a large hole in the ground. I'm also in the hole, and I can see one of the great pyramids above us. I am walking in a rectangular shape around her coffin, chanting prayers. Slaves are standing above us, looking down into the hole. I'm some kind of holy man."

The scene was as vivid as watching a TV show. Dr. Bruce then decided to move me "forward in time," and after some more breathing instructions, and counting backwards, I came up with this next one:

"I'm a farmer. I'm plowing a field along with my teenage son. It's a sunny day. I see people riding past us on a dirt road in carriages pulled by horses. It's the 1890s. I'm Amish. I can see my house. I'm walking inside. There's something wrong. I go into the bedroom. My wife is sick... very sick. She's in the bed, sweating and crying. She's pregnant. She's in labor. A woman nurse stands beside her, holding her hand. There's a great deal of blood on the bed. I stand at the front of the bed, tears in my eyes. My wife looks at me. She's in tremendous pain. Then both she and the new baby die."

I went silent. Dr. Bruce asked, "What's happening now?" Me: "I'm back outside. The townspeople are walking down the dirt road, en masse. They're heading for a celebration of some kind. I walk up to them... a beautiful woman with long, red hair turns her head to look at me. She smiles and takes my hand. We walk off together."

When this vision ended, Dr. Bruce led me again into a more recent past life, through a combination of my deep breathing and his counting. "I'm a cop in New York," I said, "It's the 1920s. I'm walking my beat along the sidewalk, watching out for street thugs. I hear someone call my name. I look up into an open window of a brownstone building. A woman with a kerchief on her head waves to me. 'He's gone,' she calls, 'Come on up.' I walk up the stairs and knock on her apartment door. She opens it and leads me into the kitchen. We start kissing passionately. I'm her lover."

The scene continued: "Suddenly, her husband walks into the room and confronts us. I take out my gun and kill him. The woman screams. I run out the backdoor of the apartment, down a flight of stairs, and into a back alley. A dozen policemen chase me and force me up against a fence. Their guns are drawn, and they want me to surrender. I take my gun, point it at my temple, and shoot myself in the head."

Time ran out on my session with Dr. Bruce. As he walked me to the door, he said, quietly, "If you believe in such a thing, Dan, I would say you're someone with a 'carry over curse' from a past life encounter… maybe even from several. I've rarely heard this many stories concerning violence and death. You're an interesting subject. Please let me know if you'd like to do this again."

The guy cost me a small fortune, so I wasn't in a rush to return. But I did believe what he said to be true. Each of these past life encounters seemed so real to me, I could still recall the colors, the sights, even the smells, during my drive back home.

****

While discussing the possibility that, perhaps my "Carrots" situation was stemmed in part by the reality of past lives, a friend suggested that I see a Shaman to learn more. I managed to find two female Shamans living in Los Angeles.

Amanda was an older woman who reminded me of Anne Bancroft in her later years. Living in a compound hidden within a Malibu forest, she spoke with me for two hours about why I'd traveled to see her. I told her about my peculiar history and unending problems with the opposite sex.

The woman had me lie down and covered my eyes with a cloth. She began to chant, shook Indian rattles, banged on a drum, and blew across my neck and chest. While completely awake, I felt as though my eyes were in REM sleep, as they fluttered rapidly beneath my lids. I saw a series of amazing images, most notably my dead grandfather Joe; my kids when they were small; and a wild deer with dark black eyes, who came out from a forest to stare at me.

At the end of the session, the woman told me that the deer was my "animal guide." She also said that she'd had a powerful vision of the ancient Egyptian Goddess, "Nut," who'd descended from heaven to visit me, enveloping me in her arms, and vowing to protect me for the rest of my life. "Nut is one of the most powerful spirits imaginable," she informed me. "I've very rarely seen her at work before. She came to continue your 'female energy download.' Apparently, it got interrupted when you were born into this lifetime. She knew you from a past life in Ancient Egypt."

I left the woman's home that day elated and joyous. Those emotions remained with me for a few weeks.

My second Shaman was a very attractive blonde woman named Erin, in Beverly Hills. Following a very similar modus operandi to that performed by Amanda, Erin had me lie down. Then she started to chant, while banging musical instruments, and blowing over me while I relaxed on her table.

This time, I experienced a series of beautiful, flowing colors, oceans of blue, red, orange and yellow vividly filled my senses. The experience was peaceful and calming. Also, during this trance, I could feel Erin clasping her hands above my chest, as though she were extracting something from me.

Afterward, Erin told me that she, too, had had a vision. Hers was the following: Dressed in a flowing white gown, Erin was walking through a forest, when she saw another version of ME as a dark-skinned, mysterious, and evil man wielding a raised knife. "Are you here to hurt me?" she asks the man, who replies, "Yes." "Why? the Erin 'as vision' asks. The man answers, "Because my soul is dead inside."

Without giving her any "hints" about my belief in a past life curse, Erin experienced what she told me was an "evil presence that has long impeded my life." She explained that during this vision, she did her best to remove the bad spiritual energy from me… the "extracting" actions she'd performed with her hands above my chest, earlier.

While my visits to both Shamans (Sha-women?) were extraordinarily interesting, I'm not sure any concrete changes were made as a result.

****

I was walking down Hollywood Blvd. killing time one day during Fall 2023, when I saw a sign on a small building that read, "Psychic Readings." In a virtually exact repeat of my story from 1979, I walked in at random, and met a short, young woman named Sarah. "Would you like a reading?" she asked. I paid her thirty bucks, and she led me into a small booth. "Hold out both hands," she said, "and let me see them."

In quick succession, Sarah told me that: I had my own business; I had two adult children, both in their 30s; my father had recently passed; and that my mother was now confined to a wheelchair.

Every single one of these pronouncements was 100% true.

Then Sarah asked, "Would you like to know about your love life?" Me: "Yes, actually… that's really why I'm here." She stared into my hands for a minute, then said, "You have the ability to find love… over and over again… but you don't have the luck TO KEEP IT."

Here I was, more than four decades after my first-ever reading by a fortune teller in New Jersey -- the one who'd said, "Many women are attracted to you, but something goes wrong with each one you meet." And now, another psychic 3,000 miles away, had delivered a corollary to that very first revelation bestowed upon me in 1979!

Sarah continued, "Do you believe in past lives?" Me: "I do." She stared again. I saw her body actually shudder: "You have a lot of very strong negative energy from a past life. I see a great many deaths and tragedies. In an ancient time, you were murdered. In another, a woman you loved very dearly accidentally drowned. Before that, I believe in the early 1800's, you were in love with an older woman named Jessica Burrows. She was a dark-haired beauty, but she left you for another man. You were so despondent, you hung yourself. Your suicide unleashed a black spirit. It's a very powerful, evil presence that haunts you, lifetime after lifetime. It prevents you from securing the true love that you constantly seek today."

I asked Sarah if there was a way to get rid of the "black spirit." She told me

that, for a fee of $10,000, she could order a rare "pink stone" for me. She and I would then sit in front of the pink stone for an hour and focus my negative energy into it. When it turned black, the evil, negative energies from my past lives would be gone, forever.

Of course, I knew the $10,000 pink stone bit was a scam.

I'm not a total schmuck!

Chapter Thirty-Eight

The Publication and Success of *After They Came* (2023)

I'd finished writing my book *After They Came* during Spring 2018, and then spent much of the next four years pitching it to virtually every literary agent, publishing house and movie producer in America.

No one cared. Zero interest. I truly thought the book was dead, so I put it in a drawer.

In Fall 2022, a friend of a friend told me about a family-owned publishing house called Genius Books Publishing, located in Milwaukee, that put out both Light and Dark Fiction stories. I pitched the book there, and it was well-received. Miraculously, I'd finally made a publishing deal for *After They Came.*

The basic storyline: Two benevolent Aliens come to Earth in the near future to "fix" all of mankind's problems, while working solely through the efforts of one human being, Jonathan Michael Tuckerman. Tuckerman, a lost and broken man, is rescued by these Aliens in chapter one, as he's purposely drowning himself in the Pacific Ocean on the occasion of his 70th birthday.

Having been saved, and quickly thereafter becoming embraced by the President of the United States, Tuckerman gains redemption over the course of the novel through a series of unprecedented acts of global heroism and brilliance, while ultimately fulfilling a life path he had no idea was predestined. Along the way, Tuckerman discovers that his late father, a scientist for the U.S. Military, was a UFO researcher, and had, 70 years earlier, saved the life of a young Alien visitor, months before Tuckerman was even born.

Obviously, I crafted the lead character's father after my own!

A few months before my book was published, I reached out to some of the world's leading UFO Researchers, to request book review quotes from them that I could use to promote book sales. I was very fortunate to get quotes from a number of these experts, including Richard Dolan, Nick Pope, Travis Walton, Dr. Lynn Kitei, Chase Kloestzke, and Kathleen Marden. I particularly loved the quote from Travis Walton -- the world's most famous Alien Abductee (and the subject of the movie *Fire In The Sky*/1993) who said, "*After They Came* could serve as the basis of an entertaining film adaptation."

After They Came was released on March 1, 2023. It was instantly embraced by many UFO enthusiasts around the world. I even hired a New York PR firm to help me secure promotional media coverage. I was interviewed by dozens of the top Paranormal podcasters and radio show hosts across the USA, UK, Canada and Australia, including the wildly popular, national American radio show "Coast to Coast AM with George Noory." During that interview, George said, "Danny, your book needs to be a movie, my friend!"

I also received countless emails from interested readers (and fans!) around the world.

Additionally, I presented the book at a number of UFO Conventions and meetings, including AlienCon 2023 in Pasadena, where I met the legendary father of "Ancient Astronaut Theory," Erich von Daniken. While gifting him my book, he said, "I haven't read this one yet," to which I replied, "Erich! It only came out three days ago!"

Also at AlienCon, I was reunited with Giorgio Tsoukalos, now the famous creator/star of the History Channel's TV series *Ancient Aliens* (2009). When I thanked him for his work in presenting the history of UFOlogy and Alien Visitations to the world, he laughingly replied, "Dan, it's all just smoke and mirrors!"

In addition, I promoted the book at UFO/Con in San Francisco, where I befriended UFO/Disclosure Activist Stephen Bassett;

Biblical scholar/author Ella LeBain; and Mark Glen Moore, a lifelong experiencer of extraterrestrial visitations.

Other promotional spots for me and *After They Came* included appearances at the Los Angeles Times Festival of Books; the LA/UFO Club; the Contact in the Desert 2023 event near Palm Springs; and the MUFON (Mutual UFO Network) Los Angeles Chapter meeting, during Summer 2023.

After They Came has opened countless doors for me within the fascinating world of UFOlogy history and research. I've made dozens of new friends, and am now considered, much to my own surprise, something of a "UFO Expert" by dozens of paranormal media outlets around the world.

I must thank my late father for the supernatural genesis of *After They Came,* which I truly believe HE bestowed upon me with that digital download from Heaven. Perhaps the most remarkable part of this story, is that this belated gift of my father's -- from beyond the grave – ONLY happened because I REALLY wanted a pastrami sandwich that day back in April 2017!

Chapter Thirty-Nine

The Hollywood Disclosure Alliance (2023/2024)

As I mentioned in the last chapter, I befriended longtime UFO/ Disclosure Activist Stephen Bassett in March 2023 at UFO/Con in San Francisco. My brother Bob and I had attended his lecture there, during which he discussed Disclosure – the day the President of the United States stands before a live TV audience of millions, and finally confirms to the world the existence of extraterrestrials who have long been visiting Planet Earth.

I'd not heard about "Disclosure" before that day -- I am certainly well aware of it now!

Steve Bassett, based in Washington, D.C., has been lobbying members of the U.S. Congress (both in the Senate and in the House) to advance the prospects for Disclosure since 1996 by sharing scientific and experiential data with its members for decades. At UFO/Con, I gifted him a copy of my book and gave him my business card. "If you ever get to LA," I said, "let's get together and talk."

At the very start of June 2023, Steve was in LA and gave me a call. We had lunch together at a noted Italian restaurant in Hollywood. There, he told me his life story and his intense, passionate desire to ensure that Disclosure happens during our lifetimes. At the end of his spiel, he looked at me and said, "Dan, you're a Hollywood publicist. You know people. What can we do together?" I thought for perhaps 10-seconds, then replied, "Steve, let's create the Hollywood Disclosure Alliance. We can put together all of your UFO connections with many of my Hollywood contacts. By joining forces, both groups can share stories and information to help create the future of science-fact based films, TV shows, documentaries and books."

The look on Steve's face was priceless. "Yes, that's it exactly!" he said. "Let's do it." We shook hands and finished our pasta.

Two days later, I became Steve's roommate at Contact in the Desert, the world's largest UFO conference, held annually near Palm Springs, CA. Steve was a guest speaker there, and introduced me to numerous, important UFO researchers and experiencers, as well as a number of his fellow Disclosure Advocates. Within the world of UFOlogy, Steve Bassett is a superstar, and walking behind him in the hallways at Contact in the Desert was like watching Moses part the Red Sea – countless people approached him to shake his hand, share their story, or get an autograph.

It was an enthralling weekend for me. I gleaned a ton of knowledge about this field, and made many new contacts which helped propel me into the next level of my UFOlogy expertise.

Over the course of Summer and Fall 2023, Steve and I shared our idea for the Hollywood Disclosure Alliance, or HDA for short, with hundreds of his contacts and mine. And together with my daughter, Anjuli, who created for us the HDA logo and website, Steve and I began to assemble a remarkable 20-member Board of Directors and 200-member group of Founding Members, many of whom are based internationally. We also designed the HDA as a 501 (c/3) non-profit corporation, and, at present, we are seeking tax-deductible donations from supporters around the world.

I serve now as the Chairman of HDA, Steve is Executive Director, and many of our fellow HDA members are renowned UFO/ET researchers, experiencers and Disclosure Activists. We also have dozens of members from the Hollywood community among our membership, including noted writers, producers, directors. As of the writing of these words, we also have four movie stars within our membership: my friend and *ET* (1982) star Dee Wallace, Thomas Jane, Shirley Maclaine and Dania Ramirez.

I was the Host and MC for the official launch of the HDA on November 2, 2023, at Musso and Frank Restaurant in Hollywood. There, we had dozens of members in person, and another two-dozen attending from various spots in the world, via Zoom. The HDA has been written up in a number of media outlets, and Steve and I have given dozens of podcast and radio interviews across North America in efforts to further promote our cause.

The Hollywood Disclosure Alliance has been another gift in my life. Of course, the formation of the HDA was a direct result of the success of my book *After They Came*.

If anyone had ever told me just a few years ago that I would one day become one of America's most in-demand UFO/Media experts, I never would have believed them!

Chapter Forty

The *Live From Hollywood…It's Paranormal Tonight*! Podcast (2024)

During early 2023, a woman named Margie Kay wanted to interview me about my book, *After They Came,* on her live podcast program called *The UnX News.* Margie is the owner of the KUNX Digital Broadcasting Network, aka The UnX Network, which is based out of St. Louis. Six months later, Margie called me again to ask if I could help her publicize her network, but said she had very little money to pay for the PR. I quickly countered with, "Tell you what. I'll handle the PR for your network at no charge, if you give me my own podcast." She instantly agreed – "Sure! Let's do it!"

I titled my podcast *Live From Hollywood…It's Paranormal Tonight!* and launched that show on Jan 11, 2024, broadcasting from my Asbury PR Agency office within my home in Beverly Hills, CA. Dee Wallace, the star of *ET* (1982) and a longtime friend of mine, was my very first guest.

Paranormal Tonight! is a live, one-hour weekly program during which I interview a variety of my friends, colleagues and past clients culled from my years in Hollywood and discuss with them their thoughts about the odd, the bizarre, and the unexplained. Of course, I also promote my various books during each telecast as well.

I am also interviewing dozens of my newer friends and colleagues on the show, primarily members of the Hollywood Disclosure Alliance, who are noted UFO researchers and paranormal experiencers. These folks include Steve Bassett, of course, along with other names in UFOlogy and related fields, such as Nick Pope, Richard Dolan, Paul Hynek, Earl Anderson, Ron James, Kathy Marden, Deb Kauble, Sev Tok, Katie Page, and many others.

Once again, I have my late father to thank. Were it not for that memorable 1970 UFO sighting, which led to me receiving my Dad's "home movie download from Heaven" in 2017, which led to me writing *After They Came,* which led to me creating the Hollywood Disclosure Alliance, I never would have been gifted the opportunity to host and produce my own paranormal podcast, which is showcased internationally over a well-established, digital broadcasting network.

None of the extraordinary things that have been happening to me during the past few years would ever have taken place, had it not been for my craving of a pastrami sandwich just a few days after my beloved father, Jack Harary, passed away.

After Word

So, let's recap, shall we?

Do Ghosts and Poltergeists exist? I'd have to say DEFINITELY YES! How else to explain the Ouija board spelling "Joseph" and "Syria" for my grandfather? What about the face of my dead grandpa superimposed over my son's face at the moment of his birth? How to explain the booming voice, "DANNY, JEANNIE CHANGED MY WILL!" or the cymbals clanging in my bedroom, or my bedroom "touch" lamp going on and off by itself in the middle of the night, other than by the spirit of my recently departed father?

And did you read about my daughter's experiences in her three different apartments?

Do Guardian Angels exist and whisper into people's ears? Duh! How else to explain the Voice telling me in 1966 to Play the Drums, or in 1980 to write *Carrots,* or the voice in the chandelier telling me to Start My Own Business in 1996, or to leave the Biggie Smalls party just minutes before his murder, or to help Supermodel Amber Smith?

Or that I'd never see my father alive again?

Per my Alaskan Psychic, I believe the latter-day voices I heard were from my late friend Paul Dorfman. But I honestly have no idea WHOSE VOICE was the one I heard prior to Paul's death! Since my first grandparent (Joe) died in 1967, I clearly had another Angel watching out for me during early childhood. Perhaps a distant relative I never even met?

Do UFOs exist? Of course, you silly. I saw three with my own eyes. I've also had lengthy discussions with dozens of the world's leading UFO Researchers, several of whom are literally geniuses. I've become personal friends with many of these characters as a result of my book *After They Came* and my involvement as the Chairman and Creator of the Hollywood Disclosure Alliance.

If more folks took the time out from their busy schedules to actually read about and study this phenomenon, they'd learn that MANY UFOs (not ALL) are piloted by extraterrestrial beings. They'd also discover that Aliens have been visiting -- and interacting with – Planet Earth and mankind for tens of thousands of years.

Look up "Ancient Astronaut Theory!" Read *Chariots of the Gods*! Watch the *Ancient Aliens* TV series! Attend a MUFON meeting near where you live! If you open your heart and mind to new ideas, the realities of extraterrestrial life long visiting Earth become truly staggering.

Did a Gargoyle save my life when I was five? My mother is convinced I dreamed this… I clearly remember this happening. Can I prove this one? Alas, not. But I wish I could track down those two little neighbor girls, Kathy and Lizzie. Perhaps they'd remember something I'm missing!

Were my two Magical Zits really "magical?" Well, given their timing at EXACTLY THE WRONG MOMENTS when I was with desirable girls, you tell me. Hormones and nerves? Yes, of course… but to happen EXACTLY at those moments and not before or after? I can't find another explanation there.

Mind reading? Hard to say, but I did see the word "STEVE" on high school girl Laura's forehead. And I did see the word "WIFE" on my OWN forehead, just before I proposed to Kim # 2. I'm really not sure how to explain those events, but they happened exactly as described. I suppose my intuition can sometimes be a powerful messenger.

Can people manifest something to happen? Well, I did, WITH HUGH HEFNER, no less! What were the odds there? Not to mention manifesting a Brand New Car! And the legendary Musso & Frank Restaurant becoming my most important, ever, PR client?

Was I Predestined to meet my wife? Let's review: Meeting two Kims on two New Year's Eves exactly four years apart to the hour? Both Kims being nurses with blonde hair and blue eyes, aged 20?

Come on now... this one really should speak for itself, don't you think?

And what about "Long Red?" It sure felt to me as if I KNEW HER already... there's just no other way to tell that story. I KNEW that our paths were meant to cross, but, in retrospect, probably only as fodder for a chapter in this book.

Do Fortune Tellers know what they're talking about? Well, if my very first reading in 1979, in which a woman told me: "Many women are attracted to you, but something goes wrong with each one you meet," wasn't the most accurate sentence I ever heard in my life, I don't know what was. I do believe that there are men and women in the world who are psychically gifted – Tom the deaf psychic and the woman in Alaska as other examples. I believe they can tap into a higher plane and sometimes see, or hear, or intuit, facts and celestial voices and images that are simply floating around up there in another dimension.

Do odd, random, offbeat things simply just happen in life. YES! Of course. But are they truly Supernatural? How else to explain my friend Steve suddenly becoming a Southern Woman? Or the girl I was making out with on the beach in Cancun suddenly vanishing? Or women in Boston my senior year of college being convinced I was a man named "Jeffrey?"

And how about meeting Leon Harary at EXACTLY the right second in time?

I suppose all of these things could "just be silly, odd things that happen." But, to me, it sure seems like they were MEANT to happen.

Can Dreams become true predictions or serve as communication to the other side? Well, my mom knew my girlfriend Sarah was pregnant WEEKS before my girlfriend did! That came from a dream, so, there's that. And how about the dream I had in which my dear friend Julie appeared to me JUST A FEW HOURS AFTER SHE DIED? I know she came to say goodbye.

The only other dreams I've had like the "Julie Dream" include visits from my dead father. These were remarkably realistic moments and conversations with a much beloved man taking place within just the first few weeks after his death. As of the writing of these words, my Dad has been gone now for seven years – I've seen him in at least 50 dreams during that time.

And what about my other "transcendent" dreams? I have no idea why I am such a prolific dreamer – I've always been. Why is it that when I first wake up every single morning, I have no idea where I am? I'm exhausted and convinced that I've just come back from somewhere else, far, far away.

Are my Life Numbers really 6-1-7? I have no idea… maybe, maybe not. But what were the odds of me waking up at 6:17 pm on June 17 after surgery in a hospital and then being wheeled into Room 617? I'd say pretty slim to none, probably.

And, finally: Am I really the victim of a Past Life Curse?

Well, if you read this book, hopefully I've convinced you of that as a hardcore fact. No other single, heterosexual man who's ever lived on Planet Earth has had more "bad luck" romantically with members of the opposite sex during the course of an entire lifetime than me.

It's not even possible.

But if you're STILL NOT CONVINCED, I urge you to read my earlier book, *Carrots: True Confessions of a Hollywood Sex Addict* from Bear Manor Media (2022.)

If THAT book doesn't prove my thesis that reincarnation is real, and that I've been the victim of a Past Life Curse since childhood -- involving every single girl and woman I've ever encountered in this present lifetime with the sole exception of my daughter -- then nothing else I could ever say or write will make you a believer!

When this book is published in Summer 2024, I will be 68 years old. I can honestly declare, right here and now, that I have truly lived a *Paranormal Life!* The off-the-wall experiences chronicled within the pages of this book have been hung upon my body like a heavy, winter overcoat.

Since the moment of my birth into this lifetime on Sunday evening, June 17, 1956, at about 11:55 pm, in Neptune, New Jersey, until the typing of these final words right now, I have been – and must diligently remain – at the ready, to embrace whatever oddball moment may next make its other-worldly appearance along my paranormal and pre-destined path.

About The Author

Born and raised near Asbury Park, New Jersey, Dan Harary is best known for his 40-plus years of work in Hollywood as an Entertainment Industry Publicist, and as the Owner (since 1996) of the Asbury PR Agency in Beverly Hills, California.

Dan has worked with hundreds of famous celebrities from movies, TV, music, and pop culture since the age of 15 (1972), including a pre-fame Bruce Springsteen, KISS, and Fleetwood Mac. Dan's first book, a Hollywood memoir entitled *Flirting With Fame: A Hollywood Publicist Recalls 50 Years of Celebrity Close Encounters,* was published by BearManor Media in 2002. The book was covered in major national media outlets, incl. The L.A. Times, Newsweek, The Hollywood Reporter, The Village Voice, L.A. Weekly, The New York Daily News, KFI Radio, and many others.

Dan had a dramatic UFO sighting in his hometown in 1970, where he shared the experience with his father, an Electronics Engineer/Physicist for the U.S. Army. He has been interviewed about that sighting by media outlets around the world - the story also became a feature article in the June 2023 edition of the MUFON Journal.

After his father's death in 2017, Dan recalled that encounter for the first time in 47 years, discovered the nature of his late father's top-secret work with radar systems, missiles, and military drone technologies, and was inspired to write his second book, a science fiction novel entitled *After They Came*. That book was published in 2023 by Genius Book Publishing. Dan later went on to experience two more UFO sightings: one near Edwards Air Force Base in 1996, and a third, in 2008, at the ECETI Ranch in Washington State, at the base of Mt. Adams.

Upon its release in Spring 2023, *After They Came* quickly made an impact within the UFO Researcher and Experiencer communities, and was endorsed by numerous top UFO experts, incl. Richard

Dolan, Chase Kloetzke, Lynn Kitei, Earl Grey Anderson, George Noory, Jimmy Church, Deb Jordan-Kauble, and Kathleen Marden, among them. The book was covered by media around the world, including *The Daily Mail* in the U.K. Said UFO Expert Nick Pope of *After They Came:* "Dan Harary's book is an entertaining and upbeat work of sci-fi that cleverly incorporates key parts of the UFO phenomenon's lore and backstory - a delightful tale of wonder and hope." Adds iconic UFO Experiencer Travis Walton, himself a famed ET Abductee, "The style of the images in *After They Came* are presented in such a graphic visual style that it could serve as the basis of an entertaining film adaptation."

Dan has been a member of the Southern California Chapter of MUFON since 2007. He is also the creator and host, since early 2024, of The UnX Network's podcast: *Live From Hollywood...It's Paranormal Tonight!* As presented in this book, Dan has been experiencing supernatural, paranormal, and highly bizarre phenomena throughout the course of his life.

In 2023, Dan conceived the LA-based Hollywood Disclosure Alliance and serves as its Chairman. His book *My Paranormal Life* was published by BearManor Media in 2024. In addition, his original, dark-fiction novel *FIVE*, was also published in 2024, by Genius Book Publishing. Please visit: www.DanHararyAuthor.com

Dan lives in Beverly Hills, CA. He is the father of an adult daughter, Anjuli.

Photo Credits

All Photos Appearing in this Book Courtesy of Author's Personal Collection, Except:

Photo of Two Girls in New York City with "Ass Shorts" 1980, Courtesy Columbia Pictures

Photo of Hugh Hefner 1984, Courtesy The Hugh M. Hefner Foundation and its Board of Directors

Photo of Playboy Playmate Kym Malin 1985, Courtesy of Sam Maxwell

Photo of Supermodel Amber Smith 2009, With Approval Of Amber Smith

Photos of Book Cover *AFTER THEY CAME* 2023, Courtesy of Genius Book Publishing

Photos of *LIVE FROM HOLLYWOOD, IT'S PARANORMAL TONIGHT!* 2024, Courtesy of The UNX Network

www.ingramcontent.com/pod-product-compliance
Lightning Source LLC
Chambersburg PA
CBHW070748160726
48004CB00001B/102